Algrove Publishing Limited
1090 Morrison Drive
Ottawa, Ontario
Canada K2H 1C2

Canadian Cataloguing in Publication Data

Main entry under title:

   Popular mechanics shop notes

(Classic reprint series)
2nd ed.
Includes index.
Originally published: Chicago : Popular Mechanics Co., 1905-Compiled from the Shop notes department of Popular mechanics magazine, and Written so you can understand it : tells easy ways to do hard things.
ISBN 0-921335-74-1 (v. 1) - ISBN 0-921335-76-8 (v. 2) - ISBN 0-921335-78-4 (v. 3) - ISBN 0-921335-80-6 (v. 4) - ISBN 0-921335-82-2 (v. 5)

   1. Do-it-yourself work. 2. Industrial arts. I. Windsor, H. H. (Henry Haven), 1859-1924. II. Title. III. Title: Shop notes. IV. Series: Classic reprint series (Ottawa, Ont.)

TJ1160.P66 1999   600   C99-900763-7

Printed in Canada
#10799

Publisher's Note

Virtually every woodworking magazine in the English-speaking world has a shop notes section and has published an accumulation of them in book form. This was all started in 1905 with the first annual issue of *Popular Mechanics Shop Notes*, a compilation of advice on jigs, fixtures, methods of work, processes and projects. The earlier issues focussed primarily on metalworking, but with tips for a variety of other trades liberally sprinkled throughout. As years went by, the contents shifted more and more to woodworking and handyman projects. Each book is profusely illustrated. The line drawings of the earlier issues were supplanted by superb engravings until photographs started to creep in during the 1920s. Each year has its charm but all issues share the attribute of being clear, concise and widely informative.

Leonard G. Lee, Publisher
Ottawa
September, 1999

This Volume is Reprinted from the

SHOP NOTES DEPARTMENT
OF POPULAR MECHANICS

As Published Monthly During 1906

Edited by H. H. WINDSOR

SHOP NOTES

TO FLATTEN AND SHAPE RAWHIDE

Warm two metal plates a little warmer than is comfortable to hold; put the rawhide between them and press solid in a

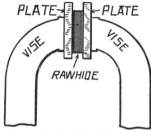

Shaping Rawhide

vise, leaving all there till the plates are cool. Be careful not to heat the plates hot enough to burn the hide.—Contributed by J. H. Jerome, Brighton, Mass.

HOW TO MAKE A SMALL ACETYLENE GAS GENERATOR

To make this machine the materials required are two tin cans, one of a size to fit into the other, a smaller can and an acetylene gas burner.

Solder the gas burner, A, to the smaller of the two large cans, B. Punch the smallest can, C, full of holes and fill it with carbide 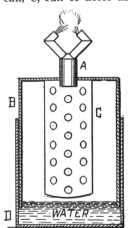 and fasten it to the under side of can B. Partially fill can D with water and place can B with its attached apparatus in can D, as shown in the illustration.

Wait a moment, then touch a lighted match to the burner. If too much gas is generated the carbide is automatically lifted out of the water, as shown, and the generation of gas ceases until more is needed.—Contributed by Fred Crawford Curry, Brockville, Ontario, Canada.

FRAME FOR HOLDING MILK CANS WHILE SOLDERING

In a shop where soldering milk cans forms an important item of repair work the frame shown in the illustration will be found convenient. Placed on this frame a 40-qt. milk can can be rotated freely so that the seams in the breast of the can may be

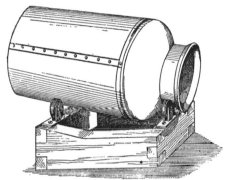

Frame for Holding Milk Cans While Soldering

quickly and easily soldered. The frame may be held in the lap of the operator, if it is more convenient. To solder the bottom seam, an arm is fastened to the frame, so as to support the bottom of the can when inclined for this soldering, says the Metal Worker, and the frame is then taken in the lap of the operator, who turns the can and at the same time solders the seam. The construction of the frame is shown in the illustration.

To renovate varnished work make a polish of 1 qt. good vinegar, 2 oz. butter of antimony, 2 oz. alcohol and 1 qt. oil. Shake well before using.

For oil gilding make an oil size of calcined red ocher ground with the best and oldest oil. Add oil of turpentine to make it work freely when ready to use.

QUICK BOILER MOVING

An engineer was given from Sunday morning until the following Wednesday at 2 p. m. to connect up some new boilers that had just been installed, and break the connections· of the old boilers and move them from the plant to the cars on which they were to be shipped. He tells in the Engineer's Review how he did it with the help of but two white men and a gang of southern negroes. He says:

When the order came, I completed my measurements for connecting the new boilers to the engine and piping system and starting up the shop, cut and fitted the two 6-in. and one 4-in. connections that were necessary. Getting in some more men these

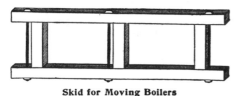

Skid for Moving Boilers

were erected in place that night and the old boiler connections broken and plugged.

The next morning the fronts and stays were taken off and the boilers stripped. A crib work of blocks was then placed under each end of the boilers, and with jacks they were raised clear of the settings and securely blocked. A gang of men then pulled down the brick setting. Meanwhile I had the carpenter get out some skids of 6 by 8-in. timber, as shown in the sketch. As soon as one of the boilers was clear enough to work on, it was lowered down onto a skid. While this work was going on, I had a hole made in the boiler room wall large enough for the boiler to pass out, and by the time I had

boiler was on a car, with all the fittings, securely braced and ready for moving.

In the meantime the other setting had been removed and the rubbish cleared away so we had a clean sweep at the other boiler, and Wednesday morning at 7:40 o'clock everything was ready for the freight. This job might have been accomplished more quickly if we had had better facilities and competent help.

BEST ANTI-FREEZING SOLUTION

The best anti-freezing solution for the use of motorists is prepared by the following recipe:

Mix and filter 4½ lb. pure calcium chloride and a gallon of warm water and put the solution in the radiator or tank. Replace evaporation with clean water, says the Motor Age, and leakage with solution. Pure calcium chloride retails at about 8 cents per pound, or can be procured from any wholesale drug store at 5 cents.

A ROPE PIPE WRENCH

A rope pipe wrench which may be operated by one man is shown in Fig. 1. The rope is wrapped on the pipe and toggle as shown, then, holding the ends of the rope in one hand, the operator pulls the toggle with the other. In operating the device shown in Fig. 2, which is used for heavier work, one man is required to hold the rope ends and another to handle the toggle. This device, says American Machinist, is called a Spanish windlass, and is used by seafaring folk.

A method of grinding a pulley on a shaft, or grinding a shaft in the boxes, is shown in Fig. 3. The ends of the rope are pulled

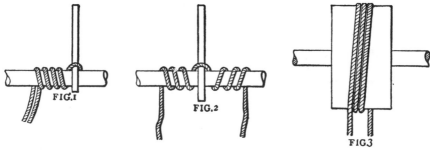

FIG.1   FIG.2   FIG3

the track ready the first boiler was on the rolls. Hitching the blocks to the skid we soon had the boiler walking out in great shape. Tuesday morning at 10 o'clock this

alternately. The hand-rails of marine engines are polished by wrapping them with emery cloth which is worked by a piece of spun yarn instead of rope, as in Fig. 3.

NEGATIVE NUMBERING DEVICE

The negative-numbering or marking device shown in the illustration is very simple in construction and will save time for the photographer using it.

To make the device prepare a brass strip by cutting into its face the inverted numbers 0 to 9 and screw the strip to the edge of a printing frame. Then construct a small pantograph of light ash strips and brass screw eyes.

To number a negative put the plate, with its dull side out, into the frame and pick out the correct figures on the brass strip and transfer them neatly to the negative by holding the wooden block to which the pantograph is attached lightly against the

Tool for Numbering Negatives

frame with the right hand and tracing the figures with the left. Slip the wooden block backward or forward to get the right spacing.

Keep the tool with the printing frame in a drawer of its own, says a correspondent of the American Machinist, so that no time is lost in preparing or assembling the parts.

WATERPROOF POLISH FOR WOOD

Put into a stopped bottle 1 pt. alcohol, 2 oz. gum benzoin, ¼ oz. gum sandarac and ¼ oz. gum anime. Put the bottle in a sand-bath or in hot water till the solids are dissolved, then strain the solution and add ¼ gill best clear poppy oil. Shake well and the polish is ready for use.

TO TEST THE CAPACITY OF AR-TESIAN WELLS

Where a weir cannot be built, the following test of the capacity of an artesian well is recommended by a correspondent of the Crane Valve.

Lay about 40 ft. of 10-in. pipe, with a 90 deg. elbow looking up from its outer end,

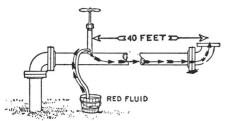

Testing the Capacity of an Artesian Well

horizontally from the well. Tap the pipe near the well and attach a small force pump. Let this pump draw from a bucket a solution of red aniline dye. One stroke of the pump will force about 4 oz. of the red dye into the water passing through the pipe. When this stroke of the pump strikes, start a stop watch, and when the colored water shows at the elbow, stop the watch. Thus the exact time taken to travel the length of the pipe may be ascertained, and with this time and the capacity of the given size of pipe the amount of water passing per minute may be figured. This test will come within three-fourths of one per cent of being absolutely correct.

CALIPERS MADE OF PINCERS

To make a pair of calipers of a pair of pincers, heat both handles of the pincers so that they will bend to meet at the ends

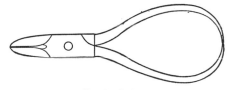

Handy Calipers

easily. Then file the tips of the bent handles to a point. This makes a very handy tool.—Contributed by Jack Wener, 2247 F St., Los Angeles, Cal.

AUTOMATIC ELECTRIC INDICATOR OF WATER LEVEL IN DISTANT DITCH

I am in charge of an electric generating plant which ordinarily operates with water-power. The water is brought in an open ditch to within 300 ft. of the station, where a waste gate is placed. From there the water is carried in a pipe. In order to carry the proper load without using too much water, it is necessary for me to know the depth of water in the ditch at all times. I am running a 90 kw. alternator in multiple with another set of alternators 10 miles away. Both plants are short of water

the ditch is 6 ft. deep. The diagram will make the construction readily understood. There should always be one of the six lights burning, and when two burn it indicates a 6-in. level. For example, when lamps 5 and 6 are burning there would be 5½ ft. of water in the ditch. If No. 6 goes out there is only 5 ft. of water; if No. 4 and No. 5 light there is 4½ ft. of water, and so on.

The contact points, 1, 2, 3, 4, 5 and 6, are placed on a wood block 14 in. x 14 in. x 1 in.

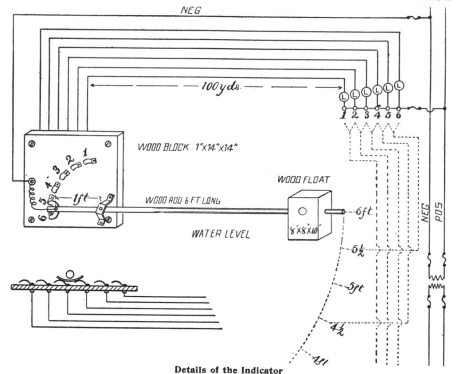

Details of the Indicator

at times and then it is necessary to use steam when the load is at the maximum. I can usually hold the load during the day. My plant has a 6-mile ditch and the other a 1-mile ditch. Both ditches cause a great deal of trouble in stormy weather.

The 100-yd. trip in the dark to get the water level was a great annoyance; even in the day time it took time, so I studied out the following plan to indicate the water. It is so simple any electrician can install one, and it has worked to my entire satisfaction. My indicator uses six lamps, as

The wooden lever is 6 ft. long, with the negative wire connected to the contact point on the lever with a flexible wire long enough to allow for travel over the six contacts. At the other end of the lever is a float which I made of a block of wood 8 in. x 8 in. x 10 in. At the station a positive bus bar connects to the six lamps, from each of which leads a wire to the contact block, where connection is made to its corresponding contact number. I used No. 16 wire for the outdoor lines, about 2,000 ft. was required. For the lamp signals I used 8-cp. 110-v. lamps. By placing the contact points at nearer or farther intervals the device may be made to indicate changes in 3-in. levels, or 1 ft., but for my purpose the 6-in. change in level is sufficiently exact.—Contributed by Lee R. Clarke, R. R. No. 2, Bozeman, Mont.

EMERY WHEEL ARBOR

An emery wheel arbor to rig on a lathe is shown in the sketch and is the device of M. C. Warnock, of Farmington, Ill. It consists of a flange coupling, C, in this

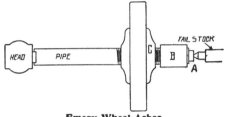

Emery Wheel Arbor

case 3½ in. in diameter, and a length of piping. A coupling, B, is put on the tail stock end, into which is screwed a plug, A, for the center to hold. If the plug were inserted in the pipe without a coupling the threads would cut through, being threaded both inside and outside. A solid bar of iron may be substituted for the pipe. The flange may be trued in the lathe.

If you want anything and don't know where to get it, write Popular Mechanics. Information free.

AIR DRILLS FOR DRILLING MARBLE

To successfully drill marble with a pneumatic drill, an ordinary twist drill is prepared as shown in the illustration. The twist is removed for a distance of about ½-in. from the point and the face of the

"The Drill is Ground Square"

drill is ground square, which gives it the appearance of an ordinary screwdriver. When running light with this drill the speed should not exceed 70 revolutions per minute, and when pressure is placed on the machine and the drill begins to cut, reduce it to 30 revolutions. In this way marble can be rapidly and economically drilled.

METHOD OF TELEPHONE WIRING

A method of wiring and connecting two short line battery call telephones is shown in the illustration. The chief feature of this method is that it permits the use of the ordinary two-contact push in place of the unreliable three-contact push generally made use of in this type of 'phone. Figures 1 and 2 show the transmitters and receivers in series with the battery when conversation is going on. Figure 3 shows induction coil in series with transmitter and having a closed secondary through receiver. This kink is contributed by a reader.

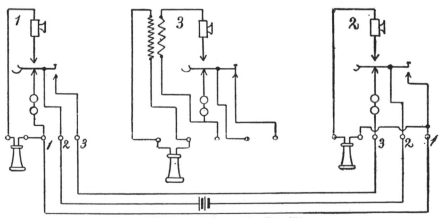

Plan of Wiring and Connecting Two 'Phones

HOW TO MAKE A PARALLEL RULE FOR THE DRAWING BOARD

A very useful drawing device, which saves time and does better work than the T-square, as by its use it is impossible to get a line out of parallel through carelessness, was constructed by C. D. Gilbert, St. Johnsburg, Vt., who tells how to make the instrument:

Unless one has a lathe the machine shop must be called upon to make six brass pulleys, four single and two double as shown in the drawing. This is the only expense, assuming, of course, that the device is to be used on a drawing board one already has.

up and down the board freely, but leaving very little end play. Screw the pulleys on the board, as shown by the drawing, and if there are cleats on the board remove them and proceed to connect up.

Beginning at Post 1 fasten the end of the line under the hexagon nut and bring it over the under side of Pulley 2 (the board being in the position shown in the drawing, face down), then to the lower groove of Double Pulley 3, to Double Pulley 4, then over the upper side of Pulley 7 and to Post 6. There it is given one turn around the post between the two nuts and starts back to Pulley 5, then to the upper groove in 4, crosses the other part of the string to 3,

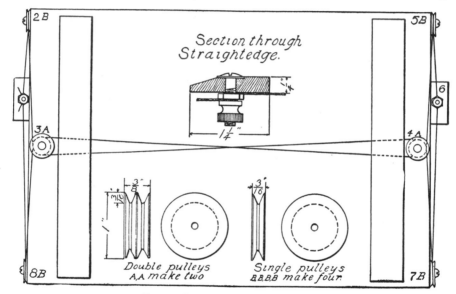

Parallel Rule for the Drawing Board

The holes in the pulleys are drilled to fit easily a 1-in. round head screw. Other materials needed are a piece of hard wood, about 1½ in. longer than the board, and suitable for making the straight edge, as shown in illustration, two brass binding posts from the carbons of some discarded dry batteries, and a few feet of good fishline.

To make, put one of the posts through the end of the straight edge, about ½ in. from one end, countersinking it slightly, and screw the check nut up snug, and with one side of the hexagon nut square with the end of the ruler, so that it will slide easily along the board.

Then lay the ruler on the board and put in the other post so that the ruler will slide

next passes to 8, and back under the milled nut on Post 1. Now if drawn snug all is ready for business unless the ruler has been pulled out of square; if so, loosen the milled nut at Post 6 and slide the ruler along the string till correct. The line will stretch at first and have to be taken up, but will soon work all right.

The cleats which were removed from the board must now be notched to allow the strings to pass and replaced, when all is complete. If one has several boards, a frame may be made which will hold the largest one, and the device attached to that, when one can readily change from one piece of work to another by simply changing boards—often an advantage to a busy draughtsman

IDEAL TOOTH OUTLINE FOR CIR-CULAR SAW

A saw expert in the Woodworker gives a sketch of what he considers an ideal tooth outline for a circular saw. He says:

Let us consider such a saw at work. Suppose the saw to be 24 in. diameter, with

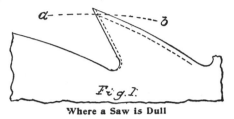

Fig. 1.

Where a Saw is Dull

48 teeth, which makes the teeth practically ½-in. space. Supposing this saw is making a 3-in. cut—that is, 3 in. of feed for one revolution. It is obvious that each tooth cuts a shaving 1/16 in. in thickness. If we could draw a circle 1/16-in. smaller than that of the saw, we should find that the saw is dull only outside of the line where the said circle crosses the face of the tooth (Fig. 1, a b).

How shall we sharpen? This dull point is but a trifle over 1/16-in. long, but is probably less than 1/124-in. deep. Consequently, if we sharpen on the back, we must grind or file 1/16 off all along the periphery

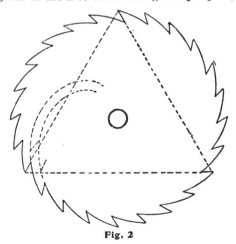

Fig. 2

line, and as stated by another, the saw is ⅛-in. smaller when we are done. On the other hand, if we grind or file on the face of the tooth, we will have less than 1/124-in. to grind to obtain a sharp point, but we sha'n't lose anything like ⅛-in. in diameter. Considering the size of

said saw, and the gauge as well, I think it obvious that such a saw will stand up and rip for a long time; and I may safely contend that every semblance of a corner will be gone when it comes up to the file room. These conditions are true in conjunction with the upset swage, only to a greater extent.

ERASING MACHINE FOR DRAFTING ROOMS

Frequently in drafting rooms, such records as street records, plat books, main records, etc., are kept which have to be changed from time to time to show new pipe lines, etc., and thus a great deal of erasing is occasioned. To do this work quickly and neatly the erasing machine may be employed.

To make this machine, procure an ordinary dental engine or machine, such as is used for drilling teeth, and, instead of the drill used by the dentist, set a circular ink eraser in the mandrel by means of a small screw. An electric motor may be attached to the machine, or it may be run by foot power. In operating it, merely guide the eraser by means of the handle.

A few points, however, should be kept in mind, says the Progressive Age: The eraser must not be pressed too hard on the paper, and the machine must be kept at a good speed.

With a good paper the erased spot will have a hard surface, and the erasing will be hardly noticeable. The time required is very short, and the operator quickly becomes an expert at erasing by machine.

NATURALIST'S PASTE

For mounting specimens make a paste of thick mucilage of gum arabic and powdered starch. Suitable for artificial flower makers' use, also, and for sticking wafers, paper ornaments, etc., to candies and cakes. For the last mentioned purpose, add a little lemon juice.

HOW TO LAY GALVANIZED IRON ROOFING

The use of galvanized iron for general roofing work has increased greatly during the past few years. It has many features which commend it as a roofing material, but difficulties have been experienced by beginners as to the proper method of applying it to the roof. The weight of material used is rather heavy to permit of

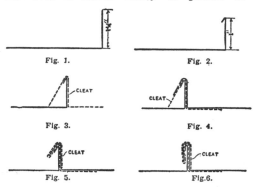

Fig. 1.   Fig. 2.

Fig. 3.   Fig. 4.

Fig. 5.   Fig.6.

double seaming, but a method that has been evolved by a correspondent of the Metal Worker is found very satisfactory. By this he says that galvanized iron roofing can be put on at low cost, that it is water tight and is subject to no buckling in the joints, does away with double seaming and is considered more suitable than the latter for roofing purposes wherever it can be laid on a roof steeper than 1 to 12.

Galvanized iron of No. 28 and heavier gauges is used, the sheets being lap-seamed and soldered together in strips in the shop the proper length to apply to the roof. After the sheets are fastened together a 1¼-in. edge is turned up the entire length of one side of the sheet, as indicated in Fig. 1. This operation is done with tongs having gauge pins set at the proper point. The second operation consists in turning a strip ¼ in. wide toward the sheet, as shown in Fig. 2. This sheet is then laid on the roof, and a cleat about 8 in. long and 1 in. wide made of galvanized iron is nailed to the roof close to the sheet and bent over it, as shown in Fig. 3.

A second sheet having 1½ in. turned up is now brought against the first sheet and bent over both sheet and cleat, as shown in Fig. 4. The cleat is then bent backward over the second sheet and cut off close to the roof, as in Fig. 5, after which the seams are drawn together by double seaming tools, as the occasion demands,

and slightly hammered with a wooden mallet. The finished seam is shown in Fig. 6. It will be seen that the second sheet of galvanized iron, cut ¼ in. longer than the first, laps over the former, making a sort of bead which prevents water from driving in. Cleats hold both sheets firmly to the roof and are nailed about 12 in. apart. Roofs of this character, when laid with No. 28 gauge iron, cost, he says, very little more than the cheaper grades of tin and do not have to be painted. Some of them have been in satisfactory use for eight and twelve years. A name applied to this seam which, though somewhat long, describes it well, is half double standing seam.

TO MAKE A SPRING FASTENER FOR A LATHE POINTER

A feeler or pointer, used for setting up work on the lathe where the work has a hole through it by which it is to be trued up, is shown in the illustration. The spring S is made of a straight piece of wire with an eye turned on each end. This spring is sprung around an arbor, A, and a pointer, P, is passed through the eyes of the spring and over the arbor. The tension is sufficient to hold the pointer in place.

When the arbor is rotated by hand, it carries the pointer around with it to test the accuracy of the setting. This device, says a correspondent of Machinery, is of the most service for heavy and awkward

Spring Fastener for a Lathe Pointer

shaped pieces, as they can be set and fastened without starting the lathe. For setting on the lathe carriage cylinders, bushings, etc., that are to be bored with a boring bar, it is handy also. For small holes in work, use a very light arbor, with a short spring and pointer. For setting to the outside of a hub, bend the end of the pointer hoop-shaped.

PLUMBERS' CEMENT

A good plumbers' cement consists of 1 part black rosin, melted, and 2 parts of brickdust, thoroughly powdered and dried

MYSTERY OF BOILER EXPLOSIONS EXPLAINED

The "Lap-Joint Crack" is the Greatly Dreaded and Unseen Danger

A locomotive standing idly on the track or hauling a train, in apparently a perfectly normal condition, explodes without warning; a great factory is busy with hundreds of operatives at work, when suddenly the structure is torn asunder and the air is filled with the cries of the injured and groans of the dying. Both disasters were wholly unexpected. Usually the engineer and fireman are among the dead, and too often blamed by an unthinking public for carelessness, when in fact they were wholly innocent.

Brockton Lap-Joint Explosion--Boiler Was Hurled 215 Ft. and Moved House 16 In.

The explanation of a very large proportion of these accidents lies in the "Lap-Joint Crack"—an insidious, unseen danger, which cannot be found save by tearing a boiler to pieces, and which may exist for years without giving the slightest warning.

The expert of a well-known boiler inspection company, in the Locomotive, goes into details of this danger, from which the following is condensed or quoted:

A "lap-joint crack," as the name implies, is a crack in a boiler plate, which follows the general course of the longitudinal lap-riveted joints by which the plates of the boiler are held together. Any kind of a crack possessing this peculiarity of position would, strictly speaking, be a "lap-joint crack;" but the name is usually applied to one particular kind of defect, which is illustrated in Figs. 1 and 2. The main thing to observe in connection with Figs. 1 and 2 is that the crack, although it may occur in either the inner or the outer plate

of the boiler, always starts from the face of the affected plate which is in contact with the overlapping plate, progressing into the metal more and more deeply until the boiler is weakened perhaps to the point of explosion; and being itself so situated that it cannot be seen from either the inside or the outside of the boiler. It is this peculiarity of position which makes the defect so dangerous, the strength of the plate being sometimes greatly reduced before there is any external, visible evidence that the crack exists at all.

One of the most unfortunate things about these hidden cracks is that they show a marked tendency to extend nearly through the affected plate for a considerable distance along the joint, without actually perforating it anywhere. Fig. 3 illustrates a well-marked case of this sort. The piece of plate which it represents was cut out of a boiler that was affected by a lap-joint crack. The crack, in this instance, did not actually perforate the plate at any point, but it extended so nearly through it that the specimen here shown was bent over by hand. The position of the edge of the overlapping plate is indicated, in this engraving, by the dotted line.

The two main causes of lap-joint cracks are the treatment the plates receive during manufacture, and the action to which the boiler is subject on account of steam pressure.

First, as to the processes of manufacture and their effects. In rolling plates into the cylindrical form, preparatory to riveting them up into shells, the rolls do not "grip" the plate as effectively near the end of the operation as they do in the middle of it; for the last end has a tendency to slip off the first roll, and spring back so as to be flatter than the desired radius would require. If the plate were solid, and had no rivet holes in it, the resulting cylinder would look something like Fig. 4, one end of the shell "standing off" from the general curve, as represented. If, on the other hand, there are one or more rows of rivet holes along the edges of the plate that is being rolled, it may easily happen that the plate takes a sharper bend along one or more of these rows of holes, owing to the weakening of the plate at these points,

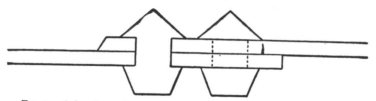

FIG. 1. — A LAP-JOINT CRACK UNDER THE OUTER EDGE OF THE RIVET HEADS.

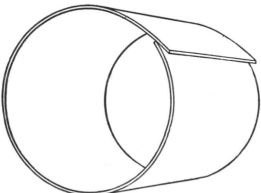

FIG. 4. — ILLUSTRATING THE "OFF-SET" OF THE LAP.

FIG. 3. — A PLATE ALMOST PERFORATED BY A LAP-JOINT CRACK.

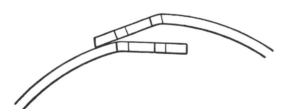

FIG. 5. — SHOWING THE ACTION OF THE ROLLS. (EXAGGERATED.)

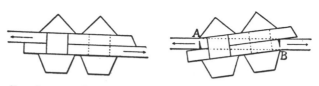

FIGS. 6 AND 7. — BEHAVIOR OF A LAP-RIVETED JOINT UNDER PRESSURE.

FIG. 2. — SECTION OF A BOILER PLATE WITH A LAP-JOINT CRACK.

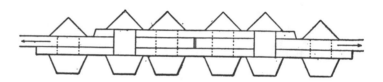

FIG. 8. — DOUBLE-STRAP BUTT JOINT

from the removal of the material in forming the holes. The ends of the plate, where they come together, may then present the aspect represented on a greatly exaggerated scale, in Fig. 5. Careless sledging produces stresses, often of considerable magnitude.

The steam stresses are shown in Figs. 6 and 7. Fig. 6 represents an ordinary double-riveted lap-joint, and it is to be observed that when the boiler is under steam, the tensions on the respective plates which are united by the rivets cannot possibly act in one and the same straight line. The plates do not abut against each other at the edges, but are laid one over the other, and the tensions to which the plates are subjected must be related to each other somewhat as indicated by arrows. It is evident, therefore, that there will be a tendency, in such a joint, for the rivets to "cock up" somewhat after the fashion shown in Fig. 7. The action will not be as violent as here represented, but the tendency will be for the joint to be deformed towards a position in which the two overlapping plates would come into one and the same straight line, as suggested by the dotted lines in Fig. 7. The parts of the plates which lie between the rivet shanks and under the rivet heads will be held firmly together by the rivets; and the bending action to which the plates are subjected will therefore be most severe immediately under the edges of the rivet heads, where it first becomes possible for the plates to bend to any perceptible extent. As the steam pressure in the boiler varies, the bending action upon the plates will also vary, and hence there will be a tendency, sooner or later, to form a crack in the plate, either at A in Fig. 7, or at B.

Inasmuch as the lap-joint crack appears only in lap joints, the use of butt joints, as shown in Fig. 8, is recommended as preventing the trouble. The use of the butt joint is increasing, but probably 85 per cent of all the boilers in use today in the United States still have lap joints and their manufacture continues.

IMPROVED DESK 'PHONE

The desk 'phone is often in a busy man's way and takes up too much space, also it is frequently knocked off with injurious effects to the instrument. An apprentice in our machine shop contrived the method

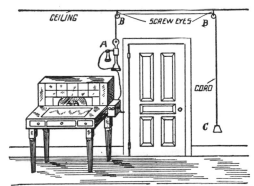

To Keep the Desk 'Phone Out of the Way

shown in the illustration for overcoming this difficulty. The device requires two pulleys, a cord, weight and two eye screws. The weight can be a shot bag of sand or shot of the same weight as the 'phone stand, A. The device has proved a great improvement over the old arrangement and is recommended to others.—Contributed by F. A. Grier, Jr., Salisbury, Md.

COMPOSITION OF BABBITT METAL FOR STREET CAR MOTOR BEARINGS

The following compositions are recommended by the Mechanical and Electrical Association:

The following babbitt metal composition makes a long-lived and tough metal, that will not pound out nor be too severe on the armature shaft: 100 lb. tin, 10 lb. copper, 10 lb. antimony.

We are using the following composition with good results: 83⅓ lb. tin, 8⅓ lb. antimony, 8⅓ lb. copper.

Our motor bearings have without rebabbitting an average mileage of 52,100, with an oil consumption costing $0.089 per 1,000 car-miles, the cars being equipped with two 125-h. p. motors.

A good composition of bearing metal for motor bearings is: 105 lb. copper, 60 or 55 lb. phosphor-bronze, 9¾ lb. tin, 25 lb. lead. Phosphor-bronze is composed of copper, 79.7, tin 10, lead 9.5 and phosphorus, 0.8 per cent.

10 parts tin to 1 part antimony.

Shop Notes, Volume II, for 1906, is a useful book for the mechanic. Price, 50 cents.

COIL HEATER MADE OF OLD CAR HEATERS

Old discarded street car heaters may be used to make a coil heater suitable for heating large barnlike structures, where doors are opened often and heating is ordinarily a problem. The kind of heater referred to is those made under Gold's patent of 1884.

Each section of the coil heater should con-

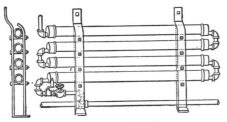

Heater for Large Building

sist of a length of 4-in. pipe capped at each end, and with a 1-in. opening tapped near the edge of each cap. Lay the section across a bench made of two barrels and some planks and assemble and connect them. Use short nipples and elbows for connections. Thread the middle nipple at each end, right and left-handed, and have left-handed threads in one of the elbows. Paint all outlets well with litharge. Fix the pitch by putting on wrought iron clamps, as shown in the illustration, when the parts are on the bench.

Make these clamps, says a correspondent of Power, of heavy ⅜-in. iron, with the back bar 1 ft. longer than the heater, and in a manner to serve as a foot and also to keep the heater free from the wall. Have the front bar shorter than the back one, and curve it at the top to hold the upper length of pipe in place. Offset the back bar at the top and bend it at the bottom as shown. Insert ½-in. bolts through the bars between each section of pipe and bolt the back bar to the wall.

Let the steam feed from overhead and put an air valve on the return line to insure circulation.

METAL FOR GONGS AND CYMBALS

A sonorous metal for cymbals, gongs and tam-tams consists of 100 parts copper with 25 parts tin. Ignite the piece after it is cast and plunge it into cold water immediately.

TO DO AWAY WITH SHIMS IN ENGINE BRASSES

In taking up the wear of engine brasses on wrist pin or crosshead pin when the key is driven clear down, back out the key and instead of putting in sheet-iron shims put in a small piece of pine wood of just the right thickness to allow the key to come even with the under side of the strap, then pour in melted babbitt. A hole must be drilled through the flange of the brasses to allow for pouring the babbitt.

Every engineer knows the trouble it is to put several shims between the brass box and the end of the strap, especially if the box is a round-end one, as many are. By using the method described, brasses may be worn up much closer, even if worn through; the babbitt will form part of the bearing. This kink is the idea of W. H. Nostrant, engineer, and will be found worth trying.—Contributed by F. A. Sustins, Stevens Point, Wis.

A CAN SHAFT OILER

To make a good shaft oiler, take a can that is opened at the top, turn the lid back and nail it to the beam. Stretch lengths of hemp packing from the can to each oil hole in the box and fill the can half full of oil. The can must be filled every two weeks.

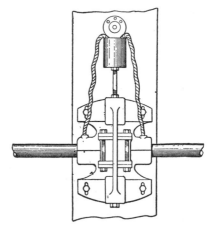

Shaft Oiler Made of a Can

This method is used by a correspondent of the Engineers' Review for oiling a line shaft 150 ft. long and a countershaft. It works successfully, and he goes over the shafting every two weeks, only; thus saving an hour's work every day.

Original Frieze, "Night"--By Percy Lancaster, London

SMOOTHING TABLE LEGS IN A TUMBLER

A good method of smoothing table legs in a tumbler is described by a correspondent of the Wood-Worker as follows:

I have a tumbler about 6 ft. long and 3 ft. in diameter, with a shaft 11/16 in. extending the entire length of it. On each end and bolted to the head is a cast iron flange 12 in. in diameter, with 3½-in. set screws in the hub of each to hold the tumbler to the shafts; bearings are close to the ends of tumbler. On one end and attached to the head is secured a rim of the necessary size to secure the proper speed, which is 36 revolutions per minute. The tumbler is filled about half full of legs, and a lot of scrap sandpaper is put in with the legs, and the whole falling about together allows the sandpaper to assist in cleaning the legs. Our legs are turned from reasonably good air-dried stock, and after turning are placed in the dry-kiln and allowed to stay two nights and a day before going to the tumbler. In this way the legs become good and dry on the outside, which aids in getting them clean in the tumbler. They are run about two and one-half hours, which in our case cleans the legs well. In this way about 1,000 center table legs may be smoothed per day.

HOW TO ESTIMATE CONTENTS OF CIRCULAR TANK

The capacity of a circular tank may be determined by multiplying the diameter in inches by itself and by .7854 and by the length (or depth) in inches, which gives the capacity of the tank in inches, and then dividing by 231, the number of cubic inches in a U. S. gallon.

Old coins may be cleansed by first immersing them in strong nitric acid and then washing them in clean water. Wipe them dry before putting away.

Original Frieze. "The Storm"--Decorator's Magazine. London

HOW TO TURN A HOLLOW BALL

As most machinists are familiar with the turning of a sphere by means of the compound rest, it will not be necessary to go into details. Assuming we have a ball 1 in. in diameter, and wish to bore out the inside so as to leave a shell 1-16 in. in thickness: A piece of hardwood is clamped in the chuck and the end turned out cup-shaped (Fig. 2, first cut) so it will extend a trifle over the center line of the ball. A little chalk rubbed into the wood will

ease. Now the gauge A is folded down and the carriage moved towards the ball until the line C-D is ¼ in. away from the nearest point of the ball and locked there, then the cross slide is moved to bring the center line of H in line with the lathe centers. If there is any difference between the diameter of the ball and the hole in the gauge plate A, allowance for such difference must be made in adjusting the tool rest. Now the carriage is backed, the gauge is raised on a level with B and the first tool in the shape of a flat drill inserted in the tool-

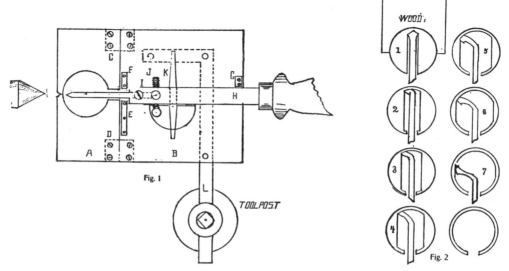

Fig. 1

TOOLPOST

WOOD

Fig. 2

help to hold the ball firmly in position. Now the tool rest (Fig. 1) is clamped in the tool post by an L-shaped piece of stock (L), riveted to the bottom, just high enough to allow the tool, when resting on the support, to come to the center line of the ball. The tool rest is made of two pieces of sheet metal, A and B, which are hinged together on the line CD, allowing A, which is only used as a gauge for setting the tool to be folded down. E, F, and G are guides for the tool holder, the former two also serving as stops. The tool holder, H, is made of ⅜ in. square stock, having a ⅛ in. hole in the end to insert the tools, which are held by means of a set-screw, I. Back of this is the guide screw, J, a piece of 3-16 in. stock is fastened to the end just long enough to reach down into the semi-circular aperture cut into B. K is a crosspiece fastened to the bottom of H to insure a wide bearing on the tool rest. To adjust the tool rest in position we measure the distance between the aperture cut in A and the line C-D, say ¼ in. in this

holder in such manner that when the tool-holder is up against the stops E-F-G the point of the drill will be 1-16 in. away from the edge of the hole (Fig. 1). Turning the gauge plate down the carriage is again moved up to the stop and locked there, the ball having been previously centered, we now take the first cut with the tool up to the stop. The chips may be removed by blowing into the hole with a blowpipe. Back up the carriage again and turn up the gauge plate and insert the second tool and turn the guide screw J to such position that both cutting edges of the tool will be 1-16 in. away from the edge of the hole in the gauge at either end. Once more the gauge is folded down, the carriage moved up to the stop and we take the second cut. In each of the subsequent cuts another tool must be inserted, shaped to fit that part of the circle to be cut away, and the guide screw J must be adjusted to the length of the cut.—Contributed by Wm. Lachmich, Chicago

MUFFIN PANS FOR SCREW CABINETS

Tinned muffin pans make satisfactory drawers for cabinets to hold screws, brads, staples, etc. Procure the required number of pans (they cost about 10 cents each), nail a couple of strips on each side of them, provide the cabinet frame with suitable ways and the arrangement is complete and ideal. This is an idea of a correspondent of Wood Craft.

DEVICE FOR LINING SHAFTING

A convenient instrument for lining shafting, described by a correspondent of the American Machinist, operates as follows:

Referring to the sketch, a b is the line to which the shaft ought to be parallel horizontally; a square, c, slides in the slit of the head d, and may be clamped by the screw e to this head; a level, f, is put at a convenient place on the longer edge of the square.

After first securing the line a b so that its two ends are at the same horizontal distance from the ends of the shaft to be lined, put the head d on one end of the shaft and slide the square in the slit of the head until its vertical edge is about 1/16 in. or so from the line a b, while by the level f keeping the longer edge of the square horizontal. Then by the screw, e, clamp the square to the head and proceed along the shaft, putting the head d on the shaft and leveling the square to see whether the line a b be just at the same distance from the vertical edge of the square as when the latter was adjusted at the end of the shaft.

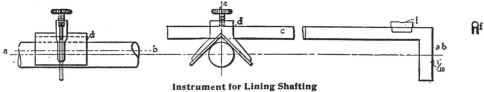

Instrument for Lining Shafting

By this method it is not necessary to know the varying diameter of the shaft, and no scale or graduation is wanted.

SEALING WAX RECIPES

To make black sealing wax use 5 parts shellac, 9 turpentine, 6½ pine resin, 4 chalk and 1¼ soot. For blue, use 7 parts shellac, 6 turpentine, 3½ pine resin, 1 magnesia, 2 chalk, 2 blue coloring matter.

SINGLE ECCENTRIC REVERSING GEAR

A single eccentric reversing gear, simple in action and efficient, is described in the Model Engineer, London.

Figure 1 is a front elevation of sheave and crankshaft; B is a disc, or cam, bored and turned diagonally as shown, and is

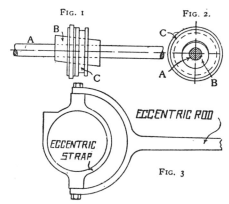

Simple Reversing Gear

keyed on shaft A, the throw at either end being equal to the travel of valve. C is a loose sheave and lever-clutch, which works on a feather-key let in B, and is operated by a forked lever, which is fitted with a pawl, and works in a quadrant placed horizontally, so that when moving the lever from right to left, or vice versa, it would operate the sheave and clutch, and thus reverse the valve from full forward to full backward or cut-off at any point of the stroke by simply notching up, as in link-motion.

Figure 2 is an end view of shaft and sheave, and Fig. 3 shows the eccentric strap with forked rod, in order to accommodate itself when thrown out of center line with valve spindle.

This attachment was fitted to a portable engine used for winding purposes at a small colliery.

Popular Mechanics life subscriptions at $10; five years for $3.

HOW TO MAKE A DOG OR GRAB

A dog or grab, easily made and without a weld, requires a piece of iron 4 in. wide, ½ in. thick and 7 in. long which is enough for one pair. Split the iron with a hot

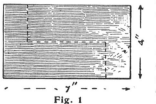

Fig. 1

chisel, as indicated in Fig. 1. Sharpen the bit, place the dog, back down, on the anvil and beat down until it is in the shape shown in Fig. 2. Punch a hole at A, Fig. 2, and round up the eye on the anvil horn so it will work easily in the link. The finished dog will look like Fig. 3. The point

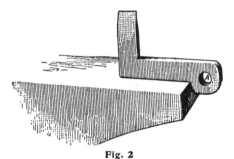

Fig. 2

should set in toward the eye ¾ in., so it will draw when driven into the log, says a correspondent of the Blacksmith and Wheel-

Fig. 3

wright. The dotted lines in Fig. 3 show how to set the point.

SUBSTITUTE FOR WIRELESS COHERER

In experimenting with wireless telegraphy, writes Everett R. Hough of Johnstown, N. Y., I have found that an ordinary telephone transmitter will answer in place of the coherer, if one of the latter is not at hand. The decoherer hammer can be arranged to strike the transmitter and so jar the carbon particles apart after they have once cohered. It works very well, and is much better for a beginner to use than are many of the home-made coherers I have seen.

CEMENTS FOR IRON

To make a good cement for iron on iron, make a thick paste, with water, of powdered iron, 60 parts; sal-ammoniac, 2 parts, and sulphur flowers, 1 part. Use while fresh.

Another consists of sulphur flowers, 6 parts; dry white lead, 6 parts, and powdered borax, 1 part. Mix by sifting and keep as a dry powder in a closed tin box. To use, make into a thin paste with strong sulphuric acid and press together immediately. This cement will harden in five days. Recommended by the American Machinist.

REMOVING STRAINS IN METAL BY HEATING

In making springs of piano wire, or, in fact any wire, if the metal is heated to a moderate degree the spring will be improved. Piano or any steel wire should be heated to a blue, brass wire to a degree sufficient to cause tallow to smoke. Heating makes the metal homogeneous; before heating it is full of strains.

If a piece of metal of any kind is straightened cold and then put into a lathe and a chip turned off, it will be far from true. Before turning it was held true by the strain of the particles on the outside, they having changed position, while the particles near the axis are only sprung. The outside particles being removed by the lathe tool, the sprung particles at the center, return to their old positions. If, after straightening, the metal is heated to a temperature of 400 deg. the particles settle together and strains are removed.

This is the case in the manufacture of saws. The saw is first hardened and tempered and then straightened on an anvil by means of a hammer. After it is hammered true, it is ground and polished a little, then blued to stiffen it and then is subjected to the grinding process. Before bluing the metal is full of strains; these are entirely removed by the heat required to produce the blue color.

Often a piano wire spring will not stand if used without heating, while if heated it will last for years.—Contributed by J. H. Beebee, Rochester, N. Y.

SHOP NOTES

HAMMER MADE OF PIPE

A very handy hammer can be made for little or nothing, provided one has a few old materials on hand.

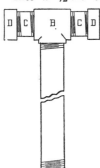

Into a ½-in. tee (B) screw a piece of ½-in. pipe (A) about 8 in. long with threads on one end and two pieces of ½-in. pipe (CC) 2½-in. long with threads on both ends. On the ends DD put ½-in. caps.

A larger hammer can be made by using pipe of larger dimensions, and the hammer can be made heavier by stopping up the tee and filling the head with lead.—Contributed by H. G. Stiebel, Jr., 3207A Olive street, St. Louis, Mo.

A HOME=MADE TRIP-HAMMER

A trip-hammer like the one shown in the illustration was used for eleven years, turning horseshoes, laying plowshares and other work without a break, says a correspondent of the Blacksmith and Wheelwright. A good sapling with considerable spring in it is secured in the wall to make the spring and the striking hammer is of 16 or 18 lb. It is operated by foot-power. One man and his helper can rig the device up in one day.

Foot-Power Trip=Hammer

GLUE=MELTING DEVICE

A handy device for melting glue is made as follows:

Tap a hole at one side in the top of an ordinary glue pot and put in a piece of ⅜-in. pipe about 4 in. long. At the opposite side drill a hole and tap it out for a ¼-in. nipple. In case it be desired to use the pot in any other way, a plug may be substituted for this nipple, says a correspondent of Power. All that is necessary to heat the

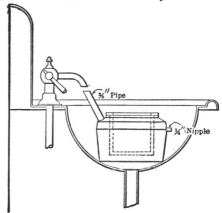

For Melting Glue

glue is to set the pot in the wash basin and turn the hot water into the ⅜-in. pipe. The hot water supply in many plants comes from the feed-water heater, which is an excellent arrangement. This is a neat and speedy method of getting hot glue.

TO REMOVE CAN COVERS

To remove a tight fitting screw cover to a can rub a little chalk on the top and wrap a piece of sandpaper around the cover with the sand side next the can. The top can then be removed without trouble.—Contributed by J. C. Fox, Sabetha, Kan.

Linseed oil and benzine, half and half, with burnt umber or Vandyke brown incorporated with the mixture, makes a good brown stain for oak or ash. Apply in the usual manner and finish as desired.

AIR SUPPLY FOR PYROGRAPHIC OUTFITS

Some time ago I purchased a wood-burning outfit such as are on the market for scorching fancy designs on wood. The outfit consists of a small bottle for benzine, a squeezing bulb for supplying air at a low pressure and a needle with a hollow platinum point, this needle is kept red hot by means of the mixture of air and the fumes from the benzine.

After using the outfit for a short time I hit upon the following arrangement for giving a steady supply of air and at a higher pressure, and so doing away with the hand bulb, leaving both hands free to hold the work and apply the needle.

The engraving shows two 30 gallon tanks,

Tank Arrangement for Air Supply

the kind ordinarily used for hot water heating. They need not be new as they are costly. They can usually be had at any plumbing shop second-hand. I paid 50 cents apiece for mine and had any leaks soldered tight.

These tanks, as will be seen by the illustration, are connected across the top by ¼-in. pipe with ¼-in. globe valves on each one and the pressure gauge placed in the middle, thus making one gauge show the pressure on either tank, independently, or on both of them.

At the rear of the right hand tank a connection is made by means of a piece of hose to the city water supply, being controlled by a ¾-in. globe valve; at the front end will be seen a ½-in. check valve, while above it is a bushing and plug to stop up the opening as this hole is not required. At the bottom of the tank is placed a ¾-in. globe valve to drain off the water.

At the rear end of the left hand tank will

be seen a length of ¼-in. pipe which is carried around on to the front porch where it terminates with a ⅛-in. globe valve and a short nipple for attaching the rubber tube and needle, the benzine bottle, of course, being connected in between the valve and needle.

The method of obtaining a supply of air is to allow the water to run into the right hand tank, the valve at the left of the gauge being closed. The water is allowed to run in until the gauge shows the pressure of the water main, in this case about 55 lbs. The resulting supply of compressed air is then admitted to the other tank, the water supply is cut off and the water drained away, being assisted by a slight pressure of air still left in the tank and then by means of the check valve which opens up, admitting air to the tank.

It will of course be understood that only enough air will pass over to the air tank to make the pressure equal in both of them. In this case, the first charge nets me a supply at 10 lbs. pressure; by repeating the process five times more I get a supply at about 40 lbs. which is the limit with the pressure available.

The waste water I use to irrigate the flower beds; the tank when charged at 40 lbs. will last for three or four days, as the supply required in burning is very small.—Contributed by Everett E. Pomeroy, Los Gatos, Cal.

HARNESS HOOKS OF OLD BUGGY STEPS

Old buggy steps make good harness hooks, much stronger than the harness hooks one gets at the stores, writes Henry J. Heaton,

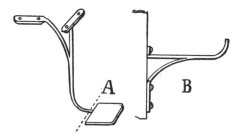

Strong Harness Hooks

of Sidney, Iowa. Cut off the step at the dotted line, A, and nail the hooked part up as shown at B.

"Mechanics for Young America," an interesting book for boys. Price, 25 cents.

HOW TO MAKE A PARALLEL CLAMP

A handy tool-maker's clamp which is self-contained and does not need a wrench is described by a correspondent of the American Machinist. The jaw A is counterbored for screws C and D—the latter a running fit, the former a driving—secured by the steady pins, G and H. The jaw B is recessed, bored and counterbored for the tapered nut F and a rather loose fit for the screw, D.

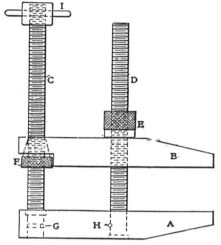

Tool-Maker's Parallel Clamp

In operation, adjust both the knurled nuts to your work and tighten up by the handle, I, and the screw, C. The tapered nut, F, grips the jaw, B, firmly without further aid while tightening by the handle. Both knurled nuts are slightly smaller than the jaws of the clamp, which lies flat with the work. All parts are drawn to scale.

MAKING A WRENCH

It is just as important that a wrench should be balanced as that a hammer should be. In making an S-wrench, do not give it too much hook, as you can not handle it so fast. The illustrations show how to make a tire-bolt wrench, called a side wrench. It is made of a piece of spring plate 1¾ in. by 6 in. Parts C and D are worked over the hardy, having care not to punch the holes at these points too far back. H indicates holes punched in material to be cut away. Part A, Fig. 1, should be beveled from the center and made as wide as the material will allow. B, Fig. 2, shows the pointed jaw

and how it is beveled on the handle. This wrench will work in places that other

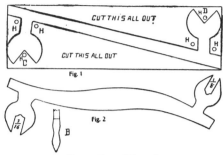

Home-Made Wrench

wrenches will not.—Contributed by James N. Keach, 803 Clay street, Bloomington, Ill.

TO REMOVE PACKING FROM A FLANGE JOINT

When the pipe can be sprung apart far enough to allow a scraper to work between the two flange faces, it is easy enough to remove old packing from flange joints, but often this is impossible. A correspondent of the Engineers' Review had a pipe running from a head which was anchored solid across the room and running down along the wall as shown in the illustration. When the flange connection in this pipe began to leak, he drove a cold chisel in at the bottom between the flanges to keep them from

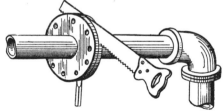

Sawing Out Gaskets

springing together, then sawed out the packing with an old hand saw. When he had sawed half way through, a chisel was driven in from the top and the rest of the gasket cleaned out. A new gasket was then inserted and the flange bolted together.

Red lead and glycerin, equal parts, kneaded to the consistency of putty is said to make an excellent cement for iron on iron. Mix fresh as needed and use quickly.

Index to Vol. VII, January to December, inclusive, 1905, is ready for distribution and will be sent free upon request.

TOOL FOR MAKING WIRE SPRINGS WITH A BRACE

Get a hardwood board (A) about 12 in. long, 6 in. wide and ⅞ in thick. At one corner bore a hole (a, Fig. 2) of the size that the inside diameter of the spring is to be. Set two flathead screws (a^1 and a^2) in the board in the positions in relation to the hole indicated in Fig. 2. At the opposite end of the board, near the upper cor-

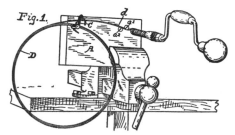

Making Wire Springs

ner, place a hook (C, Fig. 1) to receive the reel of wire (D) of which the springs are to be made. Then fasten the board in a vise or other convenient place.

Secure a rod (B) the size of the hole and 12 to 18 in. long (sufficiently long to make the length of spring desired, or several springs may be made in one coil and then cut to length). Fasten one end of the rod and one end of the wire (d) in the chuck of the brace (see Fig. 3), hooking the wire under screw head a^1 and over a^2 and hanging reel D on hook C. Proceed to turn

HOW TO ATTACH ENAMEL LETTERS TO GLASS

Not all sign painters know how to attach enamel letters, though it is a simple matter when once learned. Clean the glass and draw the lines of the lettering with chalk. If it is to be a curve use a string in the usual way. Space the lines off and you are ready for the lettering.

For this purpose a reliable cement will be required. Plaster the cement on the letters with a knife, being careful to have the part around the edge full, then place each letter in turn on the glass and press it up and down gently and firmly to get all the air out, then push to place. Be very careful not to bend the letters, says the Master Painter. Give large letters a second coat before putting them in place. It is only necessary to fill the edges of concave letters with cement; the flat letters must be pasted all over the back. Hold large letters in place, until the cement has time to set, by a bit of wax. When the cement has set remove any that may be around the edges of the letters and clean up the glass.

White lead in oil, thickened with dry lead, thinned properly with copal varnish and worked well on the stone with a spatula or elastic blade putty knife, makes a good cement.

A pocket knife and wood alcohol will remove old letters. They nearly always break, and the enterprising painter will always have a number on hand for supplying the need, at a neat profit to himself.

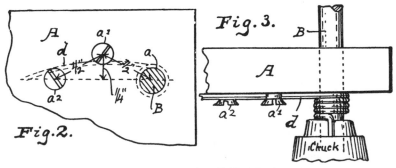

Details of the Spring-Making Device

the brace handle the same as in boring a hole, slightly pressing against board A and backing the brace out as the wire is wound on rod B. Continue this operation until the desired amount of spring is wound on the rod.—Contributed by Chas. N. Leonard, 1319 Barth avenue, Indianapolis, Ind.

REPAIRING A LEAKY GUTTER

To repair a leaky gutter, put putty in the hole, smooth it off with a putty knife and paint over the spot with a mineral or an oil paint.—Contributed by Gordon M. Backus, 32 Euclid avenue, Hackensack, N. J.

HOW A THREE=WIRE SPLICE IS MADE

Two pairs of connectors are required to properly make a three-wire splice in order to have, the joints long in the "neck" and

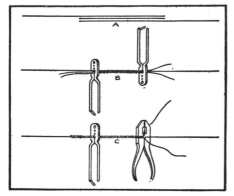

Making a Three=Wire Splice

not mar the galvanizing at that part of the joint. In iron line construction the skilfully made three-wire splice will eliminate the necessity for soldering, says the American Telephone Journal, and insure freedom from high resistance joints. The superior conductivity of these joints consists not in the cross turns at the ends, but in the spiral twist at the neck. To make the splice proceed as follows:

Overlap the ends to be spliced about 18 in. and cut a third wire 18 in. long of same gauge and lay it with the ends to be spliced (Fig. a). Clamp two pairs of connectors over all towards the center and about 5 in. apart and revolve connectors in opposite directions, slowly, so as not to "burn" the wire (Fig. b). Care should be taken to revolve connectors evenly and at the same speed. Turning one pair faster than the other will result in a "humped" joint. When the wires have been twisted to a tight lay, remove the connectors and clamping one pair on the neck to hold the work, use pliers and finish the end with six or seven cross turns the same as in an ordinary W. U. splice (Fig. c).

CLEANING WINDOW GLASS

To thoroughly clean window glass pass diluted sulphuric acid, about as strong as vinegar, over it, and let it act a moment; then throw on just enough pulverized whiting to give off a hissing sound, directs the Master Painter. Rub both over the pane with the hand and polish with a dry rag.

Rinse with clean water and a little alcohol, polish dry and clean. Treat both sides of the glass in the same way.

THE READY=MADE LATHE TOOL

Old mechanics looking back over their history as such can remember the days before the patent lathe tools. In those days they were obliged to forge their own tools into the desired shape. Modern improved tools can be ground to any desired shape and used in most any position, their use, however, requires a certain amount of judgment.

Figure 1 shows the effects on a small tool used for too heavy duty. This tool was made for a 12- or 15-in. lathe, but was used in a 30-in. lathe. The bottom at A is worn away until the pressure of the screw breaks the steel.

Figure 2 shows the effect of grinding without removing the steel. The under support is completely ground away at B. Figure 3 shows a cutting-off tool allowed to hog in and break, battering down the support, C. Figure 4 shows the effect on a small tool which was used in a large lathe. The powerful screw mashed the tool at D.

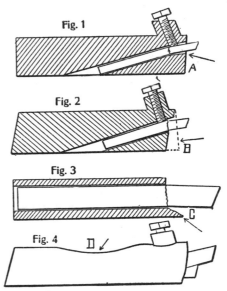

I recently looked over a number of patent tools of different makes. They had been used about one year and were a sad looking pile of junk. A lack of good judgment had sent them to the scrap heap.—Contributed by **Paul S. Baker**, Muscatine, Ia.

CONTINUOUS MIXING OF CONCRETE

[Extract from a paper by E. N. Trump, read before the American Society of Mechanical Engineers.]

Of the methods mentioned the revolving table, with a stationary spout above its center, has been considered the most accurate, and is much used in cement manufacture for feeding mills, etc. Its defect is the change in the natural slope of the material, which varies the amount cut off by the diverting blade as indicated by dotted lines in Fig. 1.

If we make the table of relatively large size and distribute the material in a uniform

storage cylinder, somewhat smaller in diameter, with its lower edge spaced a distance above the table sufficient to clear the knife and yet near enough to the table so that the material flows out from under the edge of the cylinder and takes its natural slope, we shall have the condition represented by Fig. 3.

The cylinder being supported by arms from the central spindle may be filled to the top by means of the chute, and as the knife removes the section represented by its path over the table, the material from the cylinder above will take the place left vacant, and will come out under the edge of the cylinder to the extent of its natural slope. While this slope may vary a little

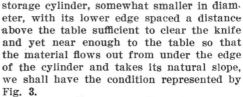

Fig. 1

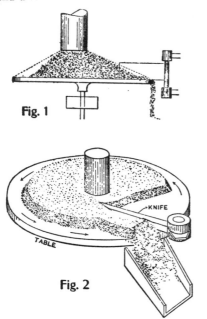

Fig. 2

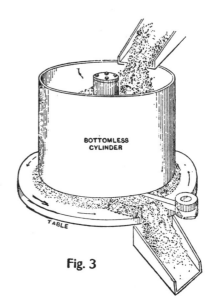

Fig. 3

layer upon it, as shown in Fig. 2, the stationary knife, or diverting blade, may be pivoted so as to take off a predetermined quantity in one revolution, and if the layer is thin, variations in the natural slope on the edge will affect the accuracy very little. As the table revolves the stationary knife will divert the material in front of it over the edge of the table and it will fall in a continuous stream into the chute. If the material is replenished on the table so that the layer taken off by the knife is restored to exactly the same shape as before, and is continuously removed by the knife, an accurately measured quantity will be diverted.

By adding to the table a bottomless

this variation is a very small part of the amount diverted by the knife, and as the material composing nearly the whole base of the cylinder is cut away the space behind the knife is filled from above with nearly uniform pressure, and in practice the natural slope angle is almost exactly the same, in spite of considerable differences in height and material within the cylinder.

After deciding on the distance between the bottom of the cylinder and the table, and the width of the knife, the other factors, which determine the amount of material measured off in a given time, are the speed and rotation and the depth of the cut of the knife, and these are both adjustable.

The depth of cut of the knife is adjusted by swinging the knife around on its pivot so that it extends a greater or less

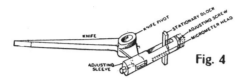

Fig. 4

distance into the material. This swing is controlled by a screw attached to an arm, cast as part of the knife, and a micrometer scale with pointer shows the amount of movement. This is shown in Fig. 4.

The mechanism described above may be employed for the feeding of a great variety of materials, varying considerably in size and consistency, and if the size of the table, the shape of the cylinder and the size of the knife and space between the cylinder and the table are properly adjusted, almost any kind of crushed material may be fed.

The variations in size may extend from fine powders, like cement, to rocks of 6 in. cube. In the case of the larger sizes the

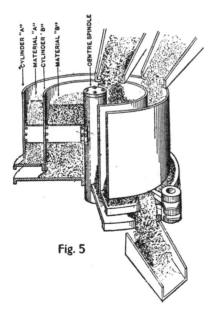

Fig. 5

space between the bottom of the cylinder and the table is made considerably higher than the height of the knife, as the space between the bottom of the cylinder and the top of the knife must be sufficient to let the largest pieces pass through without catching. The amount diverted by the

knife is not dependent upon its height, but on the height of the space under the cylinder.

LEVELING TWO POINTS WITHOUT TOOLS

To level up two or more points which are far apart, as posts, etc., without a level, straightedge or square, all that is required is a few nails, three pieces of old board, a

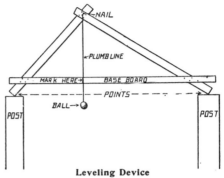

Leveling Device

piece of cord and a small weight, to be used as a plumb bob. Nail the boards together as shown in the illustration at any angle, place the two points of the boards on top of the posts and mark where the line crosses the baseboard. Turn the device about, end for end, and mark the baseboard again. Then raise or lower one of the posts until the plumb line hangs midway between the two marked lines and the posts will be level.—Contributed by Thos. McIntyre, 407 Root street, Chicago, Ill.

COUPLING A TANK-HOSE

Every engineer knows what a moist job it is to couple up a tank-hose after disconnecting it for the purpose of cleaning the strainer, says Locomotive Engineering. Very few tank valves will shut down perfectly tight; and the leakage, when attempting to connect the hose, is not appreciated by the man who is doing the coupling. Here is a simple remedy: When all ready to couple the hose, start the primer of the injector, when all of the leakage will be drawn into the suction pipe by the strong vacuum so created.

Contributions to the Shop Notes department are invited. Your experience and handy devices are valuable to others, also. Pass it on.

LAST RESORT REMEDY FOR A LEAKY VALVE

When every other remedy for a leaky inlet or exhaust valve has failed, try this:

Chuck the stem of the valve in a high-speed lathe, and with as fine a flat file as

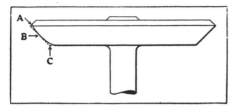

Repairing a Leaky Valve

can be obtained, while the valve is revolving in the lathe at a high rate of speed, touch lightly at A (See sketch), skip B and take off the corner C, leaving the valve with a slightly rounded instead of a flat seating surface. It has been found that this method is sure when others fail, says Motor Way, and that a valve so dressed will hold well for months afterward. It does not matter which way the stem wabbles, for the valve always finds a perfect seat, on account of its spherical shape, the action being similar to that of a ball check valve.

HANDY MARKING CHISEL

A marking chisel is a convenient tool about the engine room. One of the instances in which it can be used to advantage is in marking the eccentric so that it can be readily reset should it slip on the engine shaft.

It is often difficult to mark the eccentric and the shaft so that the lines come exactly opposite. With the tool illustrated this is

Chisel for Marking

made easy, says a correspondent of the Engineers' Review. The cutting edge is made as shown and not at right angles with the side. The point strikes first and makes a true mark on the eccentric hub. By turning the chisel in the opposite direction a mark is made on the engine shaft.

A freshly painted room should not be closed up tight, but opened to the air and light. Paint with driers in it will not dry if corked up tight in a bottle.

KEEPING SOLUTIONS IN BOTTLES

It is well known that solutions of easily oxidized substances do not keep so well in bottles which are partially empty as when they are full and The Photogram suggests the following as an excellent method of overcoming the difficulty. Keep on hand a quantity of small glass marbles, and whenever any of the solution is poured from the bottle add sufficient to bring the solution again up to the neck.

NOTES ON SOLDERING

I had not been long out of college when I was first sent out as a road engineer, so it was not to be expected that I would know very much. In those days, I even throught that a soldering iron was made of iron, writes a contributor in the Electric Journal.

When I first used a soldering iron on wire joints, I held a dry iron under a joint and waited for the wire to heat enough to melt the solder placed upon it. After floundering around at that awhile and making a bad job of it, I began to remember how I had seen others do it, and then I placed some solder on the iron and held the iron with the molten solder against the joint, which soon began to sizzle, and as it was clean and well fluxed, the solder flowed at once all through and over it.

In college, I had taken a course in physics under Professor N. and had heard all about conduction, convection and other things concerning heat, and also knew that copper is a good conductor of heat. But it did not occur to me, in the present instance that those principles had anything to do with the work in hand. After I had mastered the job, I began to see their connection with it.

A soldering iron, when in use, may be considered a reservoir of heat and the object in view is to get as much of the heat as possible into the wire. When the iron is held against the joint it touches only the high spots and there is a thin film of air between, no matter how smooth the surfaces may be. This air is a very good heat insulator, though when solder is run into this space, it unites with both iron and wire and acts as a bridge over which by the principle of conduction heat flows rapidly into the wire from the reservoir.

Clean and hot are the two essentials. One trouble with some novices is that they only half appreciate that statement and seem to have an idea that the solder is the only thing requiring heat, whereas all surfaces to be joined must be brought to the temperature of molten solder before union can take place. This mistaken idea does not lead to much difficulty when the work is confined to joining small wires, for in that case, a small quantity of molten solder contains sufficient heat to quickly raise all parts of the joint to the required temperature. But when large wires or any bulky pieces of metal are to be soldered, this idea leads to trouble.

BRASS-MELTING FURNACE

A good furnace for melting brass is built with a cylindrical fire space, lined with fire brick set in clay and provided with a grate that can be dumped, says the Blacksmith and Wheelwright. The chimney is of sufficient height to insure a good draft and is

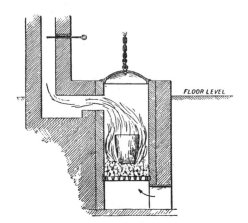

Furnace for Melting Brass

supplied with a damper to regulate the draft. Dome-shaped cast iron covers are used for the tops of the furnace and these may be raised or lowered by means of a chain passing over a pulley. The furnace may be built below the surface of the floor or ground, with a pit for removing the ashes and supplying draft, or entirely above the ground. In the latter case steps and a platform must be used to reach the crucible in which the metal is melted.

A very small furnace may be built of heavy sheet iron, shaped like a cylinder stove and lined with fire brick. Coke or coal that will burn without smoke may be used for fuel.

HOLDER FOR SOLDERING-IRON ON GASOLINE TORCH

Many gasoline torches are not fitted with a holder for soldering irons. To such torches this convenience can be attached in the shop. The illustration, from Power,

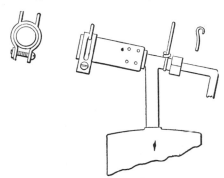

Home-Made Soldering-Iron Holder

shows how this is done. An old hose-clamp, taken from ¾-in. garden hose and two pieces of wire are the materials used.

SAW FOR MILLING GERMAN SILVER

German silver in almost any form is very hard to work, but the cutter shown in the illustration will cut it satisfactorily and outwear the ordinary cutter, says a correspondent of the American Machinist. An

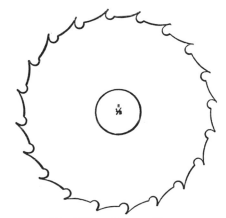

For Milling German Silver

ordinary stock cutter is used and every other tooth is ground down. The grooves are made with a narrow wheel with the periphery made round. One of these saws has cut over 2,000 pieces and is still sharp.

TESTING A CLOSED WINDING WITHOUT DISCONNECTING

A convenient device for testing a closed winding without disconnecting the winding from the commutator consists of three dry battery cells, a buzzer for interrupting the current and a telephone receiver.

To locate a short circuit, says the Electric Journal, pass the interrupted current

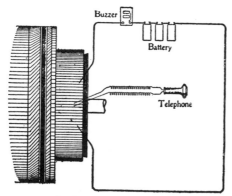

To Test a Closed Winding

from this apparatus through the winding (see sketch) and move the leads from the receiver from bar to bar on the commutator. There will be no audible vibration in the receiver if there is a short circuit between the bars of the commutator or winding; if these, however, are clear of short circuit at the point tested there will be a distinct vibration or buzzing. The vibration will be more distinct if an alternating circuit of 200 or 100 volts is handy and after attaching the leads of this circuit to almost any part of the commutator of the armature to be tested, the same method as before is followed.

CRIMSON TONES FOR SILVER PRINTS

Silver prints may be toned to a crimson or carmine color by the following process: Make a bath by dissolving 75 gr. ammonium sulphocyanide with 20 gr. iodide of potassium in 3 oz. water. Add 4 gr. gold chloride dissolved in a little water, making up as much of the bath as necessary for immediate use. Carry the printing only to the depth required when finished, then wash the prints well and immerse them in the toning solution. After which fix, wash and dry them. Let them remain in the fixing bath not less than fifteen minutes, says the

journal of the Photographic Society of India. The bath described above will produce pictures of a bright crimson by toning from a half to three-quarters of an hour.

TO MELT OLD LEAD PIPE

Having occasion to melt up a lot of old lead pipe I prepared the device illustrated.

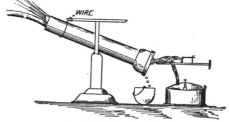

Lead-Melting Device

It consists of a boiler stand, a piece of 3-in. soil pipe about 2 ft. long and a firepot of the type shown with the burner reversed. The dross and most of the dirt are burned up in the pipe, only clear lead dropping out. It is surprising how fast lead pipe will melt in this way.—Contributed by R. Stanton, Portland, Ore.

A PIPE-THREADING KINK

Often when threading pipe with a solid die from 1 inch down, it requires considerable muscular exertion with the ordinary small stock. To save strength, make a square of wood to fit any larger stock with larger handles, or have the piece made of iron if preferred. Use the proper bushings and it will work to perfection.—Contributed by H. B. Heineman, Sheboygan, Wis.

HOISTING WITH AN AUTO

An auto which is used for passengers on Sundays and as a hoisting machine on other days, is described by a correspondent in the Automobile. He says:

The machine is a steamer with a cylindrical gasoline fired boiler and an ordinary double cylinder link motion engine developing about 4 hp. The windless attachment is carried on a special frame which is firmly clamped to the rear axle and driven by the sprocket chain which for the time being is removed from the driving sprocket of the car. The gear on the windlass gives a reduction of about 70 to 1 from the driving sprocket to the carved spool for the hoisting rope. I use the rig chiefly for installing elevators. The windlass is jacked down from the elevator entrance, or it may be fastened in any convenient place to withstand the strain. The tackle I use is about 800 ft. of 1¼-in. manila rope with a three-sheave 10-in. pulley block and a two-sheave 10-in. block, giving a leverage of 5 to 1. We generally run the engine with a boiler pressure of 50 lbs. per square inch. The boiler is tested to 300 lbs. The boiler

SUBSTITUTE FOR A TWO-THROW CRANKSHAFT

A substitute for a two-throw crankshaft which costs about 50 cents is shown in the illustration. The shaft costs about 40 cents and the floor flanges 10 cents, and the device takes the place of a crankshaft 1 in. in diameter with two cranks in center of shaft which would cost not less than $5. The outfit need not be made double and a

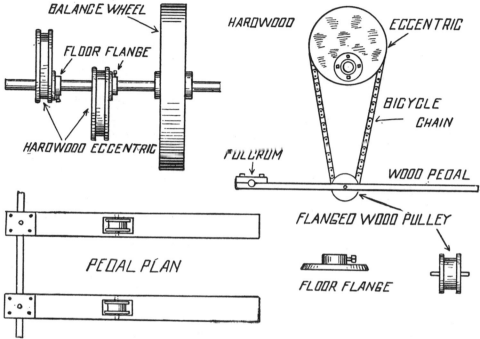

Substitute for a Two-Throw Crankshaft

is fired with gasoline, and one man operates the entire affair.

With this auto hoist we have lifted 5,000 lbs. 100 feet in forty minutes. In a recent installation of elevators at the John Deere Plow Works here, we lifted all the parts of two freight elevators—one a freight elevator of 5,000 lbs. capacity and the other a passenger elevator of 2,000 lbs. capacity—to the roof of a new eight-story building.

With the old hand method, it would take six men about six days to do the amount of work that one man can do in two days with the auto hoister.

When going out to a job, we load all the tackle and the windlass on the car, and it will carry the load to any part of St. Louis under its own steam. The fuel consumption in hoisting will average about five gallons of gasoline for 1½ days' work.

leather strap or rope can replace the bike chain, but the chain is better. A makeshift like this has been used by Stoke Richards, of Santa Clara, Cal., on an emery grinding rig for many years, satisfactorily and he recommends it to others.

PECULIARITY OF MANILA ROPE

Manila rope does not show, from the outside, the actual amount of wear that really must be present. In ropes of this character, says the Engineering and Mining Journal, the principal effect of use is shown in the grinding up of the fibres comprising the core, wearing it into short pieces, or even into powder. This is especially noticeable with ropes that pass over sheaves or pulleys of small diameter.

BREAKING STRAIN OF WIRE ROPE IN FREIGHT ELEVATOR SERVICE

The maximum safety load of a wire rope should never be exceeded even in freight

DIAMETER	CIRCUMFERENCE IN INCHES	WEIGHT PER FT POUNDS	BREAKING STRAIN TONS OF 2000 LBS	SAFE LOAD IN TONS OF 2000 LBS
3/8	1 1/4	0.23	2.50	1/4
7/16	1 3/8	0.29	3.00	3/8
1/2	1 1/2	0.39	3.48	1/2
9/16	1 5/8	0.48	4.27	3/4
5/8	2	0.60	5.13	1 1/4
3/4	2 1/4	0.88	8.64	1 3/4
7/8	2 3/4	1.20	11.50	2 1/2
1	3 1/8	1.58	16.00	3
1 1/8	3 1/2	2.00	20.00	4
1 1/4	4	2.50	27.00	5 1/2
1 3/8	4 3/8	3.00	33.00	6 1/2
1 1/2	4 3/4	3.65	39.00	8

service. The National Engineer gives a table showing the breaking strain of several diameters.

TO KEEP A WINDOW FROM RATTLING

To stop a window from rattling when the wind is high, procure some leather washers, about 1 in. in diameter, from the hardware store and nail them with one nail only, through the side (not center) to the board that fits against the window sash. When you wish to raise the sash, slide the washers around on their axes to the front; or when you wish to keep the sash from rattling, crowd the washers between it and the board.—Contributed by Gordon M. Backus, Hackensack, N. J.

A good formula for violet-colored bronze is 50 parts copper and 50 parts antimony.

STANDARD UNIT OF REFRIGERATION

F. E. Matthews, in a paper on the "Standard Unit of Refrigeration," presented at the meeting of the American Society of Mechanical Engineers, gave the following proposed equivalent standard units:

"On a basis similar to that of the present boiler horsepower of 30 pounds of water evaporated per hour from feed water at a temperature of 100 degrees Fahrenheit into saturated steam at 70 pounds gauge pressure, which requires 33,306 British thermal units of heat or 34.5 units of evaporation, each of which is equal to 965.7 British thermal units—the amount of heat required to evaporate one pound of water from and at 212 degrees and atmospheric pressure—may be established a standard ton of refrigeration, equivalent to 27 pounds of anhydrous ammonia evaporated per hour from liquid at a temperature of 90 degrees Fahrenheit into saturated vapor at 15.67 pounds gauge pressure (0 degree Fahrenheit), which requires 12,000 British thermal units of heat or 20,950 units of evaporation, each of which is equal to 572.78 British thermal units—the amount of heat required to evaporate one pound of ammonia from a temperature of 28½ degrees into saturated vapor at atmospheric pressure."

TO MAKE A 6=IN. BEAM MICROMETER

Any mechanic can make the 6-in. beam micrometer illustrated, says the American Machinist. After the forgings are shaped out holes are drilled and reamed approximately 1 in. apart, and taper eccentric pieces to fit held in position by screws as shown. The pins can easily be adjusted 1 in. apart by turning the eccentric studs.

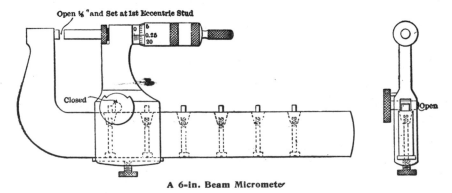

A 6-in. Beam Micrometer

PAINTING AN OLD HOUSE

In painting an old house much depends on the condition of the old paint on its walls. If pure white lead was used it can be brushed off; but if the old paint still clings here and there in scales it will have to be scraped off or have wire brushes used on it, says the Metal Worker. Then give it a coat of oil, using one gallon of turpentine and a pint of good drier to four gallons of oil. After this any remaining paint may be scraped off. Let the oil dry, then put on two coats of paint in the regular way.

INDUCTION COIL TESTING

The most accurate method for testing induction coils is to first take terminal No. 1 and put on binding post No. 1, then to fasten one side of the head telephone to the ground binding post and to touch terminal No. 3 with the other side. If you do not get the battery you will know the coil is open.

Then touch the receiver cord to terminal No. 2. If you get the battery the coil is crossed; if you do not get the battery the coil is not crossed. The other part of the coil may be tested in the same way. Bear in mind that if you are testing terminal No. 1 you must touch terminal No. 3, but if you do get the battery on either terminal No. 2 or No. 4 the coil is crossed.—Contributed by James M. Cleveland, Chicago.

(The value of this method is that a head telephone receiver is more sensitive than some test instruments. With a good test instrument the results are practically the same.—Editor.)

TO CONVERT A HAND DRILL INTO A DRILL PRESS

Secure blocks B B, Fig. 1, to wall A or some other convenient support. With screws and clips (e) fasten the drill frame (E) to block D (see Fig. 2). In order that block D be in parallel with the drill shaft, it will be necessary to let portions of the drill into the block, as shown at d, Fig. 2. Make parallel bars (C and CC) and rivet them in position so that they meet at c (Fig. 2). The drilling in these parallel bars should be equal distances apart (8 or 10 in.) and on block BB and D it should be equal distances apart, also, but nearer together, owing to the size of the drill.

To the lower bar (C) attach one end of spring b, about midway from the ends,

and attach the other end to a screw eye on block B. (Spring b can be attached at one end to the upper bar, C, near the drill and at the other end, by a link, to the ceiling, bracket or any other convenient support, if preferred.) This spring should be strong enough to lift and hold the drill off bracket H. Near the drill in the lower bar (C) at-

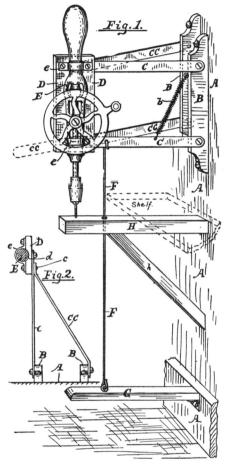

Home-Made Drill Press

tach the treadle rod (F), passing it through bracket H to treadle G.

Foot pressure on treadle G will force the drill through the metal, leaving both hands free to handle the drill and the articles being drilled. If the treadle is not desired, or it is preferred to have both lever and treadles, the lower bar (C) may be extended as indicated by the dotted lines cc, Fig. 1, and hand lever force may be used. The two pairs of bars (C and CC) will give almost vertical travel of the drill.—Contributed by Chas. N. Leonard, 1319 Barth avenue, Indianapolis, Ind.

SUPPORTING HANGERS FROM I-BEAMS

There are a number of methods of hanging shafting from structural shapes in use. Figs. 3 and 4 show hangers fastened to the lower flanges of I-beams. The method shown in Fig. 3 is common, but that shown in Fig. 4 is an improvement on it. In this a gray-iron clip (Fig. 5) with a square hole in the top of it to keep the nut from turning is used. For suspending hangers or motors from I-beams, or for eyebolts for chain blocks, the beam fastening shown in Fig. 1 is good, says a correspondent of the American Machinist.

thick and made of gray iron. Fig. 8 is not a good method unless a plate, x, is secured to the timber, as the bolt has a tendency to split the timber. Fig. 9 shows a method of supporting piping. If an insulator is put in the eye, x, it makes a good electric light wire supporter.

PAINT FOR WIREWORK

Boil good linseed oil with sufficient litharge to make it of a consistency to be laid on with a brush. Add 1 part of lampblack to every 10 parts (by weight) of litharge. Boil over a gentle fire for three hours. Let the first coat be thinner than the others.

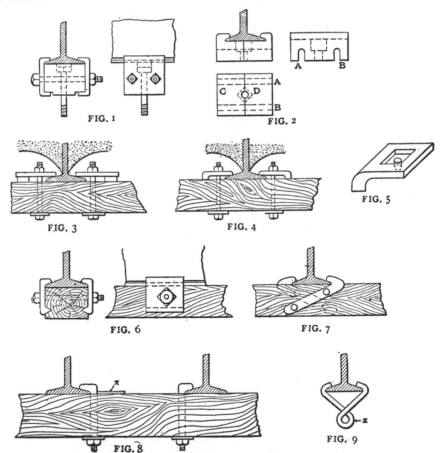

FIG. 1
FIG. 2
FIG. 3
FIG. 4
FIG. 5
FIG. 6
FIG. 7
FIG. 8
FIG. 9

A clamp for hangers or timber is shown in Fig. 2. Bolts are slipped in at A and B, holding C and D together, and cannot drop out after the hanger or timber is in place. Fig. 6 explains itself. Fig. 7 shows a method of holding a strip of wood to beams for fastening electric wires. The clip is about ¼-in.

RECIPE FOR ALGERIAN LUTE

Pass through a sieve: 2 parts wood ashes, 3 parts lime and 1 part sand. Moisten with water and oil and beat up with a wooden mallet until the compound is of the right consistency.

Frieze Design--London Decorator

STEAM FITTERS' CEMENT

The following formula for steam fitters' cement was presented by S. S. Sadtler in a paper read recently before the Engineers' Club of Philadelphia. The body of the cement consists of either red or white lead. The red lead is often diluted with an equal bulk of silica or other inert substances, so as to make it less powdery. The best way that I have found to do this, however, is to add rubber or gutta-percha to the oil as follows: Linseed oil, 6 parts by weight; rubber or gutta-percha, 1 part by weight. The rubber or gutta-percha is dissolved in sufficient carbon disulphide to give it the consistency of molasses, mixed with the oil, and left exposed to the air for about 24 hours. The red lead is then mixed to a putty. Oxide of iron makes a less brittle cement than red lead. Probably fish oils and red lead would make good cements of the class for joining pipes, as the fish oils are not such strong drying oils as linseed, and their use might be a case of permissible substitution rather than adulteration.

FEEDING BARROW FOR THE BARN

For the distribution of food, either wet or dry, to the stalls on the barn floor, a feeding barrow is convenient, says the Farm Journal. The barrow is shaped so that the food can be shov-

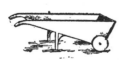

eled up easily and the sides extend to form the handles. The wheels are cut from a hardwood board. A shovel is carried along with the barrow.

A CORRECTION

On page 1239, December, 1905, issue, is an account of welding aluminum with oxygen gas which is incorrect as to the gas used. Oxygen gas alone cannot be used in this way.

NEW METHOD OF TYING LINE WIRE TO INSULATOR

An improved method for tying line wires to insulators is shown in the illustration and is suggested by a correspondent of the

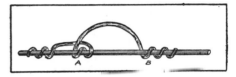

Good Method of Tying

American Telephone Journal. The wire is turned back over the loop formed around the insulator after three turns made around the wire and is then secured by three additional turns outside of the first lashing.

REINFORCING A BENT AUTOMOBILE FRAME

When the frame of your automobile begins to sag in the middle, try reinforcing the side-members of the frame by filling them with wood, recommends the Motor Way. Either ash or elm will answer the purpose. Bed the wood in a coat of white

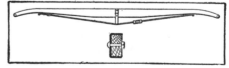

Repair for Automobile Frame

lead as a precaution against the moisture rusting the steel or rotting the wood. Fasten the wood in place with carriage bolts. In doing this you will probably be obliged to strip everything out of the frame and take the side-members off.

Another method is to put on a truss rod to support the frame where it sags. Use a ⅜-in. rod and have a turnbuckle to draw it in place. This is a cheaper and quicker way, but will not look so well.

OPERATING A STEAM PUMP BY WAVE POWER

A steam pump used for filling a tank was operated by a correspondent of the Engineers' Review without the aid of steam, compressed air or other ordinary power, but by the action of the waves of Lake Michigan.

A platform was built to fit around the top of the base of an upright pump, and then the pump was set upon a flat stone at the

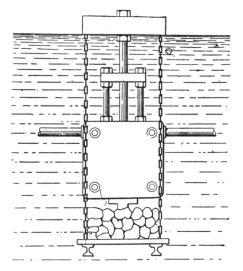

Wave Motor

bottom of the lake. Two lengths of railroad rail were placed on the base as weights, and the platform was laid on the rails; this in turn was loaded down with rock to secure the pump in place. Chains were then run from the rails to a float fitted to the plunger. These chains were of the right length to keep the motion of the float less than the stroke of the pump. With this arrangement, when the lake was calm, the float was partly submerged. Connections were then made to the tank.

The waves operated the pump successfully, supplying all the water required for the tank.

EGG-SHELL GLOSS ON REDWOOD

Put on one coat of orange shellac, sandpaper it to a smooth surface and follow with three coats of white hard oil finish. Rub the first coat with hair-cloth and the last coats with pulverized pumice stone and raw linseed oil.

INTERESTING ACCIDENTS IN THE SHOP

An accident happened in our shop a short time ago while we were getting out a hurry-up job (a job that is done in a hurry without the proper amount of thought applied to it). We had a wrought-iron eccentric yoke, hardly large enough to fit the eccentric we wished to use it on (Fig. 1). It was taken to the blacksmith to be made larger, therefore the rod, B, was left screwed fast to handle it by when hot. It had not been in the fire long until, with a loud report, it burst, forcing two great swells and parting the wrought iron marked A-A in two places.

Fortunately for the blacksmith, the rod did not blow out. He was standing squarely in front of it. The wrought iron was ⅝ in. thick around the rod and, considering the diameter of the hole, it required a very high pressure to burst. The accident was caused by oil or dampness generating steam under the intense heat.

Another accident that came near resulting fatally occurred while removing a cylinder head without due care. Before removing the head, the two valves, C C (Fig. 2), and the two cocks, D D ,were opened, creating a vacuum within the cylinder when the bolts were out and the head loosened a little. The inrush of air through valves,

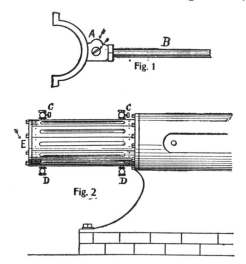

Fig. 1

Fig. 2

C C and D D, blew out the head with such force as to break a 2 x 12 plank.—Contributed by Paul S. Baker, Muscatine, Ia.

Popular Mechanics life subscriptions, $10; five years for $3.

SHOP NOTES

METHOD OF CONNECTING A BELL TO A TELEPHONE

Referring to the illustration: A is the telephone gong from which the wire is run to the extension bell and which must be

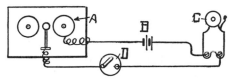

Bell and Telephone Connection

insulated; B, batteries; C, one-stroke extension bell to any part of the shop; D, switch. With this method of connecting the bell will sound the different rings, instead of one continuous ring, until the switch is turned. It will rarely be necessary to turn the switch. —Contributed by A. C. Esty, 2643 Humboldt avenue S., Minneapolis, Minn.

EXPANSION STEAM PIPES

The illustration shows a recent installation of pipe bends to take care of the expansion and contraction. Three wrought steel pipes were used of 8 in. diameter, instead of a single, larger pipe, on account of greater flexibility. A leading manufacturer makes the following recommendations: For bends 12 in. and smaller to regular dimensions and for all purposes up to 200 lbs. pressure use full weight steel pipe; 14 in. to 16 in. outside diameter up to 200 lbs., use ⅜ in. thick; 18 in. outside diameter and larger, up to 150 lbs., use ⅜ in. thick; same

This Method Gives Greater Flexibility

sizes up to 200 lbs., use ½ in. thick; if pressure exceeds 200 lbs., it is better to make the bends of extra strong pipe up to 8 in. diameter, and pipe ½ in. thick on the larger sizes.

HOW TO MAKE A BRACKET FOR LIFTING WATER CYLINDER HEADS

In the small water works plant where no traveling crane is installed, a bracket for taking off and replacing water cylinder heads will be found a convenience.

In the sketch, D shows the form of bracket necessary. Procure a piece of iron, 40 in. long by 2 in. wide and 1¾ in. thick and dress it round at the end as shown at

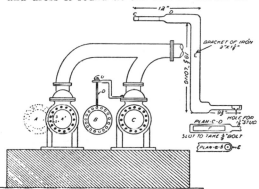

Bracket for Removing Cylinder Heads

E in plan a-b. Drill a 13/16-in. hole to fit freely over a 1⅛-in. stud, and counter-bore it to a depth of ⅞ in. to receive a 1⅛-in. hex-nut. Forge the bar to shape, as shown in the sketch, making it 9½ in. long on the lower arm, 18½ in. high and 12 in. long on the upper arm (see plan F.). Make the slot indicated in F wide enough to take in a ¾-in. bolt and about 6 in. long, in order to allow for prying the cylinder head clear of the studs while taking it off. Use a piece of ¾-in. round iron, 24 in. long, threaded on each end for 4 in. of its length, with a hex-nut and a washer, to take the head off with.

The position of the cylinder head, as shown by the dotted lines at A, represents it hanging to two studs of the cylinder A, at

S and S'. By putting the head on the studs in this manner it allows for the use of the bracket on the other cylinder, if necessary. It is also very convenient to cut a gasket for the head joint while hanging in the position shown at B, says the National Engineer, and if in any doubt as to the safety of the bolt or the bracket it is a very easy matter to place a block on the pump foundation directly under the head.

DURABILITY OF COPPER ROOFING

In commenting on copper as a roofing material a correspondent of the Metal Worker describes the capitol roof at Washington, D. C., which was placed on the building after the close of the Civil War. It is of 40-oz. copper in sheets 8 ft. long by 24 in. wide with 2½-in. corrugations. The illustrations show the mode of application, the lapping of the sheets and their fastenings.

Strap for Conductor Pipe.

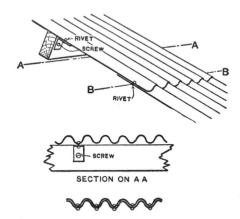

SECTION ON A A

SECTION ON B B

Fastening Copper Roofing

The cleat on the under side of the sheet is fastened to the copper by a rivet and screwed into the purlin with an ordinary wood screw. These fasteners are spaced about 2 ft. apart in every five or six corrugations. Where two sheets are brought together they are simply lapped and riveted as shown, the rivet allowing for longitudinal expansion by the sheet's buckling, while the lateral expansion is allowed for by the buckling of the corrugations. No solder is used on the main part of the roof, the protection against storms being afforded by the lapping and riveting of the sheets. In spite of the long use of this roof it is in excellent condition, and has had but few repairs.

On a building where rectangular copper down spouts were used entirely, straps designed like the one illustrated were used to hold the conductors in place. These straps in design conformed with the architecture of the house and made an attractive appearance.

CLEANING IRON BRIDGES BEFORE REPAINTING

"The sandblast furnishes the best method of removing dirt and rust from iron bridges preparatory to repainting," declares C. J. Bogardus of the Erie R. R., "but it is rather too expensive," and adds:

"The least expensive way is to scrape the iron well and to remove dust and scale by pounding it off with a special form of hammer made with a hammer face on one side and a chisel point on the opposite side. This enables one to get into many places about a bridge that could not be reached with the ordinary hammer. Of course, this tool cannot be utilized in all cases, and where such is the case, we use a tool similar to a chisel, only larger, for cleaning off the paint and rust between the ties, etc. After the metal is well hammered and scraped, it is best to use wire brushes and then dust it off before painting. It is very essential that the iron work be thoroughly cleaned in order to get the best results."

VARNISH FOR PATTERN WORK

Shellac cut with grain alcohol is the best varnish for pattern makers. Put the gum in a glazed earthenware jar and cover it with grain alcohol. For fine, light work add a little more alcohol. Never add oxalic acid to the varnish to clear it when old. Rather throw it out and prepare a fresh supply.

"A little drop of oil,
    A little bit of care;
Saves a lot of toil,
    Avoids a lot of wear."

PLAN OF PIPING FOR INSTALLING OUTSIDE GAS LAMPS

The installation of gas lighting fixtures outside of show windows so as to prevent trouble from freezing and protect the gas from cold temperatures was described in a paper read by Arthur Murray, of Detroit, before the Michigan Gas Association.

When only one or two gas lamps are to be installed in front of a store or business place, and there is a ⅜-in. drop with good supply inside the window, attach a ½-in. pipe to this, carry it out through the window and extend it down to the lamp with two 45-degree ells. Drill four 3/16-in. holes in the top of the lamp and place a 2 by 1¼-in. reducing coupling so as come on the outside of the opening in the top of the lamp.

From this reducer extend 1¼-in. pipe, or casing, back to within 1 in. of the window sash and there use a reducing tee with a ½-in. branch pointed upward, from which use a return bend to conduct heat from the inside and thus exclude water from rain or snow storms. The end of the reducing tee should fit closely around the ½-in. run.

Where three or more lamps are to be installed run a riser, cased with a larger pipe, on the outside of the building in the least conspicuous place and let it open into the basement or cellar. Place a tee "bull-headed" on the top of the casing to exclude

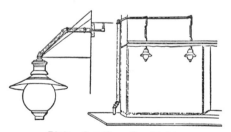

Piping Out-Door Gas Lights

water from rain. It is also necessary to case run or drops. Take a drop from side branch of the tee and where possible carry all drip water back to the riser, where a large drip is placed in the cellar. Where it is impossible to carry all drip back to the riser place an additional drip or extra riser between the store front and carry it back to the basement. Case this also and place a stop in the bottom to let out drip water.

Never use beeswax which has been adulterated with tallow or paraffin wax for pattern work. It will not adhere to the wood.

ANGLE-PLATE FOR DRILLING ANGULAR HOLES

In drilling a hole slightly angular, as is at times necessary, do not pack up with bits of metal, says The Model Engineer, London,

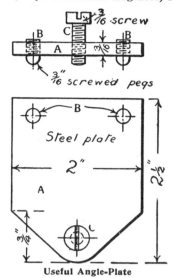

Useful Angle-Plate

but make an angle-plate which will prove useful many times. File a piece of good straight steel plate, A, to the dimensions shown, drill and tap two 3/16-in. holes and fit two pegs, BB, made from screws, with the ends rounded as shown. At the other end drill and tap a 3/16-in. hole and fit a screw, C (either an ordinary cheese-head screw, or a knurled head screw). To use, move C up and down, according to the angle wanted.

TO RECOLOR ALCOHOL THERMOMETERS

The loss of color in alcohol thermometers is not always due to fading, says a contemporary, but may be caused by the color settling to the bottom of the bulb. To stir it up well, the thermometer should be alternately plunged in water heated to near the capacity of the thermometer, or the boiling point, if the thermometer registers more than 212, and an ice bath. This will cause the alcohol to flow rapidly up and down in the tube and, of course, stir up the sediment in the bulb and color the alcohol again, thus making it easily visible against the scale. Many a thermometer has been discarded as useless when it might easily have been recolored in this way.

THE POWER OF IMAGINATION AS APPLIED TO MECHANICS

That power or faculty of the mind called imagination may seem a little out of place when brought under a mechanical heading, yet this particular power plays an important part in all occupations that produce something from an invisible design. Every person has this power to a certain extent but, like the muscles of the body, in some it is weak and in others strong, owing to lack of exercise. This power can, however, be developed to a state approaching perfection.

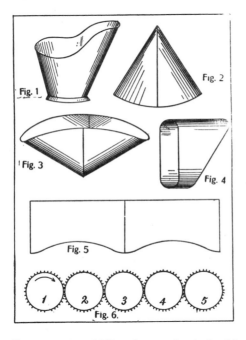

Fig. 1

Fig. 2

Fig. 3

Fig. 4

Fig. 5

Fig. 6

To judge the ability of a mechanic by his imaginative power is not wise: Some men are expert workmen with their hands after the work has been laid out for them, but are weak in head work; others have strong imaginative power and can produce great things in their minds only, but cannot produce anything with their hands.

This power or faculty may be divided into two classes, the weak and the strong. In the weak class we find the fellow who thinks that he has a machine firmly stamped upon his mind—when the machine is constructed, its dimensions are three or four times larger than he had expected them to be, and in his mind he had crowded into the space of a few square inches, enough pieces to fill a bushel basket. The weakness of this faculty has caused the downfall of many an inventor. The reason is this: The inventor, as a rule, has no means and is compelled to interest moneyed men; his invention, whatever it may be, is seen in the mind only, therefore we will call it an imaginary machine, sufficiently developed to convince the grocer or merchant, who does not understand mechanics, that his (the inventor's) idea is an assured success. The half-developed invention is constructed and the first one is a failure. The backer becomes discouraged and quits. The inventor discovers his faults, but for want of capital he cannot try again. When the imaginative power is weak, only part of a complicated object is seen. While the brain is busy with one-half of an object the other half vanishes from the mind. In the strong class we find the fellow who can picture to himself nearly correctly an object or an imaginary machine. A man of this class can construct a mechanical device and the first trial proves the value of his idea.

Those who have learned to lay out sheet iron or heavy plate work realize the value of this faculty when developed. He who follows that occupation must be able to imagine how the flat sheet will look when rolled or bent into shape. A flat plate may be laid out for bending or rolling into some irregular shape; looking at the plate one man will see just how it will look when bent, while another can form no idea at all.

Figures 1, 2, 3 and 4 are objects rolled or bent into shape. Can you imagine how they looked before they were formed? In other words, in what shape was the flat sheet cut? What would Fig. 5 make if rolled into a circle? Fig. 6 shows a train of gears. Assuming that 1 runs to the right, can you see in the mind the direction of the other four? When the mind is on 5, does 1 vanish from it? It requires practice to concentrate the mind upon each imaginary gear and control its motion. From the diagram this may be made clear. If 1 moves in a right-hand direction, all the odd numbers, 1, 3 and 5, move towards the right, while 2 and 4 run in the opposite direction.

For the benefit of those interested the next number of Popular Mechanics will contain a plan of Figs. 1, 2, 3, 4 before rolled, and of Fig. 5 after it is rolled to a circle.—Contributed by Paul S. Baker, Muscatine, Ia.

———◆◆———

Bayberry tallow applied to the surface of hot iron patterns is quite as good as the mixture of beeswax and tallow, frequently used for this purpose.

HOW TO BEND WOODEN STRIPS

In pattern shops it is frequently necessary to cover a pattern with narrow strips of wood curved to conform to the curves and angles of the surface. These strips are first heated, says Wood Craft, and then, while hot, bent on a device called a "bender."

One of these benders may be made of a length of ordinary stovepipe. Nail the pipe to a bo 'd and put a spirit lamp inside of it. That pa t of the pipe above the flame will become ery hot. Now, try taking a strip of pine, ½ in. wide, 12 in. long and ⅛ in. thick, placing it crosswise on the pipe over the heated part and pressing both ends of the strip downward. As soon as the wood is heated through, it will conform to the shape of the pipe and will remain in that shape when removed.

Benders from a tube 1 in. in diameter to 12 in. are required in the pattern shop, more particularly in putting stove patterns together. Small benders are rested on a frame and a gas jet is introduced through a slot on the under side. The illustration shows one form of bender with a lighted spirit lamp within it. This bender has a handle by which it may be held in a vise when in use. Those underneath the bench on a shelf have no handles and are handy

Bending Strips of Wood

to place anywhere. The opposite end from where the lamp enters the bender is closed by a block to which the sheet iron is nailed, holding it rigid.

These thin strips are fastened to the follow-board in the following way: The form when ready to cover is given a coat of shellac, and when this is dry it is sandpapered lightly then thinly greased with tallow or lard. This will hold the strips close. To hold a strip so that others can be glued edgewise against it, use pattern makers' tacks.

TO SLING A PLANK EDGEWISE

A plank on edge is better for supporting a swinging scaffold than a plank laid flat, says the American Machinist, as it is stiffer on edge. The method of slinging a plank edgewise by a rope so that it will stay is shown in Fig. 1. A clove hitch is made

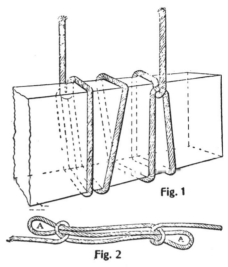

Fig. 1

Fig. 2

around the end of the plank; then one of the parts is twisted around the plank until the ends lead as shown.

To shorten a piece of rope without cutting it, try the sheep's shank shown in Fig. 2. The rope is brought back on itself, making two or more bights, and a half hitch is taken around each bight. This knot will not slip, and will nearly fall apart of its own accord if the strain is released, so that when there is a liability of this happening, it is well to pass a piece of wood through the loop A at each end and pull the rope tight on them.

HEAT LOST BY RADIATION

The amount of heat lost by radiation from bare pipes containing steam at 100 lb. pressure has been estimated to be about equal to two tons of coal a year for each 10 sq. ft. of pipe surface. It has also been found that 88 per cent of this loss can be saved by the best pipe covering.

The painter can keep the water in the brush troughs from freezing in cold weather by the addition of salt or a little glycerine. Neither will hurt the brushes.

HANDY COAL BOX FOR HOUSE

In place of the dirty coal bucket setting in the kitchen beside the range a coal box like the one illustrated may be used, eliminating a large amount of dirt and cleaning.

The box is fastened on the outside of the

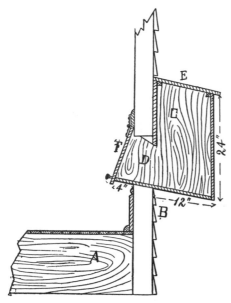

Substitute for the Coal Bucket

kitchen, within easy reach of the range. It may be of any size, but is amply large if made 12 in. wide, 15 in. long and 24 in. high. An opening, about 8 or 9 in. high, through the wall, with a slanting hinged door on the inside, admits the coal to the kitchen. The coal is deposited in the box from the outside, and is fed to the opening within by gravity. Referring to the illustration, the parts indicated are: A, kitchen floor; B, side of house; C, coal box; D, opening in wall; E, removable lid outside; F, hinged lid within kitchen.—Contributed by Wm. O. Tischendorf, Mt. Vernon, Ind.

RECHARGING DRY BATTERIES

Dry batteries can be recharged, if not too far gone, by the following simple method:

Bore two holes in the top down through the composition there, one on each side of the carbon. Pour into these holes about one gill of diluted sulphuric acid (3 parts water and 1 part acid), and plug the holes up with common soap. Let the batteries stand about 12 hours, when they will be nearly as good as new. The batteries I used were

ones thrown away by a telephone company as worthless. That was six months ago, and they are in service yet.—Contributed by Wm. J. Slattery, Emsworth, Pa.

PURITY OF SCRAP LEAD

Old lead pipe, or scrap lead, is not always suitable for the purpose to which it is to be put. Often it contains foreign matter of an offensive nature and quantities of water. Sometimes this accumulation of water causes an explosion, more frequently occurring where the water is frozen. As an illustration of this, a kettle may be half filled with melted lead and then scrap lead containing water or ice added. The steam will cause an explosion, possibly blowing out half the lead in the kettle.

Because of frequent remeltings of old lead, it gradually comes to contain a considerable per cent of tin and antimony, but these metals are beneficial, serving to harden the pipe and making it preferable to that made of pure metal, which corrodes more rapidly when exposed to moisture. Underground telegraph and telephone cables are encased in lead pipe containing from 3 to 4 per cent tin, on account of this fact.

In melting scrap lead place a stick of wood in the bottom of the lead kettle and let it boil for some time. This will reduce the oxide and a good clean metal will result when the dross is skimmed off.

WIRE TRUING DEVICE

The wire-truing device illustrated has been used by F. F. Berry, 104 Reed av., Peoria, Ill., daily on hollow tubing 3-32 in. in diameter, with satisfactory results, neither twisting nor breaking the tubing.

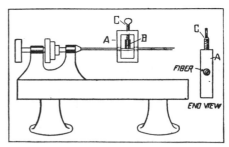

For Truing Wire

Part A is made of hard wood 2½ in. wide, 1 in. thick and 3½ in. long with holes made in the sides and plugged up with fiber which is more durable than the hard wood.

Holes for the wire are a little more than 3-32 in. in diameter. B is made of round hard wood and the screw, C, which is made of common iron, sets in loosely. This is said to be an excellent device for hand work on small wire.

STEEL SQUARE AND PIPE WRINKLE

The diameter of pipe necessary to carry the contents of two smaller pipes may be determined roughly by the use of the steel square, says the Engineer.

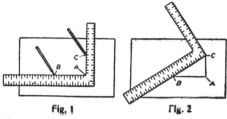

Fig. 1   Fig. 2

On a board or sheet of paper mark off the diameters of the two known pipes, as AB and AC, Fig. 1. Then measure across as in Fig. 2. The distance is the required diameter.

HOW TO PIPE WATER-COOLED MOTORS

In the left-hand illustration, showing a four-cylinder water-cooled motor, the cylinders are cast in pairs and the honeycomb radiator forms the front end of the bonnet. From the base of the radiator the water is drawn by the gear-driven pump to the base of the water jacket, surrounding the rear pair of cylinders. From the jacket it passes from the center of the top of the jacket to the base of the jacket for the front pair of cylinders and finally exits from the top of this pair to the top of the radiator. In this

way the back pair of cylinders gets the cold water and the front pair the warmed water from the rear.

This method is incorrect. It is better to have the water in both cylinders as near the same temperature as possible, says the Motor Age. Where the water is distributed to both cylinders evenly, as shown in the second drawing, the cooling is more even. Where the water is introduced to rear cylinders first, the hot water enters the front cylinders at a higher temperature than that of the water in the rear cylinders, which is cooled by the force of the air through the radiator.

HOW TO BABBITT A LOOSE PULLEY

Remove the old babbitt from the pulley and make a base a trifle larger than the diameter of the pulley, to which fasten a round piece of wood, standing vertically as shown at A, Fig. 1. Place the pulley upon the core base, and after leveling across the rim, move it so that core B stands exactly in the center of the hole in the hub (Fig. 2).

Bring a collar (previously put on), of the same size as the core, up against the bottom of the hub and secure it in place by means

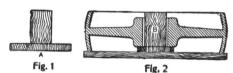

Fig. 1   Fig. 2

of the set screw, directs a writer in the Engineers' Review. Fill the crack between the collar and the hub with plaster of paris. Plug the oil hole with wood, pour babbitt metal in around the core and allow it to cool. When the babbitt is cool, remove the core, which will have shrunk some. Then scrape the babbitt until a good fit to the shaft is made.

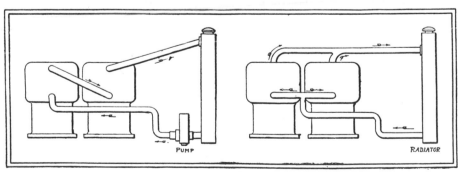

Incorrect and Correct Way of Piping in the Water System

A NOVEL CLOCK DIAL

We made a unique clock dial for our shield clock in the following manner:

Taking out the old dial, which was made of metal, we applied to it two coats of white enamel, allowing the first coat to dry before applying the second. We then painted in aluminum a circular band on the

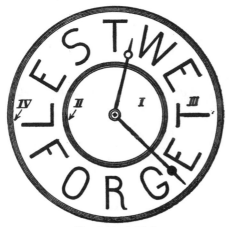

Novel Clock Dial

dial about 2 in. from the center. A band of aluminum was painted on the edge of the dial, also. Between these bands there was one of white enamel, and on this we painted in black enamel the inscription, "Lest we forget," letting each letter represent a figure. Referring to the illustration: I and III indicate white enamel; and II and IV indicate aluminum.—Contributed by Gordon M. Backus, Hackensack, N. J.

RAISING ROOF OF HAY BARRACK

An improved method of raising the roof of a hay barrack is described in the Country Gentleman. The old way has been to use a screw which was more expensive to start with and a time-consumer in operation.

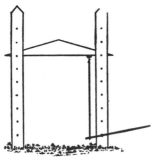

The new method is by means of a lever, the use of which is clearly shown in the cut.

REMEDY FOR SLIPPING SET SCREWS

When the set screw on the pulley of the governor shaft of a 10-hp. engine persisted in working loose, a correspondent of the National Engineer remedied the matter as follows:

The spindle was taken out and a ¼-in. hole drilled lengthwise of it, between the spindle and governor pulley—near the place where the set screw was located. A wire nail, a trifle larger than the hole drilled, was then driven into the hole and prevented the set screw from slipping again.

HOME-MADE RINGING DEVICE FOR TELEPHONE EXCHANGE

To make this device, which with ten cells of batteries will furnish sufficient ringing current for a small exchange, procure a vibrating bell, a ½ M. F. condenser, a 2 M. F. condenser, a push button switch and a kick coil such as is used in telephones in place of a generator.

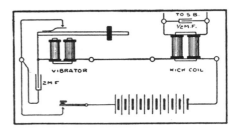

Circuit Arrangement for Ringing Apparatus

Remove the gong and tapper of the bell and solder a piece of No. 12 iron wire, 5 in. long to the tapper rod. Upon this place a light weight which can be moved up or down to govern the speed of the vibrator. Screw the vibrator and kick coil to any convenient base, says the Telephone Journal, and arrange the circuit as shown in the sketch. Place the push button switch in a convenient position, preferably near the crank of the hand generator. Connect the ½ M. F. condenser across the terminals of the secondary winding of the kick coil, and the other condenser across the make and break contacts of the vibrator.

When the operator rings, pressing the switch closes the battery through the primary circuit of the kick coil and vibrator, this causing the secondary of the coil to deliver an alternating current. The ringing cam is operated in the usual manner.

HOME-MADE LATHE RUN BY A GRINDSTONE

The boy who can find use for a lathe can make one for himself which will do for ordinary purposes. Fig. 2 shows the lathe. Make the ends 4 by 2 in., and the side pieces, 6 by 1 in. by 18 in. long, leaving between the ends 14 in. Nail the parts together securely. Bevel off the side pieces, leaving about 3-16 in. square edge to act as rests for the tools. Screw through each end, rather tightly, a coach or iag screw with the point ground conical on the grindstone; these to act as lathe centers. Cut away part of one of the side pieces, as shown, to clear for the belt.

A correspondent of Wood Craft rigged up ordinary wood chisel. Bore holes as shown in Fig. 1. These strainers can scarcely be distinguished from those bought at the stores, and are only illustrative of the work that can be done on this simple lathe.

The lathe may be fastened to anything wooden, as a house, fence, gate, etc., at a distance requiring a good long belt to maintain the right tension.

METHOD OF SOLDERING

Clean the parts thoroughly of all grease, rust or scale and wet them with prepared acid. Hold the soldering copper on each part until the article is well tinned and the solder has flowed to all parts.—Contributed by Alex. Betzer, 442 Austin avenue, Chicago.

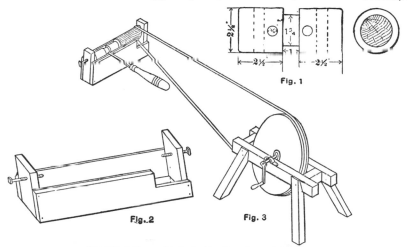

Fig. 1

Fig. 2   Fig. 3

Practical Home-Made Lathe Run by a Grindstone

a lathe like this to make some wooden wire strainers 2½ in. diameter and 6 in. long out of some 3x3-in. studding, work he would otherwise have been obliged to do by hand. Fig. 1 shows the shape of these strainers. To turn them proceed as follows:

Cut off pieces of 3x3-in. stock, 12½ in. long and chop off the corners roughly. Deeply countersink these pieces in the center of each end and put them between the centers to run fairly free. Connect up the grindstone as shown, using old reins for belting, piecing them together with wire lacing and butt joints. Run the belt around the end of a chunk of wood, before fixing the wood between the centers, and then round the grindstone. Now get a small boy to turn the grindstone while you operate the lathe. Do one-half at a time (each piece making two strainers) and then turn the piece end for end and finish. Use an

BLUEPRINTS FROM TYPEWRITTEN MATTER

When a number of copies of a specification or other paper are wanted, and none of the ordinary methods is convenient or desirable, make blueprints from the typewritten sheet, suggests a correspondent of the American Machinist.

Write the matter out on the typewriter, putting a piece of carbon paper in back of the sheet to give the printing density on both sides of the paper, then proceed with the blueprints in the usual manner. Use manifolding paper, the grade called unglazed onion skin. For white prints use new carbon paper and make the prints from that, in which case the letters will appear on a white ground. The carbon paper is more expensive than the white paper.

SCALING PIPES WITH PNEUMATIC HAMMERS

Pneumatic hammers are being used in ice and refrigerating plants for scaling condenser pipes. The method is shown in the illustration. The care of the condenser is very important in a plant of this kind, as by a few weeks' negligence the cost of production is greatly increased.

Scaling Condenser Pipes

PORTLAND CEMENT COUPLING FOR PIPE

Needing a coupling for ½-in pipe, and not having one, I used portland cement, making a thick putty and putting it on just as in wiping a solder joint. The same method can be used on bursted pipes, and the cement will hold like a coupling. I also stopped a leak in a heater with a thin paste of cement.—Contributed by Walter Weber, 643 W. 46th street, Chicago, Ill.

REMOVING HARD OLD PAINT

Hard old paint can be removed in the following manner: Dissolve 1 lb. potash in 3 pt. water and heat the mass, then add dry ochre until it is like rough stuff. Spread this on the paint and let stand until the paint softens. Then scrape off the mixture, directs the Master Painter, wash the paint clean, then dry and sandpaper.

TO MEND AN OLD SHINGLE ROOF

Cut pieces of tin about 7 in. by 2 in. from old cans that are not too rusty and slip these pieces under the joints and cracks in the shingles. Do not nail the tin, as the nails would split the shingles. In this way an old roof can be made to last several years.—Contributed by Gordon M. Backus, 32 Euclid avenue, Hackensack, N. J.

RE-BORING A GAS ENGINE CYLINDER

An 8-hp. gas engine cylinder which was solid with the bed and entirely too large for any of the machines in the shop, was re-bored by a correspondent of Canadian Machinery, by the following method, which proved economical, accurate and a time-saver.

Three hardwood collars were put on a long, true boring bar, as shown in the sketch. The front end of the cylinder was true, the piston not traveling to within 1½ in. of the end of the cylinder. The back end was not worn on account of the counter bore. A hardwood collar (maple), A, was made to fit the boring bar on the inside and a tight fit in the counter bore outside. Close to that was put another collar, B, to fit bar as before, only this was turned to the size the cylinder was to be re-bored to, and as close to this as possible was the cutter, the hardwood collar, C, was fitted at the other end, a tight fit to act as a guide or steadier to keep the bar in perfect alignment. On getting a cut started it was found that the bar had a tendency to feed ahead of itself, so a long rod was threaded and a check nut put on, and the same slacked off steadily, and with a crank on the end of the boring bar what had seemed an impossible proposition was accomplished in about one hour.

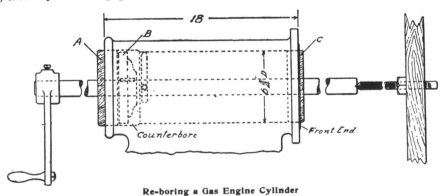

Re-boring a Gas Engine Cylinder

DO YOUR OWN BINDING

The subscriber who wishes to bind his Popular Mechanics or any other paper may do so himself at practically no cost. The illustrations are almost self-explanatory and the sizes given are for six numbers of Popular Mechanics which make a very handy size book, it being 1¼ in. thick, 7 in. wide and 9¾ in. long allowing the cover to overlap ⅛ in. at top, bottom and right side.

Figure 1 shows the size and shape of the cloth covering which can be of book bind-

shown and then pasting the complete cover over this, thereby hiding the rough stitches and giving it a finished or book-like appearance. A good flexible back can be made by substituting leather, oilcloth, etc., for the cardboard backs. The writer has used this idea in many cases with very satisfactory results and hopes that many Popular Mechanics subscribers will take the time and pains to avail themselves of this very easy way of preserving their papers.—Contributed by C. M. Shigley, 676 N. High street, Columbus, Ohio.

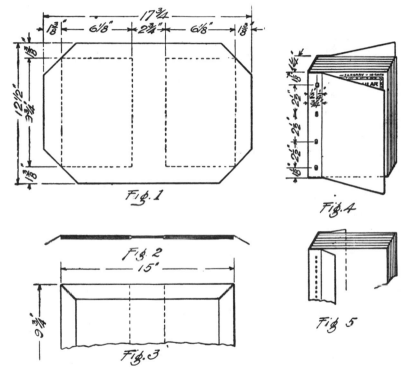

ers' cloth, thin table oilcloth, old window curtain or other material in this line on which paste or mucilage can be used. It also shows the position of the two pasteboard or mounting-board backs each 6⅛ by 9¾ in., which are to be firmly pasted in place. Fig. 2 shows the outside cover, the backs and an inside cover 9¾ by 15 in. of same material as outside, all in place to be pasted together as shown in Fig. 3.

Figure 4 shows the completed job, where the cover is mounted on the magazines and firmly secured by means of good strong paper fasteners, cord, or whang. Fig. 5 shows another way of attaching the cover which is in some respects neater. This is done by first sewing on a good firm piece as

HOW TO ESTIMATE THE HORSE POWER OF A GAS ENGINE

The horse power of a high grade four-cycle gas engine may be closely estimated by the following rule:

Each square inch of the area of the piston head will give you about 7-16 of a horsepower. This contemplates the engine in perfect condition, igniting at just the right point, etc., running at a speed of 250 R. P. M. The ordinary cheap gas engine sold in the market today will do but little better than ¼ hp. to each square inch of piston head surface. The Prony brake is the only thing where accuracy is required.

AN EMERGENCY WRENCH

When on a break down job it is necessary to make a wrench in a hurry, the one illustrated is a good one, says a correspondent of the Blacksmith and Wheelwright.

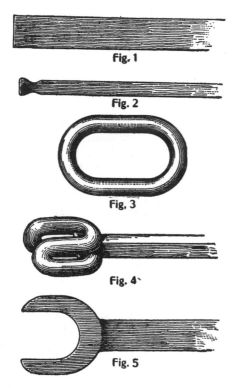

Fig. 1

Fig. 2

Fig. 3

Fig. 4

Fig. 5

Take a piece of iron 1¼ by ½ in., or according to the strength of the key required (Fig. 1) and upset the ends a little. With a pair of fullers make the iron like Fig. 2 which shows the edge. Of ¾-in. round iron make an ordinary link like Fig. 3 and weld one end on the bar (Fig. 4.) Then cut the link half through and bend it over to lay on the other side. This makes a good strong wrench (Fig. 5) for any class of work.

WATCHMAKERS' OIL

In a bottle about half full of good olive oil, put thin strips of sheet lead. Expose to the sun for a month's time. Then pour off the clear oil. This is a cheap method of making a first-class oil for any light machinery. The oil will not corrode or thicken.—Contributed by Alex. Betzer, 442 Austin avenue, Chicago.

ENCAUSTIC PASTE FOR COPYING PHOTOGRAPHIC PRINTS

Encaustic paste may be bought ready prepared or made at home, as desired, and few photographers realize with what excellent results it may be used, says the Camera and Dark Room. To make the paste, melt 1 oz. of white wax and add to it 6 dr. oil of lavender. When thoroughly mixed, add 1 dr. gum elemi and stir the mixture until it is quite cold.

For copying prints in which there is a tendency to show grain, put a little piece of the paste in the center of the print and rub it in well with a piece of cotton wool, working in a circular direction and rubbing until the wax apparently is all removed. Use the paste in the same way to brighten a print.

HOW TO MAKE A SANDPAPER BLOCK

The block may be made either wide or narrow. For ordinary use a piece of wood 6 in. longer than the width of a sheet of sandpaper and 2 in. wide by 1 in. thick will do. Round off the back side leaving 1 in. at one end. Out of a piece of heavy tin or sheet metal make a piece to fit the rounded side and hinge it to the square end of the wood. On the flat face of the wood fasten a piece of heavy cloth or ingrain carpet. Work the rounded end down to a good handle. Fasten a button on the handle end to hold the metal clamp down. Now by wrapping the sandpaper around the wood and clamping the edge on the back, you

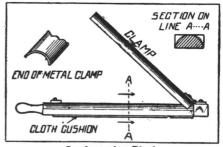

Sandpapering Block

have a rasp that will last longer, do better work and is more easily handled than most blocks.—Contributed by Wm. F. Hoag, Judsonia, Ark.

In hardening small tools that are liable to warp, heat carefully and insert in a raw potato, then draw the temper as usual.

HOW TO MAKE A SIMPLE LANTERN CARRIER

A lantern carrier, made as illustrated, has been in use in my horse stable for nearly a year, and has been very satisfactory. This carrier can be made at little or no expense. The parts are: A, small grooved wheel about 1 in. in diameter with ¼ in. hole through it; B, ¼ in. by ¼ in. bolt; C, weight hook of an old steelyard scale; D, piece of soft pine grooved so that it will fit in the weight hook, as the weight hook is too wide inside for the wheel; E, heavy wire hook bent at one end to hang the lantern on and

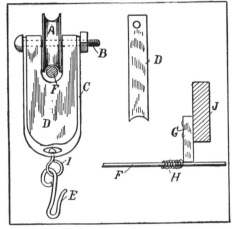

Lantern Carrier for Stable

with the other end put through the swivel loop, I, and bent around; F, heavy wire track, stretched tight, upon which the carrier runs; G, stopping block, which is pushed down a few inches and nailed to a joist, J; H, coil spring slipped on the track in front of the stopping block for the carrier to bump against; should it run farther than is desired, the spring will prevent breakage.

The stopping block should be placed far enough away from the wall so the lantern cannot swing and strike it, and the carrier should be equipped with a swivel, I, as the lantern sometimes turns one way or the other, and without the swivel would twist the carrier on the track so that it wouldn't run well. This carrier is a good one, as the lantern cannot be knocked down by loose stock.—Contributed by J. C. Mannel, Lincoln, Kansas.

Dry ochre or any other dry pigment is too coarse for priming.

HANDY SOLDERING IRON HOLDER TO USE OVER A GAS JET

From 1-in. hoop iron cut one piece 7⅛ in. long to make the top part and another piece 4¼ in. long. Bend these pieces as shown in the sketch and then rivet them together. Make two holes in the ends (A, B) for putting the device on the gas jet.—Contributed

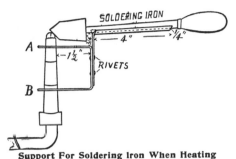

Support For Soldering Iron When Heating

by Wm. T. Ackerman, 1311 N. Stockton street, Baltimore, Ind.

CEMENT FOR PIPE JOINTS

Grind, wash, mix and regrind to a fine powder, 15 parts chalk and 50 parts graphite. Add 20 parts ground litharge and mix to a stiff paste with 15 parts boiled oil. This preparation, says Domestic Engineering, will remain plastic for a long time, if stored in a cool place.

DISK FOR TURNING LAMP WICKS

Many times the disk that is used to turn lamp wicks, becomes unsoldered and is lost.

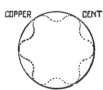

In this case, take a copper cent and file it with a small rattail file to the shape shown in the sketch. Drill a hole in the center and solder the cent to the stem. If the wick is hard to turn up or down, this gives a better grip than the original disks with their finely milled edges. I have also used this to advantage on hand bike pump connections.—Contributed by Stoke Richards, Santa Clara, Cal.

Do not use varnishes that contain resin in any quantity for exterior work.

HOW TO MAKE A DESK LIGHT

From an electrical supply dealer get some office cord, a socket and bulb.

To make the plug which is to fit into the wall socket, get a burnt-out bulb and break the glass; inside there is a small glass tube, break this also, being careful not to break the wires inside of it. To these small wires attach the cord. Cut a piece of rubber to the shape shown in Fig. 1, and fit it in to keep the wires apart. Then bind the wires with tape, to keep them away from the brasswork and prevent short-circuiting.

Cut some pieces of wood, about ¼ in. thick to the following dimensions: One piece, 8 in. by 4 in. (back); two pieces, 8 in. by 3½ in. (top and bottom); one piece 8 in. by 2½ in. (shade); two pieces 4 in. by 3½ in., with a hole in one piece for the socket (ends); one piece 8 in. by 1 in. by ½ in. (standard); one piece 5 in. by 3 in. (base

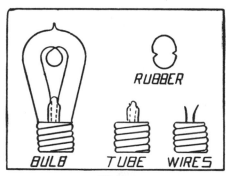

Fig. 1

of standard). Fig. 2 shows the back, Fig. 3, the socket end and Fig. 4, the base for the standard, the other pieces are used just as cut.

Of these pieces of wood make an oblong box as shown in Fig. 5. Fit a piece of tin in the back for a reflector. Bevel one edge of the piece for the shade and fasten it on so as to throw the light downward. Cut two pieces of tin, C, to fit over the ends and hold the shade firmly.

Attach the socket to the cord, when you will have the plug at one end and the socket at the other. Put the socket through the hole cut in one end of the box and fit a rubber washer around it inside the box. Then insert the bulb, put the plug in the wall socket and turn on the light.

If the device is too low, bend two pieces of tin about 1 in. wide in the form of the standard and fasten them to the back of the box as at A and B, Fig. 2, so as to let the box slide up and down on the standard cut from the wood, which is fastened to its base (Fig. 4.)—Contributed by R. W. Purdy, Chicago, Ill.

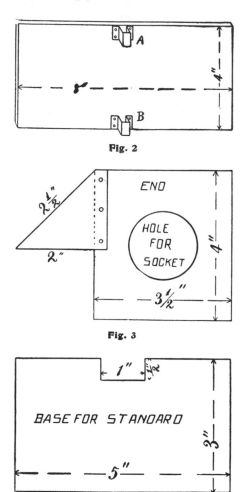

Fig. 2

Fig. 3

Fig. 4

Fig. 5

HOLE JEWEL FOR A WATCH

When the jeweler requires a hole jewel and has not one to fit, he can make one out of a small chip from a glass rod.

Put the chip of glass on a piece of charcoal and heat it with a blowpipe until it draws up into a round ball; then stick it on the end of a match with sealing wax and rub it on an oilstone until it is flat; turn it over and rub the other side until you get the required thickness. Then, with a small drill and turpentine, drill a hole the size of the pivot. Polish the hole with diamond dust on a copper wire and countersink with a large drill for the oil cup. The whole jewel can be polished with dust on a piece of peg wood.

I have drawn down a glass rod and broken off roller jewels, also. Either of these jewels can be bought cheaply, but the glass jewels are better than the brass ones commonly soldered in.—Contributed by Henry F. Shaw, jeweler, Dalton, Mass.

IMPROVED SOLDERING OR TIN-NING ACID

Into 1 lb. muriatic acid put all the zinc it will dissolve and 1 oz. sal ammoniac. Add as much clear water as there is of the acid.—Contributed by Alex. Betzer, 442 Austin avenue, Chicago.

FASTENING A ROPE TO A RING: A DEFENSE

Regarding the discussion of the methods of fastening a rope to a ring, which appeared in our September, 1905, number, Joseph B. Keil, of Marion, O., writes:

Mr. Joannis has not correctly analyzed the operation of the fastening, as described by me, when in use. It does provide two wearing surfaces in that the two thicknesses of rope passing through the ring are worn simultaneously, and not separately, as Mr. Joannis seems to think. Moreover, the simple knot in which the ring is tied does not bend the rope so short as in the round turn of Mr. Joannis' method, and hence does not strain the rope so much locally.

For tightening screw connections, dissolve powdered shellac in 10 per cent ammonia and paint the mass over the screw threads after they have been thoroughly cleaned; then screw the fitting home. The joint will be impervious to hot or cold water.

HANDLING PIPE OFFSETS

While installing some 8-in. pipe, a correspondent of the Engineers' Review used the offset fitting shown in Fig. 1 to overcome an offset caused by the 8-in. flange being riveted crooked to a new return tank for the elevator. Fig. 2 shows the elevation of the two elevator pumps and tank which, being crowded well together, required the use of close nipples; it also shows how the piping was run and what fittings were used.

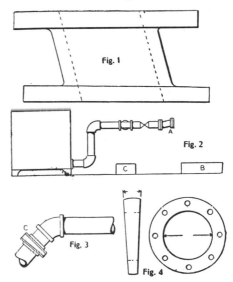

Flange connection was made to pump B, and when trying to connect to the same, it was found that the center of the pipe was 1/16 in. lower than the center of the suction opening of the pump, caused by the crooked thread in the flange pitching down. Cutting a crooked thread on a nipple was tried but the nipple was too short to give enough pitch. Then the special casting, Fig. 1, was made and used as at A, Fig. 2, making a connection without undue strain.

In turning an 8-in. pipe line to make an angle less than 135 degrees and more than 90 degrees (Fig. 3) a 45-degree ell, a short nipple and a flange union, between which was inserted the dutchman shown at Fig. 4, were used to get the right angle. The holes in the casting were drilled large enough to allow the bolts to pass through. The slant was ¾ in. in 11½ in. of pipe.

To render rough woodwork almost noninflammable, two heavy coats of ordinary lime whitewash is recommended by a painters' journal.

METHOD OF TEMPERING AN ANVIL

Have ready a tub with a good force of water coming up through a pipe from the bottom so that it will boil, and bend some irons for the anvil to rest on and let them hang in the tub (See illustration). One of these irons should go into the water deeper

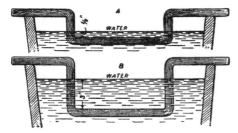

Supports for the Anvil

than the other (A and B), says a correspondent of the Blacksmith and Wheelwright.

Let the horn end of the anvil in deepest to give the thin end a chance to draw the temper. Have the thin end ½ in. in the water, but let the horn end go in 3 in. deep. Heat up to an even cherry red. Lay on the iron in the water and let it remain there until the face is cold. If not hot enough so that you can touch it with the file set it on the fire block side down.

FOR ROUGH HANDS

This is the season when the machine operator's hands are liable to become sore and stiff from exposure. A correspondent of Machinery recommends this: Take a four-ounce bottle and put in same three ounces glycerine, one ounce alcohol, and from twenty to thirty drops of carbolic acid. After washing the hands, and while they are a little damp, apply a few drops and thoroughly rub it in. A good time to use it is at night.

PACKING CAST-IRON PIPES FOR HEATING

Place the pipes in the desired position and put a roll of oakum around each and pack it firmly into the hub of the pipe with a calking tool. Use either of the following preparations, recommended by the Florists' Review, for filling the remaining space:

Sal ammoniac, 2 oz.; sulphur, 1 oz.; clean iron filings or borings, 12 lb. Add water to form a paste. Or,

Iron filings, 4 lb.; fireclay, 2 lb.; powdered potsherds, 10 lb. Make a paste with strong brine.

ASPHALTUM PREVENTS RADIATION OF HEAT

Painting pipes with asphaltum insulates them sufficiently to keep considerable heat from radiating, declares a correspondent of the National Engineer. In a plant where the exhaust steam was used in the heating system, the pipes of the system had been given two coats of asphaltum, and it was impossible to keep the building warm all that winter. That it was the asphaltum that caused the trouble was not discovered until later.

In another plant the writer had re-arranged the cylinder lubricating system by substituting a central oil reservoir for individual cups, as shown in the sketch, with a marked saving of oil. This reservoir was constructed of boiler plate to safely withstand a pressure of 120 lbs. Overhead in the engine room were a number of small

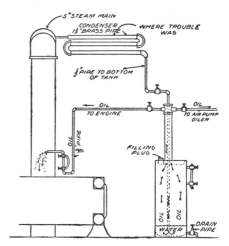

Trouble With Asphalt Painted Pipes in Oiling System

pipes, including the condenser pipes shown in the illustration. These pipes were painted with asphaltum one Saturday afternoon when the plant was not running. Then the trouble began with the sight feeds. No change had been made except in painting the pipes, and on examination these were found to be too hot to furnish the condensation necessary for the proper working of the sight feeds. The paint was scraped away and there was no further difficulty.

SHOP NOTES

SCREW-PLUGS MADE OF OLD BULBS

Screw-plugs, though not expensive, can be made of old burned-out bulbs, in the following way:

Break the glass off even with the screw base (A) and also the little cap through which the wires are admitted to the lamp. Be sure to leave the wad of felt in to prevent short-circuiting. Connect the wires or cord (B) to the wires on the base (C) securely. Wrap some rubber tape (D) around the connection to keep the wires from touching.

Mix a little plaster of paris and water to

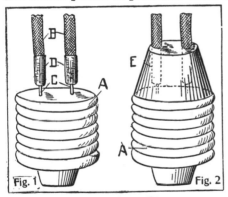

Inexpensive Screw-Plugs

the consistency of putty and fill in the hollow of the base and just high enough to cover well the connections (E, Fig. 2). Round off the top smoothly and leave until perfectly hard.—Contributed by Leslie Peto, Carmi, Ill.

PASTE FOR PAPERING PAINTED WALLS

To make wall paper stick to painted walls, prepare a batter of flour and water in the usual manner, only a little thinner, and for each gallon of batter add 1 oz. powdered rosin. Set the kettle on a moderate fire and stir until it boils and thickens, and the rosin is melted into the paste. When cool, thin down with a weak solution of gum arabic.

HOW TO MAKE A BENCH BRACE

To make a handy brace and a cheap one take 3 pieces of ⅜-in. pipe 5 in. long (AAA); three ⅜-in. ells (BBB); one ⅜-in. nipple 3

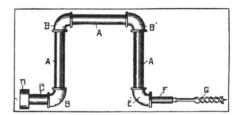

Brace Made of Pipe Fittings

in. long (C); one ⅜-in. cap (D); one ell ⅜ in. by ¼ in. (E) and one nipple 3 in. long by ¼ in. square (F) to fit the shank of the bit (G). Screw all these parts together as illustrated.—Contributed by Scott H. Phillips, Fairmont, W. Va.

HOW TO REPAIR A 20-IN. CAST-IRON PULLEY

One day whilst a large planer was running, a fellow workman threw an 18-lb. sledge hammer across the shop as he thought, but instead it struck the belt and

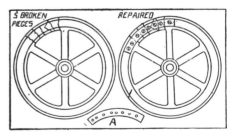

Mended Pulley

falling, knocked five small pieces out of a 20-in. cast-iron pulley. We could not get another pulley of the same size for the planer in less than a week, so I mended the broken one.

I drilled a hole in each of the small pieces

and two or three in the large pieces. Then in a piece of iron, A, 4 in. wide and the length of the opening between the spokes of the pulley, I drilled holes to correspond with those in the pieces. Then with some flathead stove bolts with nuts and washers bolted the parts together through the holes and tightened all up. The pulley ran all right for that week until we could get a new one.—Contributed by Thomas McGuire, Baltimore, Md.

DEVICES FOR GETTING ENGINES OFF OF CENTER

In Fig. 1 is shown a starting bar for getting engines of 100 to 300-hp. off the center. This is a simpler method than the old way of getting a block and piece of timber and prying the engine over a little at a time, says a correspondent of the Engineers' Review. On a large engine, however, even this wrench will not work.

For engines not too large, try the device

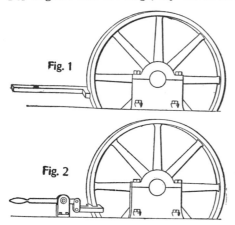

shown in Fig. 2. A clamp grips the rim of the wheel and is connected to a long lever by a short link. The long lever is supported by a stand. When the engineer forces the long lever down at the end, the clamp grips the rim of the wheel and the engine is turned from center.

TEMPLATES FOR PATTERN WORK

Use sheet aluminum, the thinnest hard stock made; lay out the template with a sharp knife. For circular work use a pair of dividers with sharp points, then by working the sheet back and forth, it will break sharp and clean on the line.—A Reader.

REPAIR FOR LEAKY VALVE

We had a 2-in. valve on a line of pipe, carrying a pressure of 40 lb. The valve was practically new, but dripped all the time. We faced up the original disk and poured an old disk with babbitt, but to no purpose,

Mending a Leaky Valve

as I suppose there was some roughness on the inside of the valve.

We then burned out the original composition in the disk and replaced it with a leather washer, marked by clamping disk and leather together in a vise, cutting to a driving fit and driving the washer into the groove with a small hammer. Now the valve holds, without any leak whatever, against a cold water pressure of from 40 to 60 lb.—Contributed by Stoke Richards, Santa Clara, Cal.

HOW TO MAKE A BLOWPIPE BELLOWS

A good blowpipe is made of a foot-ball and a bicycle pump connected up as illustrated. The whole apparatus is carefully packed in a 10-in. wooden box in the shape

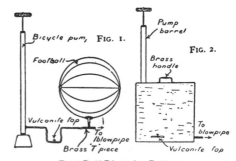

Foot-Ball Blowpipe Bellows

of a cube (Fig. 2). A hole is bored in the top to exactly fit the pump barrel, and the pump is wired down to the bottom of the box. The tube leading from the pump is fitted with a small vulcanite tap, brought outside the front of the box. When a very small pointed flame is being used, as in certain glass-working operations, a sufficient pressure can be easily stored in the football to last a considerable time without further pumping. The tap is then turned off, and none of the air can leak out through the pump (for, however good the pump may be, under the great pressure a slight quantity of air tends to work out backwards through it). Good thick rubber must be used for connections. A correspondent of the Model Engineer, London, uses a blowpipe like this for soldering and melting metals for glass working and for chemical experiments, requiring a higher temperature than a Bunsen burner will give.

SACK HOLDER MADE OF A HORSE RAKE TOOTH

A handy sack holder can be made of a horse rake tooth. Make one full turn as at

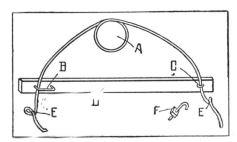

Handy Sack Holder

A to form a spring and bend each end like a pig tail (EE) about 4½ in. from the end; then flatten and shape. Place a strip of hardwood (D) on one side of the spring, and fasten it stationary at one end with a hook (C) having a threaded burr as at F on the other side. Make a strong wire loop about 2 in. wide to fasten the hardwood strip at B and to give the spring play for adjustment.

One of these holders can be hung on a nail in the granary while filling the sack and, as they are very light, it can be hooked or unhooked readily without removing the sack until it is full.—Contributed by Nathan Syverson, Stewartville, Minn.

To lace a driving belt for a high-speed machine, hold the ends together and sew them with tough, strong wire, using the shortest stitches possible. This method is recommended in Practical Pattern Making, as excellent for fast-running belts.

SIMPLE GATE HINGE

To make this hinge two pieces of round iron will be required. Heat the pieces and twist them around twice as illustrated, then bend the ends out and flatten them for

Made of Round Iron

screw holes as at A and B. The twisted part will act as a screw, says a correspondent of the Blacksmith and Wheelwright, and the weight of the gate will cause it to close itself.

TO DRAW A PERFECT ELLIPSE

The following is a very easy way to draw a perfect ellipse 3 in. long, using a pencil, two pins and a piece of thread.

Draw A-B 2 in. long and place a pin upright in the drawing board at each end of A-B. Double a strong thread and tie the loose ends together to form a loop exactly 2½ in. long. This may necessitate several trials. Place the looped thread over the pins and with the pencil point draw the string straight as at C. Then move the pencil around in the direction indicated by the arrow, always keeping the thread tight. The

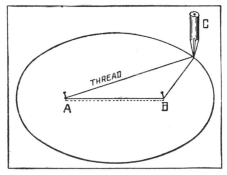

Easy Way to Draw an Ellipse

curve traced by the pencil will be a perfect ellipse.—Contributed by Harry E. Hoyt, 109 Cross St., Malden, Mass.

Contributions to this department invited. If you have a good kink, send it in.

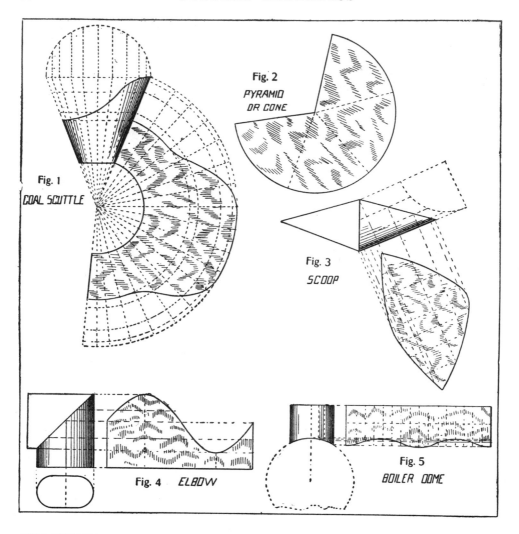

Fig. 2
PYRAMID
OR CONE

Fig. 1
COAL SCUTTLE

Fig. 3
SCOOP

Fig. 4   ELBOW

Fig. 5
BOILER DOME

IMAGINATION AND MECHANICS

In the accompanying illustration the figures correspond with those in the March number under the title "The Power of Imagination as Applied to Mechanics," and answer the question propounded therein. How many had it worked out right?—Contributed by Paul S. Baker, Muscatine, Iowa.

CHIPPING LARGE KEYWAYS

Some time ago I had the opportunity of bidding on a job of removing a wood split pulley, 5 ft. diameter, 20 in. face, from a 6-in. jack shaft and cutting a keyway 24 in. long by 1 in. wide by ½ in. deep, and placing a large 4-ton pulley on same. Several different shops figured on the job, the offers ranging for from two to four days' work on the same. I was given the job to complete in 15 hours and the general opinion was that the keyway alone would take 10 hours.

I rigged up an old man and after laying out my keyway, took a 15-16-in. drill and drilled 24 holes along the keyway, each about 7-16 in. deep, leaving 1-16 in. in sides and bottom to clean up in. In this manner the keyway was cut and key fitted in seven hours, where if I had chipped all of it, it would have taken all of the 15 hours. This is not a new kink, but it goes to show how easy we can forget the simplest things and sometimes to our disadvantage.—Contributed by Norman Baker, Hoopestown, Ill.

HOW ONE MAN BECAME A SIGN PAINTER

It takes incessant practice to become a good sign painter and no inconsiderable part of the training comes from watching signs and advertisements, picking out their good and bad points and deciding where you would improve them. Effects and wording are important particulars to watch. It is also well to watch sign painters work, when one has opportunity. A correspondent of the Master Painter tells how he began in this way while on the rounds of his daily occupation, not having opportunity to learn in a shop.

At last he secured a good plate of the Roman letters and numerals and began practicing, formulating rules for himself from measurements made by himself. After mastering this, which took a long while, he advanced to the Egyptian alphabet, and so through patient toil worked his way on to the fancy letters he had admiringly watched others make, and at last felt himself competent to tackle a billboard. He finds his occupation agreeable and well paying and names perseverance as his ladder to success.

DEVELOPER FOR SNOW SCENES

A good single-solution developer for snow scenes, says a writer in the Queen, is as follows: Soda sulphite, 90 g.; potassium carbonate, 15 g.; soda carbonate, 45 g.; hydroquinone, 7 g.; metol, 5 g. Dissolve these ingredients in the order given in one litre of boiling distilled water and then put the mixture in two half-litre bottles, labeling one "old" and the other "new." Use the "old" over and over again for developing, and as it is used up add some of the solution marked "new."

SEWER CLEANING DEVICE

The sewer cleaning device illustrated can be used successfully up to 150 ft., says the Metal Worker. When once the device is in

TOOLS MADE OF OLD BUGGY TOP JOINTS

A number of useful tools can be made from the long joints of a discarded buggy top. Any amateur blacksmith can hammer out the tools to suit himself. In the illustra-

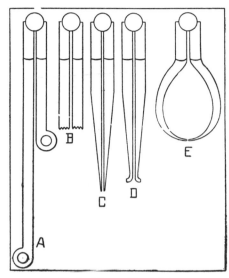

Made of Buggy Top Joints

tion, A shows one of the joints; B, joint after it is cut off; C, dividers made of joint; D, inside calipers; E, outside calipers.—Contributed by John R. Black, Jefferson, Iowa.

CEMENTS FOR MENDING CELLULOID

Broken celluloid articles, such as triangles, etc., can be mended with a cement consisting of 3 parts alcohol and 4 parts ether mixed together. Apply to the fracture with a brush until the edges become warm, then stick the edges together and leave to dry for 24 hours.

Another cement, recommended by Machinery, is: Camphor, 1 part; alcohol, 4 parts.

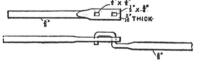

For Cleaning Pipe Sewers

the pipe the joints cannot unlock. The construction is clearly shown in the sketch.

Dissolve and add equal quantity (by weight) of shellac to the solution.

CONNECTING WATER SUPPLY TANK TO GASOLINE ENGINE

There will be no more trouble from freezing if the water supply tank is connected up to the gasoline engine as shown in the dia-

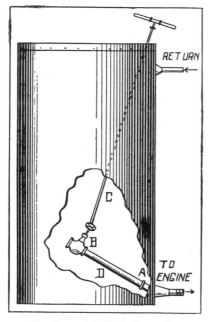

Non-Freezable Tank Connection

gram. Extend the intake pipe, D, to the center of the tank and use a 45° ell at A, in order to raise the pipe from the bottom. Use a good brass valve at B. The operating lever, C, can be made of ⅜-in. pipe. Ice may form on all sides without closing the water supply. When running in the day time the warm water will melt most of the ice that forms during the night.— Contributed by Paul S. Baker, Muscatine, Iowa.

CAUSE OF FAILURE OF BOILER FURNACES

The collapsing of boiler furnaces is almost always the direct result of scale or of oil in the feed water, the latter being a particularly prolific source of trouble, according to a recent paper before the Northeast Coast Institution of Engineers. No ordinary furnace fails for lack of strength if clean and covered with clean water, says the Journal of the Franklin Institute. A very thin smear of oil, however, has an effect totally out of proportion to what might be expected. In a furnace having a normal factor of safety of five, this factor rapidly decreases after the temperature reaches 650 degrees F., and entirely vanishes at a red heat. Steam at a pressure of 200 pounds has a temperature of about 380 degrees, or 270 below the point at which the tenacity of the steel begins to be affected, but a clean furnace, rubbed over with a very clean and thin coat of mineral oil, will soon rise above 650 degrees even under light duty, and often reach 1,200 degrees, at which point 75 per cent of the strength has departed. With the use of high-grade mineral oils the danger is less than with low-grade oils, due to the fact that the latter emulsify and hence cannot be removed from the feed water except by chemical treatment.

DIFFICULTY IN WASTE-PIPE TRAPS

In a factory where the boiler feed facilities consisted of a feed-pump, an ordinary injector and an exhaust injector (which last did the feeding) a new sink was installed so as to catch the overflow from the injector, caused by variation of load. Both injectors were put together and the sink placed under them. The waste-pipe from the sink was connected to a pipe that received the drips from the engines, pumps, heater, etc., and provided with the usual trap under the sink.

After everything was piped up, it was found that the steam pressure in the main drip-pipe forced the water out of the trap under the sink, thereby breaking the seal and allowing the steam to back up into the engine-room. In order to overcome this, a

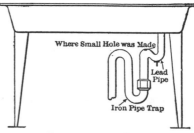

Traps in Waste Pipe

trap was placed in the iron pipe below the trap in the lead pipe. This arrangement was successful in holding back the steam, but after a few minutes' operation the water in the sink refused to run off. A ¾-in. hose with 30 lb. water pressure was run down the pipe to force out any obstruction. As long as the hose was in operation the sink worked splendidly, says a correspondent of Power, but when the hose was removed the pipe instantly clogged. The suggestion was made that the trouble was due to air being trapped between the two traps in the waste pipe. A small hole the size of a pin was made, and the sink immediately emptied and worked all right.

TIME GAS LIGHTER

This device can be used for either lighting or turning off the gas. Take the alarm

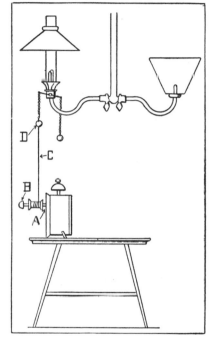

Lights the Gas at Any Hour

winding thumb screw off of an ordinary alarm clock as at A. Get a piece of ⅜-in. round iron 2½ in. long; drill a hole in one end and tap it out to fit alarm winding screw. Fasten a spool to the rod so that the spool will not turn; at the opposite end to where the rod fits the alarm screw, fasten the alarm thumb screw, B, so the alarm may be wound. Run a stout string, C, from the spool to the chain of a self-lighting gas lamp, D. When the alarm goes off the gas will light or go out according to which chain the string is attached.—Contributed by Oliver H. Bradbury, Jr., 142 Grainger av., Knoxville, Tenn.

HOW TO MAKE A CIRCULAR GUN HAMMER

A circular gun hammer may be made from ½-in. round steel without welding. Fig. 1 shows the iron flattened two ways. At A it

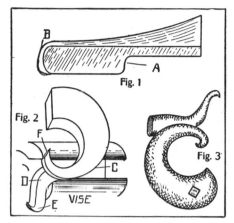

Circular Gun Hammer

is made thick enough to make the nose of the hammer; at B it is thinner. It is then placed in the vise (Fig. 2) and split with a chisel at C and D and the points are turned each way as at E and F. It is then filed to finish as in Fig. 3. This is left hand; to make the right hand work on the right side of the vise.—Contributed by Nathan Syverson, Stewartville, Minn.

ANTI-HUM DEVICE FOR TELE-PHONE WIRES

To make the anti-hum device shown, take flat brass, A, 7 in. long, ¾-in. wide and ⅛-in. thick, and hold it in a monkey wrench to bend it to shape. Then drill a ⅜-in. hole in the back and pass a ¼-in. round brass rod, B,

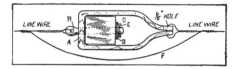

Anti-Hum Device

through. Get a thick old rubber heel and cut out two pieces with the holes in the center and take the rubber washers out and cement them together. Take the ¼-in. round brass rod 1½ in. long, flatten it at one end and drill a hole large enough for telephone wire to pass through in each end. Put the rubber washer on the rod where it passes through the ⅜-in. hole, then push the rod through the pieces of rubber heel, C. Put a brass washer, D, on that end of the rod and a wire pin, E, through the hole. Then put the device on the telephone line as shown in the illustration. I used electric light cord, F, to bridge across.—Contributed by Edward A. Pinkham, Kennebunkport, Maine.

HOW TO MAKE A STEP GRAIL

Many different styles of grails, as well as three-cornered scrapers, flat scrapers and hand chisels, may be made from old files. The illustrations show a goose neck or step grail used to get into a cavity. The cutting end, shown square here, can be made in any shape to suit the need. The tool may have teeth on the bottom side only, or on two or more sides; the corners may be round or square, but round is best, says a correspondent of Wood Craft, because it leaves a fillet of solder on the pattern.

To make this grail, draw the temper out of an old square file, grind off the file teeth and forge it to the size of the largest part of the grail—5-16 in. Bend it to shape and at point A, flatten it out. This gives strength just where needed and prevents it breaking readily. In width the file is now 7-32 in. at the largest part, tapering to ⅛ in.; the step is 1 3-16 in. down; when the teeth are resting on a flat plate, the small end on which the handle fits is 1¾ in. up.

After flattening out at A, forge out the long end to just a little larger than drawings call for and to the desired shape. Now make it very soft and file it up true and smooth. With a three-cornered file make the cutting teeth ⅛ in. apart and 1-16 in. deep. Harden it again and brighten it up with emery cloth. Using alcohol torch, draw the temper on the cutting edge to a dark straw color. Soften all other parts. Make a handle and carefully fit it on the pointed end. You then will have a tool that will last for years.

A SIMPLE SPRING WINDER

The handy spring winder shown in the illustration can be made of almost any kind of flat stock. The hole should be of proper size to fit loosely on the mandrel; the screw must be heavy enough to hold the wire and be placed a distance equal to the diameter of the wire from the mandrel hole.

To wind closed springs, hold the bar or handle at right angles to the mandrel and to wind open springs, hold the mandrel to-

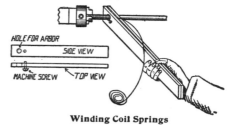

Winding Coil Springs

wards the rear end of the lathe. A little practice will make one expert at winding with this method. Springs of any length up to 100 ft., if the wire is long enough, can be wound in this way.

I have frequently used this method for winding springs to slide over rubber tubing used in laundries on gas irons for protecting the tubing and to keep it from kinking, the springs ranging from 25 to 30 ft. in length.—Contributed by W. J. Barber, North Adams, Mass.

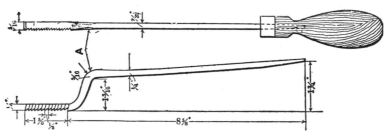

Step Grail Made of Old Files

CUTTING WIRE CABLE WITH A HACK-SAW

To cut a wire cable or a thin pipe with a hack-saw without breaking the saw, it is only necessary to turn the blade end for end in its frame, so that the saw will cut when pulling it toward you.—Contributed by Thos. McIntyre, 407 Root St., Chicago, Ill.

Two persons were electrocuted in New York recently by electric light wires that broke under the weight of sleet.

HOW TO MAKE DOUBLE PIPE HANGERS

A hanger such as is used to support ammonia coils is shown in the illustration. The coils are hung at distances of, say, 7 and 14 in. from the ceiling, two coils in a row, one directly over the other, says a correspondent of the Engineer. This method saves space and makes the parts easy of access in case of accident. Two small hangers riveted together so as to form two hooks about 8 in. apart form the hanger, the remaining portion of which is straight, having a ½-in. hole near the end to receive a lag screw. Good pipe hangers to fit any size pipe can be patterned after these.

Place one end of a piece of wrought iron 2 in. wide, ¼ in. thick and 24 in. long in the fire until red, then bend it to receive, say, a

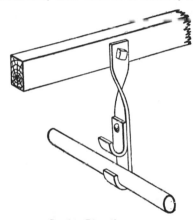

Double Pipe Hangers

2-in. pipe (grip the pipe in the vise and shape the iron around it with the hammer). When the bend is cool, place the straight end in the fire, heating it for about 6 in. from the end. Run the heated end through the vise for 6 or 7 in. and tighten the vise. Place a square wrench on the heated end and make a half twist. If the pipes run in an opposite direction to the beams, this half twist will cause the hanger to fit against the beam better, if not, the twist can be omitted. At a point 8 in. from the top of the hook place another hook of the same size and style, but not more than 4 in. long and with a hole 1 in. from the straight end. Cut another hole in the long hanger, 12 in. from the twisted end, then rivet the two together, one directly over and in a line with the other.

Any section of pipe can be removed without molesting the others.

SETTLING WALL CAUSED LEAKY PIPE JOINTS

A leak occurred in joints A and B in a supply pipe, which with the cylinder of a steam engine is shown in the illustration. After the joints had been taken apart, says

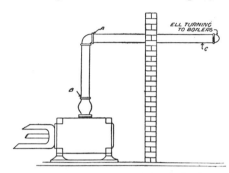

Settling Wall Causes Pipe to Leak

a correspondent of the National Engineer, it was found that the trouble was caused by the settling of the wall separating the engine and boiler rooms and which originally had supported the pipe. When a hanger was placed at C to support the weight of the pipe, there was no further difficulty.

ALARM FOR A SOUND SLEEPER

Referring to the sketch: A is a copper wire; B, brass or copper rod; C, standards;

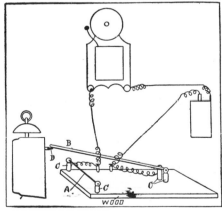

Electric Alarm

D, alarm key. When the alarm key, D, turns, the brass or copper rod, B, drops on copper wire, A, and so completes the circuit, ringing the bell.—Contributed by Eddie Evans, Hudson, S. D.

COMBINATION BACK TABLE FOR BOX SHOPS

A handy back table for use in box shops is shown in the' sketch. It may be either level or tilted. The front legs are 1 in. by 4 in., with the lower halves a little longer

wire is first laid lengthwise of the rod, and each turn of the wire goes around both wire and rod. Let the wrapping proceed away from the top end of the rod. Make not fewer than twelve turns, then twist together the end of the wire laid against the rod and the main length.

Adjustable Back Tables

than the upper ones and slotted about 10 in. A bolt, with a thumb screw, passes through a single hole in the upper leg into the slot of the lower one and a couple of large washers on each side permits of great strain in tightening. The lower leg may be vertical or slanting.

The back table is used behind the pony planer to receive the stock as it comes through. This saves rehandling the pieces so many times. When there is no one behind the planer to take away, says the Wood-Worker, the table described may be tilted so that boards, fed one behind the other, in a single or double line, will pile themselves.

ATTACHING WIRES TO GROUND RODS

To solder a heavy wire on a half-inch ground rod is not an easy matter to one who does not know the right way to go about it. Either steel or copper wire may be used for the ground, and should not be smaller than No. 14 gauge (.080 in.). Heat the rod red hot for about 1 ft. at the top end. A

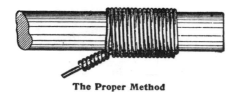

The Proper Method

combination of blow torches, a coal stove, or a forge may be used for heating, says Telephony. Scrape the heated portion quickly with a file, and wrap the wire on it as in the illustration. The end of the

The wire will have become somewhat heated by this time. Bend it down along the rod, out of the way, and lay the heated end, joint and all, in a box of granulated sal ammoniac, rolling the entire joint in it. Dense white fumes will rise, and when a stick of solder is held against the rod it will melt in a pool in the sal ammoniac. The sal ammoniac will clean both wire and rod, and the solder will flow smoothly on both. When the joint is filled smooth with solder, shake it free of any excess metal and allow to cool. Cooling suddenly in water does no harm, but washes away excess sal ammoniac that would cause wire and rod to corrode. The joint should be made a few inches from the end of the rod, so that the end will not break off when the rod is driven. No ground rod should be less than 7 ft. long.

TO REMOVE OLD PAINT AND VARNISH

The following method is good, if the surface is to be repainted, says the Painters' Magazine.

Dissolve 4 lb. caustic soda, 98 per cent, or as many pounds concentrated lye, in 1 gal. boiling water and allow it to cool. In another vessel mix ½ lb. each of starch and china clay in 1 gal. of hot water. Beat this well, so as to have no lumps, and when cooled off some add it to the soda or lye solution, stirring well in the meantime, when it forms a thick, smooth paste. Apply this paste with a fiber (not bristle) brush to the surface in a heavy film, and when the paint or varnish is raised wash with warm water. To remove any traces of causticity give the surface a coat of vinegar and allow to dry before repainting. This method will raise the grain slightly, but that is not objectionable where the surface is to be repainted.

For removing varnish from wood that is to be refinished in the natural, a mixture of 3½ pints American fusel oil and ½ pint turpentine will lift the varnish without raising the grain or discoloring the wood.

WHEN DRILL STICKS IN ROCK

When a drill-bit sticks in a hole, the usual remedy is to strike the shank violently with a sledge until the bit is loosened. It is better to strike a moderate blow on the shank, near the hole, and never so high up as to strike the chuck, because then a bent piston or a broken chuck is likely to result. Small pieces of cast-iron, nuts or other fragments are used to keep the drill straight and prevent sticking or "running off."

TO MAKE HARD PUTTY

A little red lead added to oil-whiting putty will make it hard but not brittle, says the Master Painter. Rub varnish makes putty both tough and hard.

TOOL FOR CUTTING JOINTS ON CIRCLES

The tool illustrated does away with the necessity for drawing so many lines in order to find a joint on a circle. The device will cut any circle by placing the pin on the radius. It is marked off like a rule in inches and twelfths on the inner edges and may be provided with the slide or not, as liked. The pin runs through the hinge about ⅛-in. to hold the instrument in place while measuring the distance from A to B.—Contributed by Chas. Walters, Mt. Vernon, Ohio.

SIMPLE TANK GAUGE

A handy tank gauge consists of a gear wheel set on a pinion to which is attached the hand A. A rack gear, B, meshes into the gear wheel and slides on the seat C. The hand A moves around a dial, D, with as many inches marked on it as it is desirable to let the water fluctuate up and down in the tank.

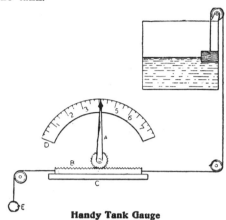

Handy Tank Gauge

When the float in the tank falls, the rack gear is drawn toward the right, causing hand A to move to the left. When the float rises with the water in the tank, weight E draws the rack toward the left and the hand moves in the opposite direction till it reaches 7, or whatever the number may be, indicating that the tank is full. This device is recommended by a correspondent of the Engineers' Review.

Heavy manila paper coated with shellac on one side makes an excellent substitute for glass for the sign painter, says the Master Painter. The prepared paper can be carried in the kit easily, does not break and is cheaper than the glass.

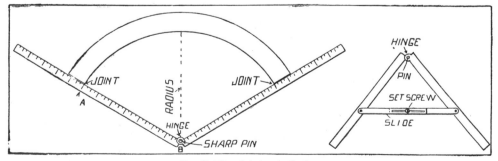

For Cutting Joints on Circles

DRILLING MACHINE MADE OF SCRAP

A small drilling machine may be made of scrap material by any one with a little ingenuity. For the one illustrated a piece of an old fret machine was used for the head (A). An old lathe head stock will do as well. Screw the part to a piece of wood 1 in. thick and then screw the wood to the workshop wall. Take a band over pulley B at the end and over the small pulleys, C, C₁, C₂, and over flywheel D at the bottom.

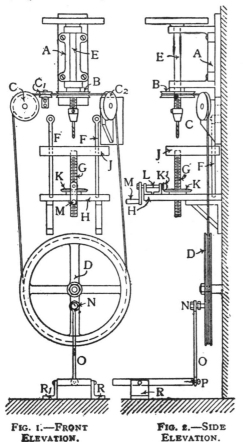

FIG. 1.—FRONT ELEVATION.

FIG. 2.—SIDE ELEVATION.

midway between the end of spindle E and the top of the flywheel. Drill a hole through one end of each of the guide-bars, and let the other end into bracket H about ½ in. from the wall. Do not let them go quite through. Bore two holes through table J, ½ in. from the edge, and put a brass plate each side of each hole to allow the ¼ in. guide-bars to slide through easily.

Tap the third ¼-in. bar and make two nuts to fit it. Screw one nut up to within ¾ in. of the top; square the end above this nut and drive it into the table J, so that when the table is put on to the guide-bars and they are in their places, screwed to the wall by a screw through the hole before mentioned, in one end, the feed-screw G comes exactly under the end of the spindle E. Before putting the table in its place get an egg-beater (one of the bevel wheel kind) and take off the large cog-wheel and one of the small ones. Bore a hole through the large wheel so that it will slide easily over the screw G. Now turn a wooden disk the same size as the large wheel and cut a hole in it to fit the nut on the feed-screw.

Screw the large wheel on top of this disk (cogs upward) and put the nut into the square hole in the wooden disk, and screw a small brass plate on the opposite side of the cog-wheel to keep the nut in its place. Bore a hole in the bracket at the same distance from the wall as the hole for the feed-screw in the table J. Screw the cog-wheel and disk on to the feed-screw G, and pass the guide-bars through the hole in the table J, and pass the feed-screw through the hole in the bracket and screw the guide-bars to the workshop wall, but put a ½-in. washer on the screw between the wall and guide-bar. Take the small cog-wheel off the egg-beater and fit it to an axle. The best way of doing this is to get a piece of wire slightly larger than the hole in the cog-wheel. Tap this for 1 in., so that it will screw into the cog-wheel, and make two nuts the same thread. These nuts must be slightly smaller than the cog-wheel. Screw one as far as it will go.

Next screw on the cog-wheel and a nut outside that. These nuts must be screwed up fairly tight to keep the cog-wheel from revolving on the axle. Now cut off the axle about 2 in. from the small cog-wheel and fix a piece of brass about ⅛ in. by ½ in. by 2 in. This should be fixed as follows:

Square the end of the axle and drill two holes in the brass plate about ¼ in. from each end. Into one of these secure a small handle; drive the other end on to the square

Place the small pulley C₁ horizontally to give the band a good grip on pulley B. Tap the end of spindle E to fit a drill chuck off of a small level-wheel drill. Arrange the table feed of the drill as follows:

Procure a piece of hard wood to project about 3 in. beyond spindle E, which may be of any convenient length; also, procure three pieces of ¼-in. iron—two to form the guides, FF, and the other to form the feed-screw, G. Screw a small bracket to the wall, end of the axle and screw on a small nut outside it. Get two small brass plates, and bend over the bottom about ½ in., L-shaped, and drill two small holes through the bottom of the L to screw down to the bracket H. Drill another hole on the other side of the angle to take the axle L. These holes should be drilled so that when the brackets are screwed down the small cog-wheel meshes with the large one K. Put a small washer outside the plate between the handle and plate, and cog-wheel plate. Now screw these plates to the bracket so that one comes up against the small cog-wheel and keeps it in place. Screw the other one up against the handle, so that axle L has no end play.

If, when handle M is turned to the left, table J will not come down of its own accord, pass a piece of brass over the large cog-wheel, K, and screw down at each end. The flywheel may be taken from an old sewing-machine, and if it is not quite heavy enough, put a lead weight on it. Pass a bolt through the center of the flywheel with a shoulder on behind. This bolt should run through the workshop wall and a nut put on from the outside.

Put a bolt, N, into one of the spokes of the wheel and put a piece of thick iron wire around this and connect it to the end of the treadle by a screw at P. Make the treadle of wood, 9 in. by 4 in. by 1 in. Screw the iron wire on at one end, not tightly, but so it can move a little each way. Swing the treadle in the middle by two screws, passing through small metal plates, R, R₁, at each side. A machine like this was rigged up by a correspondent of the Model Engineer, London, and worked very satisfactorily.

TO GILD ON GLASS

Thinly coat the places to be gilded with a saturated borax solution on which lay the gold leaf and press down well and uniformly with cotton wool. Heat the glass over a spirit flame until the borax melts and allow to cool off.

If the glass is to be decorated with gilt letters or designs, paint the places to be gilded with water-glass solution of 40 degrees, lay on the gold leaf and press down uniformly. Then heat the object to 86 degrees Frahrenheit, so that it dries a little; sketch the letters or figures on with a lead pencil, erase the superfluous gold and allow the article to dry completely at a higher temperature.

HOW TO MAKE A CHIME STEAM WHISTLE

Procure a piece of seamless brass tubing 8 in. long, 4 in. in diameter and 1/16 in. or less, thick. Have cast a bowl, B, 4 in. in diameter, and with a place in the bottom for inserting a 1-in. pipe. Also have cast, or make yourself, a disk, A, 3⅞-in. in diameter, allowing 1/16 in. between the edge of the disk and the bowl for the escape of the steam that strikes the bell. Then get a ½-in. bolt, C, 10 in. long, threaded on both ends and with three slots, just wide enough to

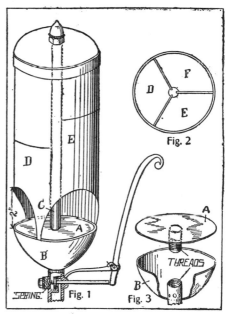

Home-Made Steam Whistle

fit sheet brass partitions for cells running its entire length into.

Cut the tubing into thirds by dividing it up as indicated in the sketch, and use sheet brass for forming the cells, soldering it in. Let one cell be 4½ in. high, D; one 5¾ in. high, E; and the other 8 in. high. Put a brass cap 4 1/16 in. in diameter, threaded, on the top and use an acorn or other ornament to finish it.

To make the valve drill a hole through the bottom of a 1-in. check valve, and stick the stem of check through the hole, as shown in the sketch. Put a brass spring in behind seat or valve disk to force it closed after using, then fasten the lever around the valve, as shown, and your single bell chime whistle is complete. This whistle makes a beautiful sound and can be heard much farther than the ordinary whistle. Fig. 2 is an inside view of the bell, looking down from the top; Fig. 3 shows how the disk is fastened into the bowl.—Contributed by Thos. McGuire, Baltimore, Md.

TO SAVE A GIRDLED TREE

When a valuable tree is girdled it may pay to try to save it. The following method has been successful. When, in the spring,

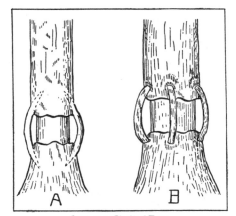

Saving a Girdled Tree

the tree is found girdled, drive a small chisel into the bark above and below the girdled portion as shown by the dotted lines in A. Then cut some large healthy twigs of the preceding year's growth from the top of the tree, each a little longer than the distance between the opposite cuts in the tree. Sharpen both ends of the twigs and bend them until the ends can be placed in the cuts as shown at B. Press the twigs in until they are as near straight as possible, so that there is a perfect union between the inner bark of both twig and tree. Four or more twigs, according to the size of the tree, should be placed around it. Then cover the whole with grafting wax. If the work is skilfully done, says the Rural New-Yorker, the tree will be completely cured in a few years.

To render ivory flexible, immerse in a solution of pure phosphoric acid, sp. gr. 1.13, until it partially loses its opacity; wash in cold soft water and dry. It will harden again if exposed to air, but may again be made pliable by immersing in hot water.

TANK TO KEEP WATER FROM FREEZING

To keep water from freezing make a tank of galvanized iron two or three inches narrower at the bottom than at the top, says the Rural New-Yorker. Set the iron tank in a bottomless wooden box and place the whole directly on the stringers of the well and plank up to it on each side. Provide a cover to the box. Warm air from the well striking the bottom and sides of the tank will keep the water warm.

WELDING A PALM ON AN ANCHOR

Sometimes an anchor with the palm broken off as shown at A, comes into the shop for a new palm or the old one to be welded on. If the break is not even, trim it a little with the chisel, fit a good pair of tongs to the palm, swing the anchor in the crane (this applies only to heavy anchors 500 lb. and up) and put both ends of the break in the fire and heat them up.

Have a piece of iron or any old metal about 4 in. by 1 in. heated in another fire, and when ready bring them all out, place the anchor and the palm together and weld the flat piece across the break. This saves lap-scarfing or rigging. Turn the anchor over and cut out a V-piece as shown at B. Now place the anchor in a clean fire (not a hollow fire), get a good heat, fill in with

To Repair an Anchor

the V-piece and finish off that side. Then turn your piece over, cut away the flat piece and cut a V into this side. You now proceed the same as on the other side, says the American Blacksmith, heating the part where V was cut, placing a wedge in and welding and finishing. You will have a good job by this method if the heats are right.

HANDY DARK-ROOM LAMP

For those who use glass trays the diagram shows a convenient way to rig up a dark-room lamp. S is a shelf with a

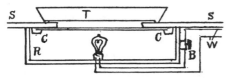

Ruby Lamp for Dark Room

square hole about 1 in. smaller each way than the tray cut in it; C is a piece of ruby glass held by clamps to the shelf; R is a box which encloses the electric light; Ŀ is a switch, which may be placed anywhere convenient; W are wires leading to the light. When the light is turned on the negative will show up plainly.—Contributed by Harold W. Moffat, 476 Main St., Orange, N. J.

TO MEND A GRINDSTONE

A piece broken out of a grindstone can be replaced by covering the surface of the piece and the broken surface of the grindstone with a strong solution of pure Portland cement and water, then pressing the piece firmly in position. Give plenty of time to dry.—Contributed by G. W. Gander, Nappanee, Ind.

BEVELING STAVES FOR ROUND TANKS

Many workmen make an elaborate process of getting the bevel of staves for round tanks. Much of their work is unnecessary, says a correspondent of the Wood-Worker. A simple method is illustrated. Take one of the pieces intended for a stave, set the

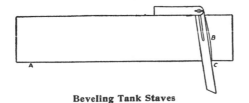

Beveling Tank Staves

trammel to the radius used in striking the bottom, or to be absolutely accurate, to that of the outside of the tank and from a point A at one edge of the stave strike curve B. Set the bevel to touch the two ends of this curve and it will be correct; the usual practice is to set it back a little at C, so the staves will be slightly open on the outside. When the tank is wet the openings close and the staves spring to the curve of the bottom.

TO PREVENT CRACKS UNDER WINDOW SILLS IN CEMENT BLOCK BUILDINGS

In erecting buildings of cement blocks, the blocks under window sills frequently crack. This is because proper provision for settlement has not been made, says Municipal Engineering. In most cases the trouble is probably due to the settling of the sills in full bed of mortar when they are first set. To prevent the cracking, in either brick or concrete construction, set the sills at first with joint full of mortar only at the ends, leaving a space under the sill for the whole width of the window space. The settlement of the

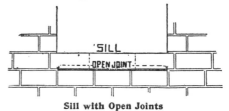

Sill with Open Joints

wall can then occur during the construction without bringing the breaking strain upon the sills. After the work is completed and the settlement is presumably all done fill the open joints under the sills with mortar and thus finish the wall. No cracks will then appear in either blocks, bricks, wall or sills under ordinary circumstances, and unless there is a great settlement, such as would come from insufficient foundation and bad design.

TO KEEP WATER PIPES FROM SWEATING

Wipe the pipe dry with an old cloth, then wind it with two or three thicknesses of good heavy paper. Cover this wrapping with 4-in. strips of heavy cotton cloth. This kink was tried on 100 ft. of pipe and there was no further trouble from dripping.—Contributed by Fred Connor, Hydeville, Vt.

To prevent the annealing of metal above the place where heat is to be applied, stick the rod or band iron in a potato.—Contributed by E. M. Atkinson, Portland, Ore.

LOCOMOTIVE TIRE AS FIRE ALARM

Inexpensive--Effective

In many of the smaller cities where an electric fire alarm has not yet been installed worn out or cracked tires from the driving

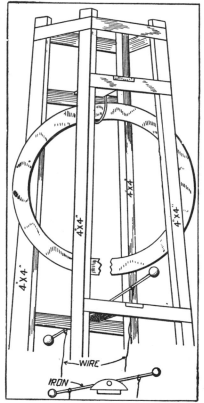

Novel Fire Alarm

wheels of locomotives are used in place of fire bells. The cost is less, the sound is very penetrating and is unlike a bell. For many years Marengo, Ill., used one of these tires before alarm boxes were put in. W. F. Mead of that place furnishes a sketch which will indicate the manner of erecting the tower, which in this case was on top the fire engine house. The tire was hung by an iron ring from a cross piece, but some towns erect a 20 or 30 ft. tower on the ground. The striker has an iron ball at each end, with two wires passing down to the ground floor one of which is grasped by each hand. By this means more rapid strokes can be sounded than on a bell.

Shop Notes for 1905 and 1906 are a gold mine of information to any mechanic.

PRESERVING OLD SCREWS

Do not place old nuts, screws, etc., which you save in tin boxes. They will soon become rusty and unfit for use. A better way is to keep them in small large-neck bottles, says Machinery. Always sort the screws, etc., according to size and provide the bottles with corks and labels.

WHEN TO VARNISH GOLD LETTERS

When gold leaf is very thin or largely alloyed varnish will protect it and make it wear longer, says the Master Painter. But for leaf of good quality and stout the varnish is undesirable. It impairs the lustre and is apt to crack.

WHEN THE HANDS OF A CLOCK COME TOGETHER

Having worked out the little problem involved in ascertaining the exact time at which the two hands of a clock come together in making their respective circuits, and thinking the information might be sufficiently novel to merit space in your columns, I submit the following table.

I say this seems novel, because I do not remember ever having seen it in print, or heard the matter discussed.

				12 o'clock	
5 min.	$27\frac{3}{11}$ sec. past	1	"
10 "	$54\frac{6}{11}$ "	"	2	"
16 "	$21\frac{9}{11}$ "	"	3	"
21 "	$49\frac{1}{11}$ "	"	4	"
27 "	$16\frac{4}{11}$ "	"	5	"
32 "	$43\frac{7}{11}$ "	"	6	"
38 "	$10\frac{10}{11}$ "	"	7	"
43 "	$38\frac{2}{11}$ "	"	8	"
49 "	$5\frac{5}{11}$ "	"	9	"
54 "	$32\frac{8}{11}$ "	"	10	"

Contributed by J. Raymond Campbell, Frick building, Pittsburg, Pa.

LOCATING BEARINGS FOR SHAFTING

Every master mechanic knows how troublesome it often is to tell in advance the exact location of the bearings for a new line of shafting. To overcome this have the shafting keyseated the entire length and then fill the keyways where the bearings come with babbitt, after the line is in place. Another advantage in this is that additional pulleys can be placed at any time. Use babbitt of a different grade from that in the boxes.—Contributed by F. C. Perkins, Harkness, N. Y.

SHOP NOTES

A BOLTING KINK

A good way to bolt a plate or angle iron to some other structural piece, having bolts in it but so short that the nuts come just flush with the ends, and where you cannot take the bolts out to put in longer ones, is as follows:

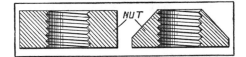

Using Short Bolts

Countersink the holes in the plate or angle to be bolted on, then screw the nuts on an old bolt and grind them down taper to fit the countersunk holes.—Contributed by Thos. McIntyre, 407 Root St., Chicago, Ill.

GOOD FLOOR POLISHES

1. Put a small quantity of spermaceti in a saucepan on the fire and mix with it enough turpentine to make it fluid. Apply to the floor a thin coat, using a piece of flannel for the purpose. Rub with dry flannel and brush the same way oak stains are brushed. The rubbing and brushing process, says the Practical Carpenter, take a long time, if properly done.

2. Dissolve ½ lb. potash in 3 pts. water in a saucepan on the fire, and when the water boils throw in 1 lb. beeswax cut up into small pieces. Stir until the wax is melted. If the polish is too thick when cold, add more water. Apply with a brush, painting the boards evenly, and when dry rub with flannel tied on the end of a broom.

TO MAKE A RIVET SET

To make a useful rivet set, take a square head bolt, cut it off 4 in. from the head and drill a 7/16-in. hole in the bottom. —Contributed by Wm. T. Ackerman, 1311 Stockton St. Baltimore, Ind.

HOW TO CUT A BELT

If one lacks the regular tools for cutting a belt a good job may be accomplished with only a knife, a vise and a block of wood. The wood should be the same width as the belt or a little wider and should be fastened in the vise about ⅜ in. below the top of the jaws. Drive the knife in the wood making the distance between the jaw of the vise and the knife blade, the re-

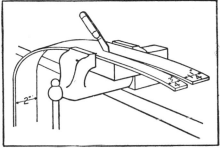

How to Cut a Belt

quired width of the belt. Then draw the belt through as shown.—Contributed by J. J. Hunziher, Cleveland, O.

A JIG FOR FILING SMALL WORK

For the benefit of bench men or any one who has to file small work requiring a perfectly flat surface, the following device is described.

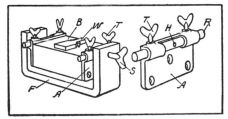

Jig for Filing Small Work

A block B, similar to those generally used for filing small work, is mounted in a frame F by thumb screws S which allow the block to swing and thus prevents rounding the ends of the work. The adjusting plate A has a sliding rod R with a hole in the centre H to receive the pointed thumb screws S, the rod R being adjusted and held in place by the thumb screws T.

The frame F may be either of wrought or cast iron, and should have screw holes in the bottom to fasten it to the bench. The wood block B is fitted with pins to hold the work. The adjusting plate A can be made of brass or cast iron and the rod R and thumb screws S, T are made of steel.— Contributed by G. D. B., Springfield, Mass.

SOLDERING IRON HOLDER FOR BLOW TORCH

A device for heating soldering irons very quickly and with little fuel consists of a sheet iron pocket A, Fig. 1, and a $\frac{3}{16}$-in. stove

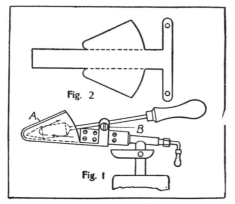

Fig. 2

A

B

Fig. I

Holder For Heating a Soldering Iron

bolt B for fastening to blow torch. Cut a piece of No. 18 sheet iron to the shape shown in Fig. 2 and drill holes for the $\frac{3}{16}$-in. stove bolt as shown. Bend the sheet iron as shown in Fig. 1 and fasten to the burner, and the heater is complete.—Contributed by G. L. Housman, Prattville, Mich.

HOW TO SENSITIZE SILK

Prepare a solution by pouring 10 oz. boiling water on 50 gr. ammonium chloride and 30 gr. Iceland moss; allow to become nearly cold, then filter. Soak the silk in this solution for 15 minutes, let it dry, then sensitize it by soaking for another 15 minutes in a silver nitrate solution (20 gr. to the ounce) with a little nitric acid added. Dry the sensitized silk in the dark room and treat precisely as P. O. P. To obtain good results the printing should be very dark.

HOW A STEAM TURBINE WORKS

The turbine mode of propulsion, which is so rapidly finding favor as a marine propeller, is most aptly described by the well-known figure of a pinwheel, says Marine Journal. The turbine, in fact, is a series of pinwheels, one behind the other, fixed to a shaft which turns with them. Now everyone knows that when a pinwheel is blown upon it revolves. For this motion in the turbine a jet of steam is employed. Fixed to the inside of the cylinder in which the propeller revolves is a series of stationary blades projecting into the space between each wheel and set at such an angle that they will deflect the stream of steam to strike the propeller at an angle which will give the most force.

The Parsons turbine consists of a cylindrical case with numerous rings of inwardly projecting blades. Within this cylinder, which is of variable internal diameter, is a shaft or spindle, and on this spindle are mounted blades, projecting outwardly, by means of which the shaft is rotated. The former are called fixed or guide blades, and the latter revolving or moving blades. The diameter of the spindle is less than the internal diameter of the cylinder, and thus an annular space is left between the two. This space is occupied by the blades, and it is through these the steam flows. The steam enters the cylinder by means of an annular port at the forward end; it meets a ring of fixed guide blades which deflects it so that it strikes the adjoining ring of moving blades at such an angle that it exerts on them a rotary impulse. When the steam leaves these blades it has naturally been deflected. The second ring of fixed blades is therefore interposed, and these direct the steam on to the second ring of rotating blades. The same thing occurs with succeeding rings of guide and moving blades until the steam escapes at the exhaust passage

TO REMOVE BROKEN SECTIONS FROM A MOWER SICKLE

Place the sickle in a vise with the points of sections down. Screw the vise up tight enough so the sickle bar will not go through. Then with a heavy hammer drive the broken sections straight down. One stroke will remove each section, if properly made. —Contributed by J. J. Hogan, Parnell, Iowa.

SIMPLE TELEPHONE LINE USING RECEIVERS FOR TRANS·MITTERS

An ordinary telephone receiver—the ear piece—can be used for purposes of transmitting and receiving on lines of reasonable distance. In this case a push button and

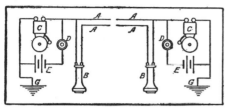

No Transmitters Used on This Line

call bell must be installed at each end of the line with which to make the call. A reader writes as follows: "I have always been interested in your shop notes and am sending you a diagram for a simple telephone. It consists of two receivers, into which the words are spoken and heard alternately, and a ringing attachment. It gives very good results, as I have one to a friend's house some 500 ft. away, which works as well as the larger, complicated telephones. Anyone can easily put up a line and make the connections by following the diagram shown. A 2-wire line is required, also grounding at each end. In the diagram, A, A, are the line wires; B, B, receivers which also serve as transmitters; C, C, call bells; D, D, push buttons; E, E batteries; and F, F, the ground connections. The cost of such a line, say 500 ft., is about as follows: 1,000 ft. No. 14 galvanized iron wire, 75 cents; 2 receivers, $1; 2 sets call bells,

Reduces Hard Work to a Minimum

push buttons and four batteries, $1.02; 18 insulators and 100 ft. No. 18 annunciator wire, 66 cents. Total, $3.43.—Contributed by Edward Band, 1232 Wrightwood Ave., Chicago.

REPAIR FOR LARGE HOLE IN OUTER CASING OF AUTO TIRE

The materials required are a piece of old outer casing for the patch, of length and thickness according to the size of the hole; a lacing needle, and a piece of cord or tape to lace the patch on with.

Trim the ends of the patch so it will fit evenly on the tire and punch lacing holes in the sides so it can be laced over the tire. The outer casing and patch should be the same diameter. Put the patch over the tire and lace as tight as possible, then

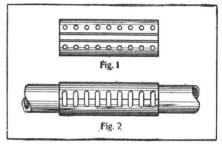

Fig. 1

Fig. 2

Repairing an Auto Tire

put the tire on the wheel. Fig. 2 shows the patch laced on the tire.

HOME-MADE FOOT-POWER SAW

Instead of being a back-breaking, tedious hardship, sawing wood may be made a pleasant exhilarating exercise. Any person with even a slight knowledge of tools can make a foot power saw. The illustration will sufficiently explain how it is done. My machine was constructed from an old bicycle frame and buck saw, the reciprocating motion being obtained by the use of a crank pin and connecting rod as shown. The upper lever raises and lowers the saw and the lower lever clamps the wood in position.—Contributed by E. Ponton, Northampton, Mass.

SHOOTING OFF AIR PISTONS

When stripping an air pump for over-hauling, it is often difficult to remove the air piston. A correspondent of Railway and Locomotive Engineering shoots it off.

The device which was used with 8-in. and 9½-in. air pumps consists of a block of machine steel 2½ in. square by 7¼ in. long,

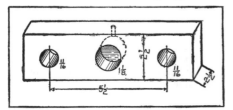

For Shooting off Air Pistons

having two ⅝-in. holes 5½ in. apart for ⅝-in. bolts and a hole 1⅛ in. in diameter and 1½ in. deep, with fuse hole drilled through in the center of the block to hole for the end of the piston rod to slip in. Then a thimble full of gunpowder and a leather wad with some paper, if necessary, is rammed in. The block is bolted up to the air piston, some powder is put in the fuse hole and touched off with a heated rod.

The piston will be removed without burring the threads or breaking anything. It is well to set up a block to keep the piston from going too far.

AN UNBREA' ABLE S-WRENCH

Forge down piece of old buggy spring as at A, ther work it on the edge of an anvil to a diamond shape by stoving as at B. Punch a hole in each diamond-shaped part a little in front of the center and cut out to edge. Drive in a punch to spread the

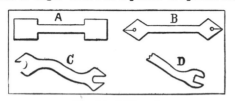

Durable S-Wrench

jaws, and bend one each way sideways and work to shape on the edge of the anvil. Bend back straight and finish on the hardy, leaving jaws with a diamond corner as at C. This wrench will not break as those made in the usual way (D) often do. I find that old springs make the best wrenches.—Contributed by O. V. Simpson, Hersman, Ill.

HOW TO GALVANIZE IRON

The two general methods of galvanizing are the dipping process and the electro-plating process. The dipping process is the one generally used, as it protects the iron and prevents it from rusting to a greater extent than the electro-plating method. There are some articles, however, which require electro-plating, especially when a very thin coating of zinc is required.

In the dipping process the article is first dipped in a solution of sulphuric acid. It is then placed in a solution of hydrochloric acid, and after drying is immersed in the molten zinc. Compressed air lifts are generally used for handling large work, and small articles are sometimes placed in perforated ladles. The troughs for holding the acids are usually made of wood, and the tanks for melting the zinc are made of steel 1 in. or more in thickness. The melting is usually started with lead, which melts first and surrounds the zinc. This saves time in melting and prevents over-heating the tank.

This process is very wasteful, as the amount of zinc deposited on the work is only about 53% of that put into the tank. Of the remaining zinc about 30 to 40% is converted into dross; 15 to 20% oxidizes and rises to the surface; and 5% or more evaporates.

The dross is an alloy of zinc and iron and, being heavier than zinc, sinks to the bottom of the tank and is often very difficult to remove. It is sold at a considerable loss and is used in making zinc oxide for paint. The skimmings are also sold, but the evaporated portion, of course, is a total loss.

A new process for galvanizing has been perfected lately which will probably be less wasteful than the one described. The new process is as follows: Pickle the article to be galvanized for a few hours in a solution of 1 part of sulphuric acid (concentrated) in 100 parts of water. Use a wooden or porcelain vessel for this process. Then scour the article with a brush, wash well and place in a solution of lime and water until ready for the galvanizing process.

Just before galvanizing immerse the article in a solution of zinc chloride and ammonium chloride until bubbles appear on the surface of the metal. To make this solution place zinc in hydro-chloric acid until no further action takes place, decant, and add sal ammoniac. Dry the metal with the film of bubbles on it on a heated iron plate, then place in a bath of heated zinc. "Be very careful not to overheat or 'burn' the zinc," warns the Model Engineer, London, and to prevent the oxidation of the metal place either some sal ammoniac or charcoal on the surface. Withdraw the article from the molten metal and beat it to remove the excess of zinc.

This process is excellent for fittings used for yachts, water motors, etc., as iron castings thus treated will resist the action of water for a considerable time.

TIME FIRE KINDLER FOR COOK STOVE

An alarm clock can be connected up to light a fire in the cook stove at the time desired, and thus save one getting up before the kitchen is heated.

Drill two holes in the stove and screw in two eyes (A A), then place a rod (B) with a spring in the eyes as shown. In the end of this rod drill a hole to receive the match. If the match is too small to stay in, use a wedge to hold it. On the eye in the middle of the stove solder a piece of

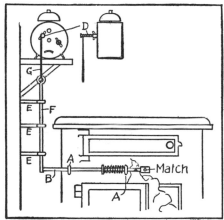

Time Lighter for Cook Stove

stiff tin, so that the match will be drawn against it when the rod is thrown by the spring.

Solder a nail (D) to the key of an alarm clock and place the clock on a shelf near the stove. Under the shelf use three screw eyes (E E E) to hold a perpendicular rod (F) connected with the stove rod as shown, and with the alarm key by a stout cord (G).

Set the alarm for the time you want the fire kindled and have the kindling device in readiness, as illustrated. When the alarm runs down it will wind the cord G on the nail D attached to the key and thus pull rod F off of the end of rod B, which

will be thrown by the spring and so strike the match. A piece of paper, or other easily inflammable material, should be placed near the match so the flame will catch.—Contributed by O. E. Vessels, 313 E. Yorwood St., Indianapolis, Ind.

TO KEEP SHAFTING BRIGHT

A good way to keep shafting bright is to cut rings either of fibre or leather and put two between each hanger and pulley— or three if they are very far apart. The ring (A) can be put on the shafting (C)

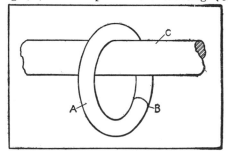

Leather Rings Keep Shafting Bright

by cutting a slit (B) in one side. When the shafting is in motion the rings travel back and forth on it.—Contributed by W. J. Slattery, Emsworth, Pa.

TO ENAMEL ALUMINUM

A coating for aluminum ware, aiming to produce a coloring of durable character or in rendering the surface adapted to enameling can be obtained by a process patented in Germany, according to Metallurgie, by a Mr. Lang. The surface is covered in the first instance with a solution of a quicksilver compound—as, for instance, chloride of mercury—and by this means a coating of aluminum amalgam is obtained. After this is removed a very active process of oxidation of the surface is said to take place, which action may be interrupted by strong heating, and the aluminum oxide will serve as a foundation for the enamel. If during the process of oxidation the metal is exposed to the action of chromic acid or other suitable chromates or to some other readily reducible substances, these compounds are at once reduced. The action of heat may also be employed to give different colored coatings, and the colors obtained may be gray, green, brown or black. They are said to resist the action of fire and render the aluminum more difficult to melt.

DEADENING THE SOUND OF AN ANVIL

If the anvil block is wider than the base of the anvil, hew it down to fit, then bore a ¾-in. hole through the block 10 or 12 in. from the top. Make four ⅝-in. bolts with ¾-in. eyes and a ¾-in. bolt long enough to go through the block and take two eyebolts on each side. Make yokes of ⅝ by 1 in. stock and punch or drill ⅝-in. holes in each end. Measure the anvil so as to have the bolts hug it closely; put the ¾-in. bolt through the block, slip on the eyebolts, put on the clamps and nuts and tighten up. A correspondent of the American Blacksmith who devised this method, says, that it will both hold the anvil securely and effectually deaden its ring.

CUTTING WINDOW GLASS

When a pane of glass is broken and you have no light to fit, a larger glass can be cut to size by the following method:

Moisten a cloth with vinegar or turpentine and wet the light where you intend to cut it. Break off a piece of a triangular file and proceed as with a glazier's diamond. Double A glass can be cut successfully in this way.—Contributed by F. Knospe, Clyman, Wis.

TO KEEP STEAM HOSE FROM BLOWING OFF WHEN TUBES ARE BLOWN

Thread one end of a piece of ¾-in. pipe, 6 or 8 in. long, and heat the other end as hot as possible without burning. Put the pipe over the horn of an anvil and pein with a light hammer to a bell shape, as at A in

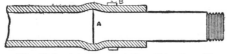

Pipe Peined to Prevent Hose Blowing off

the sketch. Work the pipe into the hose and put on a good fitting clamp, as at B. The harder it pulls, says the Engineer's Review, the tighter it will get. Couple the hose to the steam pipe with a dart union, which makes an excellent hose coupling, and can be screwed tight with the hands.

CONTINUOUSLY RINGING BURGLAR ALARM

A continuously ringing burglar alarm is a very simple affair, the only addition to the ordinary alarm being a one-point switch (which may be home-made) and a little wire, so if one has an alarm, this may be made without extra expense.

Connect up the alarm, battery and bell in the usual manner, but shunt in the one-point switch, A, as shown in the sketch. Then nearly close the switch and fasten the movable end to the tapper of the bell by means of a small copper wire soldered to it and a piece of string. (The string should not be omitted, for the switch, which works very easily, might be pushed off connection by the stiff copper wire.)

The arrangement that starts the alarm ringing is seen at the left. If a burglar in entering pulls the string the pivoted lever B will make contact with terminal C at one side and the bell will ring; and if in endeavoring to stop the alarm, he cuts the

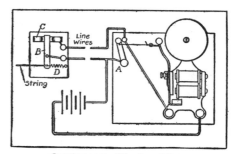

Continuously Ringing Alarm

string, spring D will move the lever so that it contacts at the opposite side of the terminal and the bell will ring on. With the ordinary alarm, should a burglar hear the bell he need only step back from the string or close the door or window, if the string is attached to either of them, and the chances are that the bell would not be heard; but a loud bell ringing continuously is sure to awaken someone.—Contributed by Jack Stair, 258 E. Market St., York, Pennsylvania.

Before putting screws in soft wood fill the holes with thick glue, or if glue is not convenient, put powdered resin around the holes and heat the screws before driving. The Practical Carpenter says this will keep the screws from working loose under strain.

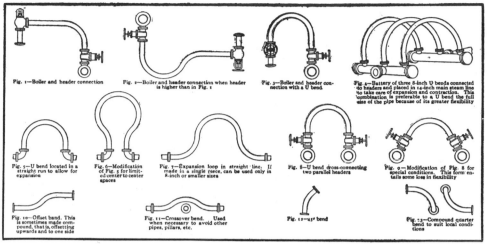

Fig. 1—Boiler and header connection

Fig. 2—Boiler and header connection when header is higher than in Fig. 1

Fig. 3—Boiler and header connection with a U bend

Fig. 4—Battery of three 8-inch U bends connected to headers and placed in 14-inch main steam line to take care of expansion and contraction. This combination is preferable to a U bend the full size of the pipe because of its greater flexibility

Fig. 5—U bend located in a straight run to allow for expansion

Fig. 6—Modification of Fig. 5 for limited center to center spaces

Fig. 7—Expansion loop in straight line. If made in a single piece, can be used only in 8-inch or smaller sizes

Fig. 8—U bend cross-connecting two parallel headers

Fig. 9—Modification of Fig. 8 for special conditions. This form entails some loss in flexibility

Fig. 10—Offset band. This is sometimes made compound, that is, offsetting upwards and to one side

Fig. 11—Crossover bend. Used when necessary to avoid other pipes, pillars, etc.

Fig. 12—45° bend

Fig. 13—Compound quarter bend to suit local conditions

Common Forms of Pipe Bends

Courtesy Valve World.

COPPER PLATING WITHOUT A BATTERY

Make the plating solution by dissolving 1 oz. sulphate of copper (blue vitriol) in 6 oz. water and then adding ½ oz. sulphuric acid. Get a piece of zinc about ⅛ in. thick and 2 in. square and solder to it at its center one end of a piece of copper wire 18 in. long. Then wrap a thick rag around the zinc, tying it close. This is the plate.

Carefully clean the tin, iron or brass article to be plated, so that it is free from grease; sand and soda is good for this pur-

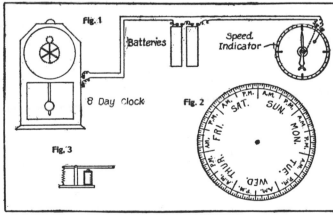

Time Indicator for Plants

pose. Now fasten the other end of the wire to the article. The wire must be bright in order to make a good connection. Dip a sponge in the plating solution and rub it over the article. Wherever the solution

touches it will immediately coat the metal with copper, and the longer you rub the heavier the coating will be.—Contributed by Ira Emery, 12 E. Simpson St., Dayton, Ohio.

TIME INDICATOR FOR PLANTS

The time indicator illustrated was originally used in a mill to show the actual number of hours the mill ran throughout the week. The device could be adapted to other plants for the same purpose.

Figure 1 consists of a speed indicator, two batteries and an eight-day clock. When the mill is shut down the hand of the indicator points upward and when the mill is at proper speed the hand points downward. A small cog-wheel, having eight cogs is fastened on the hour stem of the clock, says a correspondent of the American Miller, and the other cog wheel has 112 cogs. The small wheel turns around twice in 24 hours, and the larger one makes one revolution in seven days. A chart (Fig. 2) is fastened on the large wheel and is punctured by the magnet (Fig. 3) every time the hand on the indicator passes the button in either starting or stopping.

SUBSTITUTE FOR BATTERY INSULATOR

Sometimes the porcelain insulator which insulates the zinc from the carbon in a carbon cylinder battery becomes lost or broken,

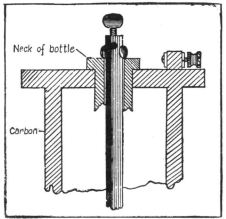

Improvised Battery Insulator

and if one cannot be procured right away, here is a good substitute. Get a bottle with a flange on the neck, break the neck (A) off and insert the zinc (B). This insulator will be just as good as a porcelain one.—Contributed by W. J. Slattery, Emsworth, Pa.

HOLDING PISTON RINGS WHILE FILING

In filing piston rings to fit, the following scheme for holding them will be found convenient:

Lay the ring on a 12x14x1½-in. board as shown in the sketch, mark holes A and B

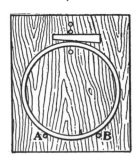

To Hold Piston Rings

and drill for ¼-in. pins, snug fit. Do not drill clear through the board. Make three ¼-in. pins large enough so that when in place they will be ⅛ in. below the top of the ring. Make a wedge of ¼-in. stuff 3 in. long with ¼ in. taper on that length. Lay the ring on the board, touching pins A and B, and drill hole H so that in placing the wedge the ring will be forced against A and B.

By having several holes ¼ in. apart, rings of different diameters can be held in place on the board while filing.—Contributed by F. Clausen, 121 Vine St., Ravenna, Ohio.

TEST WIRES IN BOX ANNEALING

Where the method of annealing by packing the pieces in an iron box with powdered charcoal and subjecting the whole to the heat of the furnace for a length of time suited to the work and then allowing to cool slowly is employed, test wires should be used to determine when the contents of the box are red hot. The wires should be $\frac{3}{16}$ in. in size and run down through ¼-in. holes at the center of the cover of the box.

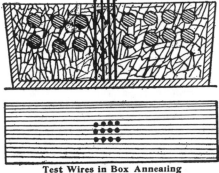

Test Wires in Box Annealing

None of the pieces should come nearer than 2 in. to the box at any point, for if the box is cast-iron it will take the carbon from the steel, says the American Blacksmith.

When the last layer of pieces is packed in the box so they do not come too near the box nor less than ½ in. of each other, fill the box with charcoal, place the cover in position and seal with fire clay. Run the test wires through the cover to the bottom of the box and when the fire clay is dry, place the box in the furnace to heat. Give it time to heat through, then remove one of the test wires. If the wire is red hot for its entire length, the contents of the box are of the right temperature. If the wire is not red hot, let the box remain a time, then draw another wire, proceeding this way until you pull a wire that is red hot. After a few trials one will be able to gauge the time required without the use of the wires.

TEST POLE FOR RURAL TELE-PHONE LINES

A test pole at the city limits for testing rural lines when there are many of them connecting with the city wires is a great convenience, says the American Telephone Journal. When heavy iron wire is used for the farmers' lines it is very difficult to make a test when the line has to be opened and later a splice made for closing the connection.

The test pole should be located at the city limits and to separate the farmers' lines from the city leads definitely, the wires should be dead-ended upon double grooved insulators. In making the dead end

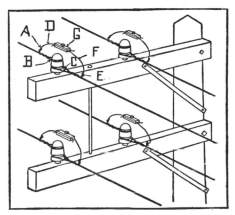

For Testing Rural Lines

leave the end of the wire about 1 in. long projecting from the final turn of the spiral used for fastening. To this projecting end solder a soft copper tie wire 14 in. long. Arrange each of the four ends terminating upon the two insulators in this way. Then join the copper wires for the city and country ends of the line by means of test connectors, to allow the line to be quickly opened and closed again after the test is finished. The copper tie wire is flexible and can be bent into any desired form. It is also easy to make a transposition at this pole, if necessary. Referring to the illustration the arrangement of the connections on the test pole is as follows: Line ties B, C, have long ends A, E, to which are soldered copper extensions D, F. The line is carried through by connector G.

To keep plaster of paris from hardening so quickly mix it with vinegar instead of water.—Gordon M. Backus, Hackensack, N. J.

TOOL FOR REMOVING DENTS IN GUN BARRELS

A good tool for removing dents in gun barrels is made of two pieces of ¾-in. half-round iron, one piece (B) 3½-in. long and the other piece (A) 5 in. long. Put the

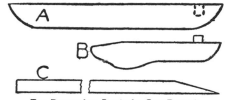

For Removing Dents in Gun Barrels

pieces together and file them down until they are slack at the muzzle of a 12-oz. gun barrel. Put a $\frac{3}{16}$-in. rivet in the longer piece ½ in. from the end, and in the short piece drill a hole in which the rivet will fit loosely to keep the pieces together in the barrel.

File the 3½-in piece oval, as in the sketch, and make a short taper wedge so as not to stick too tight in the spreader. Now place tool in the barrel opposite the dent (short piece next to dent), warm the barrel on a hot iron at the dent, put oil on the wedge and drive with a light hammer. The dent will come out very easily. A good size for the wedge is about 18 in. long and made of a suitable stock.

With a little care and good judgment, writes a correspondent of the American Blacksmith, very bad dents can be removed with this tool.

SCREW CLAMP WITH SPHERICAL BEARING

For holding objects that do not present parallel surfaces, such as I-beams, etc., the clamp illustrated is useful. It is made of a steel casting, says Machinery, and has an I cross section with stiffened back, and if sprung can be brought back to proper shape when hot, like forged ones. The spherical bearing on the under jaw allows all the adjustment out of parallel that is ever likely to be called for.

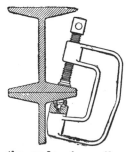

CHISEL FOR CUTTING ON A LINE

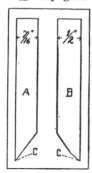

A very good cold chisel can be made of $\frac{7}{16}$ or $\frac{1}{2}$ in. square tool steel with the slope on one side only. The bevel may be in one angle or two, as shown in the sketch. C in each case indicates the cutting edge. This chisel is especially useful for cutting on a line. In cutting sheet metal the workman can see his line perfectly as he proceeds.— Contributed by Cecil Marshall, Dowagiac, Mich.

SUCCESSFUL LUBRICATING SYSTEM

The illustration shows a self-lubricating system rigged up by myself for an engineer who has used it successfully for the past

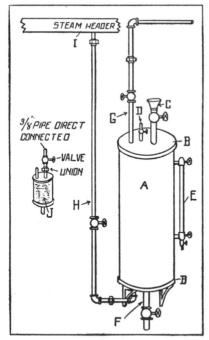

Simple Lubricating System

five months and claims that it works like a charm. The reservoir is filled with oil, then the steam is turned on slowly and as there is no perfect circulation, it condenses at the bottom. The oil, being lighter than water, floats on top, while the pressure

keeps raising the water and at the same time forcing the oil through the feed pipes to the lubricators and oil cups. The connections to the lubricators and oil cups are made with ⅜-in. pipe with a valve close near cup.

The parts indicated in the sketch are: A, piece of 4-in. pipe, threaded on ends, used for reservoir; B, caps for 4-in. pipe tapped for fittings as shown in the illustration; C, funnel connected to valve and nipples, for filling reservoir with oil; D, aircocks; E, gauge for oil; F, drain for drawing water from reservoir when filling; G, oil feed to cups and lubricators; H, steam feed to reservoir; I, steam feed from boiler; J shows how the connections are made to lubricators and cups.

The reservoir has to be filled about once in every two or three weeks.—Contributed by Joseph A. Burkhart, Emsworth, Pa.

CONVERTING A GAS ENGINE INTO AN AIR COMPRESSOR

An old automobile gas engine was converted into an air compressor by a correspondent of the Engineer's Review, who found it all that was required for his needs. He drilled and threaded a hole through the head and screwed on a check valve as at A, Fig. 1. Then, as the combustion chamber destroyed the efficiency of the compressor, he placed a piece of hard wood al-

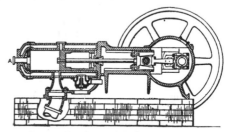

Fig. 1--Gas Engine Converted into an Air Compressor

most as thick as the combustion chamber was deep, behind the crank brass nearest the cylinder. This caused the piston to move nearer the head of the cylinder giving the minimum clearance. Small clearance is essential in a compressor, as the compressed air remaining in the clearance must expand to atmospheric pressure before more air can be drawn in; and by the time this has taken place the piston has traveled a good part of its stroke.

Another time, at a stone quarry where a large engine had just been installed in place of a 50-hp. engine, the same writer converted the smaller engine into a compressor to supply air for running drills and hoisting engines.

The engine, for the purpose of starting, had its combustion chamber connected to a tank

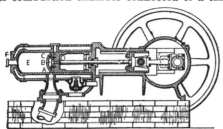

Fig. 2--False Head Bolted to Piston

containing compressed air. This pipe was closed at the engine by a hinge valve, having an opening and closing lever attached. The "locking sheet" arrangement was taken off and a coil spring substituted. On account of the spherical form of the combustion chamber, E, Fig. 2, clearance could not be reduced, as in the other case, by using a block behind the crankpin brass. Instead a hollow hemisphere, B, was cast and bolted on to the end of the piston with the balls A and C, packing the joint so no air could get in. The expense did not exceed $5.

ROOF HOOK FOR SHINGLING

An old hack tire will make the best hook as it is flat and will lay down on the roof out of the way of the chalk line, but a rod of iron may be used, if preferred.

Make the middle part 5½ ft. long; turn a hook 1¼ in. each way at the upper end and

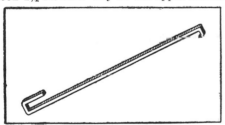

Roof Hook for Shingling

make the point sharp so it will hook over the comb, when the top of the roof is reached. At the lower end turn down 2½ in. and up 6 in. so that it will hold a 2x4 in. timber for a scaffold, says the Practical Carpenter. To use, merely hook end A in the shingle lath.

A HANDY PENCIL POINT SHARPENER

This device, which will be especially appreciated by draughtsmen, consists of a metal holder A, which can be made out of

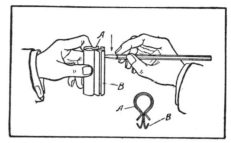

an old Spencerian paper clip, and a piece of fine emery cloth B, with the edges folded over as shown. To use it the pencil is placed in the crevice and moved up and down, giving a sharp chisel point. A round point may be made by revolving the pencil between the fingers while sharpening.—Contributed by J. R. Sourby, Chicago.

HEAT=RESISTING BRONZING LIQUID

For a liquid to mix with the bronze mix one part clear baking varnish with from two to three parts turpentine. When the surface is to be sized and the dry bronze rubbed over it, mix any good slow-drying varnish of the same nature as baking varnish with an equal quantity of turpentine, and when the surface is sufficiently tacky rub on the bronze. A fair bronzing liquid to mix with either gold or aluminum bronze, says the Plumbers' Gazette, may be made of any light-colored varnish and two to four parts of turpentine.

HORIZONTAL SCREW DRIVER

A screw driver for use in a corner or other awkward place may be made of sheet steel as shown. In the one I made the

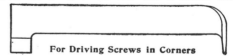

For Driving Screws in Corners

length was 4 in., the width ⅝ in. and thickness ⅛ in. The screw blade is ⅜ in. wide.
—Contributed by Gordon M. Backus, Hackensack, New Jersey.

HOW TO BUILD A SMALL PILE DRIVER

In many cases where a pile driver is needed it is cheaper to build one than it would be to buy or rent one. Such a driver can be built by four men in two days at a total cost of $102. This estimate is for a driver with a 1,200 lb. cast-iron hammer, t h e "leads" or "gins" that guide the hammer to be made of 4 in. by 6 in. sticks 30 ft. long, and the rope that raises it, 1-in. manila.

One end of the hammer rope is fastened to the nippers that clutch the lugs on the hammer; the other end of the rope passes through a pulley and around a wooden drum 12 in. in diameter. At one end of this wooden drum is fastened a wooden "bull wheel" 60 in. in diameter. Another rope is wound around this bull wheel and a horse hitched to the rope. The horse can easily raise the hammer to the top of the leads where the nippers are automatically tripped, allowing the hammer to fall. Only one pulley block is used. The use of the drum and bull wheel not only reduces the number of the blocks required, but does not consume the power of the horse in friction to such degree as pulley blocks would.

To build this pile driver the following bill of lumber will be required:

Piece. in. in. ft.   ft. B. M.
  2— 4x 6x30 (leads) 120
  1— 6x 6x 4 (cross-piece)........... 12
  2— 6x 6x16 (base) 96
  2— 2x 4x32 (ladder) 43
  2— 2x 4x 2 (ladder rungs) 24
  2— 4x 4x26 (sway braces)........ 64
  1— 2x 4x20 (long front sill)........ 13
  1— 2x 4x14 (short rear sill)........ 3
  1—12x12x 4 (drum) 48
 30— 1x12x 6 (bull wheel)..........180
                                      ———
      Total 603

Also about 24 bolts, ½ by 8 in., and a few pounds of nails. Shape the drum out of a 12 in. by 12. in. stick and leave it square

where the bull wheel is to be fastened on. At each end cut out a wooden axle 4 in. in diameter and 6 in. long, and fit them to wooden bearing blocks, daubing well with grease. Make the bull wheel by spiking together five layers of 1 in. by 12 in. planks,

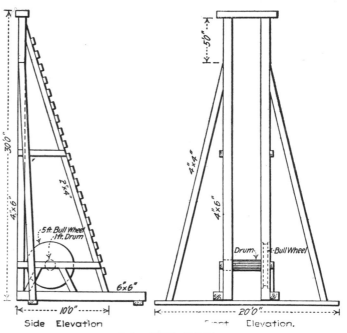

Side Elevation

Front Elevation.

A Small Pile Driver

each layer running in the opposite direction to the one under it. Spike three of these layers together and mark a 5-ft. circle on them, then cut out the 5-ft. wheel with a keyhole saw. Spike another layer of plank on each side of this wheel and saw to a circle 5 ft. 8 in. in diameter. These outside layers form the rims of the wheel and keep the "bull rope" from sliding off.

The items of expense for the driver should be, approximately, as follows:
700 ft. B. M. lumber at $20..........$14.00
Bolts and nails 2.00
Labor 18.00
1,200-lb. hammer 50.00
1 pair nippers 5.00
1 snatch block 3.00
240 ft. 1-in. rope 10.00
                                      ———
      Total $102.00

To operate the driver three men, a horse and a boy to drive the horse will be required, the daily cost, counting the horse at $1, being $9. Nine piles per day with an average penetration of 6 ft. can be driven with it, says Engineering-Contracting. A driver of this kind must have a level runway on which to work, and if the ground is irregular, scaffolding must be put up.

SPEED AND POWER TRANSMISSION

The factor of safety for a pulley may be greatly above the speed at which the belt will transmit power, owing to centrifugal force, says the American Machinist. At 5,250 ft. per minute, laced leather belts transmit a maximum of power; and riveted belts at 6,325 ft. per minute. Supposing a belt could be run safely at a speed of 9,250 ft. per minute, it would transmit an amount of power scarcely appreciable.

STEAM FITTERS' CEMENT

Dissolve 1 part, by weight, rubber or gutta percha in sufficient carbon disulphide to give it the consistency of molasses, then mix with 6 parts, by weight, linseed oil and leave exposed to the air for 24 hours. Then mix to a putty with red lead. A less brittle cement is made by using oxide of iron in place of red lead.

AN ADJUSTABLE SANDPAPER BLOCK

A good sandpaper block, which is especially useful for pattern makers, can be made from a pine block about 1 in. thick and a piece of new leather belting. Glue the leather to the block and, after it has dried, saw the wood in narrow strips as

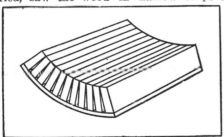

Pattern Makers' Sandpaper Block

shown. This makes a block which can be held straight or curved.—Contributed by R. B. Gregg, La Fayette, Ind.

When on a hurry-up job your belt will not pull the cut you desire, says Machinery, just hold a piece of tar soap on the inside of the belt while it is running and it will soon pull all right.

SIMPLE PRINCIPLE USED IN MAKING DIES FOR SMALL WIRE

How to Make a Hole 1/1000 of an Inch in Diameter

Those who are not familiar with the operation of drawing glass tubes will understand how it is done from the illustration. The glass is first heated in the flame of the Bunsen burner, Fig. 1, and then stretched out as shown in Fig. 2. A small tube may be

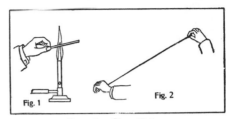

Drawing Glass Tubes

stretched several feet in this way and so reduced in size that the diameter at the middle is no larger than a fine thread, but the hole through the center is not closed in doing this. By placing the broken thread in water and blowing in the other end, bubbles are seen to come from the small end, showing that the bore has not been closed.

In making dies for fine wire it is found impossible to make a drill small enough, so the smallest size jeweler's drill is used and the steel is then heated and drawn the same as the glass. In this way dies have been made for drawing wire 1/1000 of an inch in diameter.

MAKING OVER PHONOGRAPH RECORDS

Owners and users of phonographs and the amateurs who enjoy making records will find the following kink of interest:

For scraping the record or making a blank of it a knife is usually furnished with the machine, but a simpler and more convenient way is to rub the outside of the record with kerosene oil, then rub with a cloth or the bare hand until all of the cuts are erased and the cylinder is perfectly smooth. Then wipe it with a dry cloth and leave a few minutes to dry. Remove any rings from the hand before rubbing so as not to scratch the record, and do not try to record on the cylinder until it is perfectly dry.—Contributed by W. Carey Smith, 5 S. Fulton Ave., Mt. Vernon, N. Y.

EASILY MADE SAFETY DEVICE FOR BOILER

The water level in a boiler gage is often very indistinct as the light in a boiler room is usually not very bright. Add to this the fact that rings of dirt often form on the inside of the glass, due to the water

level remaining nearly constant, and it will easily be understood how the fireman sometimes allows the water to become too low, as the rings of dirt thus formed appear quite like the water level.

In looking at the gage the fireman usually gives a quick glance at the place where the water level ought to be. If the water is only a little too low the ring of dirt would not be misleading, but if the water is way down in the bottom of the glass he seldom thinks to look there and mistakes the ring of dirt for the water level and fatal results

Fig. 1   often occur.

To avoid this danger make a screen, Fig. 1, and fasten to the glass at such a distance that the rays of light in passing through the water will be focused on the screen as shown in Fig. 2. The screen may be made of thin wood, card board or tin painted

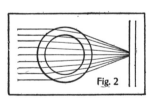

white, and the clips can be made of wire or sheet metal. The rays of light are not refracted very much in passing through

the glass above the water level but in passing through the water are converged to a bright white line on the screen which can be seen from the farthest end of the boiler room. An occasional wiping of the dust from the screen will keep it in order.

ENAMELED SLIDE IN FURNACE DOOR

Sometimes in tending the furnace I have thought that the slide in the ashpit door was open when it really was not. To avoid this mistake, I enameled the part that slides back and forth white, and the rest of the door I enameled black.—Contributed by Gordon M. Backus, Hackensack, N. J.

TO PAINT STEEL CEILINGS

For painting a metal or steel ceiling, do not use a gloss paint, warns the Carter Times, because it becomes dirty and looks worn as soon as a flat paint.

A good method is as follows: Dust off all dirt and clean any grease spots from the metal. Put on a first coat of pure white lead, half raw linseed oil and half turpentine, tinted to the color you desire to finish with. When dry, coat with a mixture of pure white lead, thinned to the right consistency with pure turpentine, and tinted as before. Stipple this coat as you proceed. Let the decorative work be according to the price to be received. Cheap work will not pay on a steel ceiling.

TO MAKE TRACING CLOTH LAY FLAT

The reason tracing cloth curls up at the edges so inconveniently is because when manufactured it is rolled with the concave

CONCAVE SIDE OF TRACING CLOTH IS THE GLOSSY SIDE AS IT COMES FROM THE MAKERS

RE-ROLL SO CONVEX SIDE IS GLOSSY SIDE

side the glossy side. The drawings are made on the glossy side, and then when they are filed away in drawers they will not lay flat, and when put into the printing frame the edges are apt to get folded down and look bad on the prints. If the tracing cloth is rerolled with the dull side out, says a correspondent of Machinery, and then left for a time the edges will curl down instead of up, which is much more convenient.

KEEPING SHOW WINDOWS FREE OF FROST AND MOISTURE

A simple and effective way to keep frost out of show windows is to bore a small hole—½ in.—in the framework directly below and another directly above the glass. For a very large window bore two holes top and bottom. The holes give free circulation of the air and make the temperature of the glass outside and in more nearly equal. If it is impracticable to bore holes, rubbing the glass with alcohol frequently will help.

For moisture in windows, place a small box of lime directly under the glass. The lime will absorb all the moisture.

PORTABLE SAW HORSES

In moving from one job to another the carpenter will find portable saw horses a great convenience. The usual form of saw

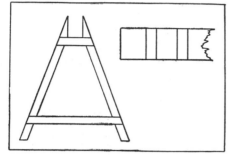

Portable Saw Horse

horse is very awkward to stow away or to move. The sketch shows the construction of a portable horse recommended by a correspondent of the Practical Carpenter.

GRAIN OF LUMBER IN PATTERNS

Quarter-sawed lumber is the best stock to use for thin patterns that have no ribs to hold them straight, but it is not always easy to get. Quarter-sawed boards are cut radially (Fig. 1) and to cut more than a few from each log would waste the material. One can tell a quarter-sawed piece by examining the grain at the end, says the American Machinist, and it pays to use it if possible as it will not warp under many changes of atmospheric conditions.

Lumber for patterns should be carefully selected. A board like Fig. 2 will not stay straight long. Fig. 3 shows how to lay two pieces with regard to the grain when gluing them together. The warping of one piece will counteract that of the other, and the joint will not open readily on the edges as it will if the pieces are laid as in Fig. 4, or Fig. 5. If one piece is glued across another the effect shown in Fig. 6 will result, unless the glue does not hold or the piece splits in shrinking. Board A pulls enough in shrinking to bend board B in its length. With absolutely dry lumber of four or more thicknesses cross grain is effective.

A pattern like Fig. 7 is more serviceable made with length of the bottom piece running from one rib to the other, as the bottom will stay straight and the side will always draw. If made like Figs. 8 and 9 you will get the effect shown, which will distort the ribs so that the pattern will not draw. When the grain of the wood can be put in to run in the same direction as the line of draft, a slight warping will not affect the drawing of the pattern. This cannot always be done, because patterns so made would be weak in vital parts.

HOW TO CLEAN FELT HATS

To clean felt hats use weak ammonia. Brush the hat thoroughly while dry, then brush over with the ammonia, using a sponge for the purpose. Treat the whole of the outside and the leather lining as well. Renew the ammonia solution when it is made dirty by the sponge being dipped in so frequently.

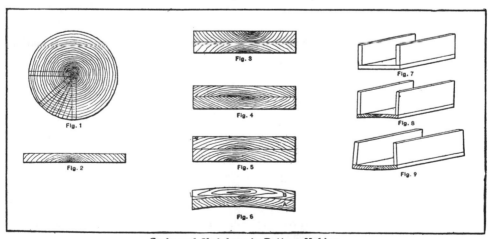

Grain and Shrinkage in Pattern-Making

HOW TO MAKE A GLUE SCRAPER

Nearly every wood-worker has a glue scraper, which is generally made from a

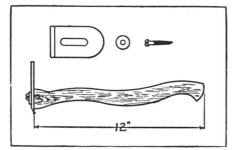

Handy Glue Scraper

strip of iron or a flat file, but a better one can be made as shown in the illustration. The handle is made from a piece of hard wood 1¾ in. by 1½ in. long by 12 in. The blade is made of an old plane bit and is fastened to the handle by means of a screw and washer.—Contributed by R. B. Gregg, La Fayette, Ind.

CLAMP FOR LEAKY PIPE

Having had considerable trouble with a pipe that was leaking badly, I used the clamp illustrated to remedy matters. The pipe was 3 in. diameter, screwed into the side outlet of a tee, partly broken off, and

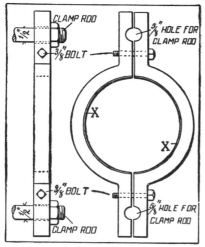

Good Pipe Clamp

about 4 ft. under ground. The pipes could not be taken up very well for threading (had no dies) as one piece was under a rail-road track and the other under a building. The clamp has been in use satisfactorily for three months.

Referring to the sketch, Fig. 2 shows the two pieces of the clamp held together on the pipe by two ⅜-in. bolts. The ⅝-in. holes are for the ½-in. clamp rod to go through as shown in Fig. 1.

To apply the clamp put Fig 2 around the leaking pipe and clamp rod (Fig. 1) around back of tee and through ⅝-in. holes (Fig. 2). Use some good packing between the shoulder of the tee and the clamp, and screw up on clamp rod. Next screw up the two ⅜-in. bolts. If the clamp is beveled on inner edges, X, it will hold the packing better. The pressure on the leaky pipe was 5 lb. per square inch. The clamp was made and put on in three hours.—Contributed by Fred. Wm. Keller, Mannheim, Ill.

METHOD OF TINNING A SOLDER-ING-IRON

Dress the iron down with a smooth file in the usual way, then heat it warm enough to melt a tallow candle. Rub a candle over the surfaces of the iron and it will be found to work fine.—Contributed by C. E. Faulks, 65 Block F, Pueblo, Colo.

COLORING SHELLAC VARNISH

To color shellac varnish black, add lamp-black; for red, use Chinese vermilion; and for blue, use Prussian blue. A very good quality of blue cannot be obtained. Have all coloring matter dry and finely pulverized. To mix, add the coloring matter to a little of the varnish and work to a smooth paste. Then add varnish, and alcohol if necessary, in proper quantity to make the mixture spread nicely.—From Practical Pattern Making, by F. W. Barrows.

MALLEABLE CASTINGS RUST MORE THAN STEEL

Malleable castings buried in the earth will rust even more than steel, says the Iron Age. The skin and immediate interior of a malleable casting is practically a rather open steel. It is crystalline in structure also, due to the original placing of the crystals of the white iron, before annealing, perpendicular to the surfaces; and so moisture can penetrate it quite a ways.

SHOP NOTES

EASILY MADE LAWN ROLLER

A good lawn roller can be made from a piece of sewer pipe, A (see sketch), with very little expense. The greatest difficulty is removing the flange, which has to be chipped off unless one has a piece of plain

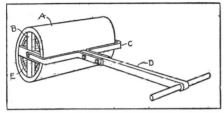

Lawn Roller

pipe. The bricks, E, are to give weight, and are fastened in with cement. The cross pieces, B, are 2 in. by 4 in. wood, and the forks, C, are made of wrought iron. The handle, D, is of wood, with a piece of pipe or broomstick driven through the end. The roller I made cost only $2 and does very good work.—Contributed by Warren M. Morse, 50 Elmore St., Newton Center, Mass.

HOW TO MAKE A PLUMB=BOB MOLD

Make a small hole in the center of the large end of an egg, and another in the side, and blow out the contents. Dry the empty shell in an oven, and then fasten a small screw eye, A, in the end hole, by means of a piece of clay, B. Place another piece of

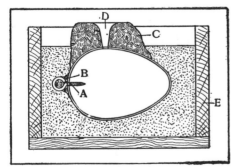

Mold for a Plumb-Bob

clay, C, over the side of the egg, leaving an opening, D, to pour in the melted lead later.

Place the egg, with the clay on it, in a box, E, and pack with sand, having the opening, D, on top, as shown.

Having thus prepared the mold, melt about a pound and a half or two pounds of lead and pour in the opening. Allow plenty of time to cool, and then break away the egg shell, and you will have a good plumb bob.—Contributed by W. J. Slattery, Emsworth, Pa.

HAMMER WITH LUBRICANT COM= PARTMENT

In driving wire nails into hard wood they are not so apt to bend if lubricated with soap. A good way to have the soap always on hand for this purpose is to bore a hole in the end of the hammer handle, as illustrated,

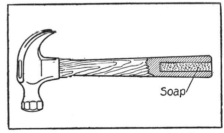

Lubricant for Nails in Hammer Handle

and fill it with soap. In driving small brads into hard wood this will be found particularly useful.—Contributed by J. Weldon, 433 Columbia St., Brooklyn, N. Y.

GOOD WHITEWASH FOR OUT= B'JILDINGS

Place 1 bu. good fresh lime in a barrel and add 20 lbs. beef tallow; slake with hot water. When the lime is slaked the tallow will have disappeared, having formed a chemical compound with the lime. Dry colors may be added to make any color desired. Add the color before slaking the lime, or, if after slaking, mix with alcohol and then add to the strained wash. Thin to flow nicely from the brush. A coat of this wash will last as long and look almost as well as much of the lead paint used, and costs a mere trifle to make.—Contributed by H. W. Kennicott, Palmyra, Va.

REMOVING OBSTRUCTIONS IN DRAIN PIPE

When a drain pipe becomes stopped up unscrew the plug, A, and remove the lint or other substance with a bent wire or old button hook. If the trouble is not remedied by this operation, it shows that the stoppage is at the other side of the plug. In this

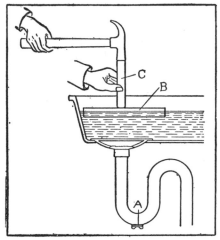

Clearing a Drain Pipe

case draw 3 or 4. in. of water in the sink, and lay a board, B, over the outlet as shown. The board should be about 8 in. square and about 1 in. thick. Hold a stick, C, on the board and strike the end of the stick with a hammer. The shock of the hammer blow is transmitted through the drain pipe for a distance of many feet and will nearly always remove the obstacle.

HOW TO MAKE A GAS ENGINE MUFFLER

The use of a gas engine in a residence district is often objectionable, as the noise of the exhaust, even when greatly reduced, is very annoying, but by using the following apparatus, which only slightly reduces the power of the engine, the exhaust may be muffled down to absolute silence.

The muffler (see Fig.) consists of a 4-in. pipe 24 in. long, F, with a 4-in. by 1-in. re-

ducer screwed on each end, E. The 1-in. pipes, AA, project through far enough to

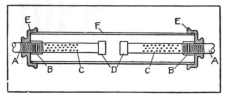

Gas Engine Muffler

hold the couplings, BB, and are each drilled with forty-eight 3-16-in. holes and fitted with caps, DD. One of the pipes, AA, connects to the engine and the other to the exhaust pipe, which is reduced at each connection until it is ¼ in.; eight 3-16-in. holes are drilled in the ¼-in. pipe near the end, which is covered with a cap.

This muffler is being used with a 3-in. by 4-in. engine, making about 400 r. p. m., and the only noise produced is a slight hissing sound, which cannot be heard 10 ft. away.—Contributed by Edgar L. Drinkwater, 51 N. Ada St., Chicago.

TO CONVERT A DRAWING BOARD INTO A TABLE

Make two legs about 30 in. long, and buy two stiff springs about 8 in. long. Fasten the legs to the drawing board with hinges, and attach the springs by means of screw eyes. Screw two hooks in the bottom of the window casing and attach springs, as shown in the sketch. The springs hold the drawing board against the casing and also hold the legs down firmly on the floor, thus making the whole apparatus solid. The front edge of the board may be lowered by inclining the legs. When not in use the springs can

Drawing-Board Table

be detached and the apparatus may then be folded up and put away. I have been using my board in this way for a long time, and find it very convenient, and its use does not mar the window casing in the least.—Contributed by Chas. A. Prickett, Auburn, Ind.

TO DRAW AN ELLIPSE: GIVEN THE LENGTH AND WIDTH

A previous article in "Shop Notes" shows how to draw an ellipse having a required length, but the following method will give the required width as well. This method is as follows: Draw line A B—the required length; and line C D—the required width intersecting line A B at right angles at the middle point O. With C as a center and radius O A describe arcs E F and H J intersecting line A B at G and K, the foci of the

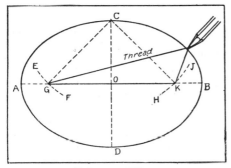

To Draw an Ellipse

required ellipse. Drive pins or tacks in these points and form a loop of thread, just long enough to enclose the triangle G C K. Then place a pencil in the loop and trace in the ellipse, as shown.—Contributed by W. J. Slattery, Emsworth, Pa.

DOUBLE CORN CRIB AND FEEDING FLOOR

Select your site and lay out a space 30 ft. square—or whatever dimensions you may decide on; dig trenches 8 in. deep and 8 in. wide around the square and two crossways the square on either side the driveway. Board up these trenches and box up to a height some 6 in. above the ground and fill them with concrete.

As soon as this concrete has set put a layer of concrete 4 in. thick over the whole surface as a floor for both corn crib and driveway. While laying the concrete, along

the trenches set ½-in. bolts 6½ in. long upright every 5 ft. and bolt on 2x6's the flat way to use as sills. Toe-nail 2x6's upright

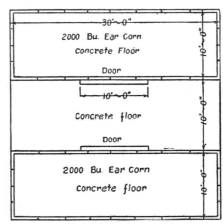

Plan of Rat-Proof Corn Crib

every 2 ft., 14 ft. high to eaves and 20 ft. high along the driveway, making the crib 23 ft. high. The rafters should be 20 ft. long and the roof shingled.

The crib will hold 6,000 bu. ear corn if the driveway is filled. Or one could have an oat granary of 5,000 bu. above the entry and need not scoop the grain out, but let it run into the wagon when loading. I use the driveway (30 ft. by 10 ft.) as a feeding floor and put ear corn on either side and use a portable corn elevater with horsepower. A door 10 ft. wide opens horizontally on each side of the driveway to let corn out to feed. My crib cost $225 painted and complete, not charging anything to my own work. Used 20 cu. yds. of gravel and 116 sacks of cement. The concrete floor does not cost more than sills and board floor and my crib is rat-proof and will not rot.—Contributed by M. D. Johnston, Danvers, Ill.

A GOOD GUTTER PAINT

Put all old paint skins, cleanings of buckets, siftings and pieces of dry putty into an old iron kettle with raw oil and boil until all is dissolved. Then add fine, dry sand until the mixture is as thick as will spread under the brush. Apply quite warm — a heavy coat. When dry it will form an enamel like granite and can be colored to match the cornice. If properly prepared this paint should be as smooth as glass. It is also good for patching old tin roofs.—Contributed by H. W. Kennicott, Palmyra, Va.

PONTOON WATER ELEVATOR

There are many ways of raising water from a stream, by utilizing the power of the current, but probably the simplest and most efficient method is obtained by using the apparatus here illustrated, which I made myself at very little expense.

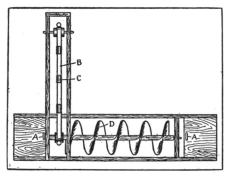

Pontoon Water Elevator

This device consists of a helical water wheel, D, which, in revolving, operates the bucket elevator at the left. This elevator consists of a belt, B, with several tin cans attached, as shown. I used two floats in making my machine, but in some devices of this kind three or four are used. The device is fastened by ropes, passing through the screw eyes, AA, and is set in the water at an angle of 45°.

I have only used this device for irrigating, on a small scale, but think that larger ones could be made to take the place of pumping stations, as there is no expense in operating. It could also be used to advantage in dredging and gold mining.—Contributed by Millis Knickerbocker, New Lenox, Ill.

TOOL FOR DRAWING SPIKES

For material take a piece of an old buggy axle, flatten and split both ends, and bend as illustrated. The claws of the rounded end

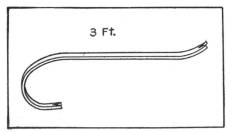

3 Ft.

For Drawing Spikes

can be driven under the head of the spike by striking with a hammer.—Contributed by Leander Manning, Akron, Iowa.

TO WRITE ON METALS

To write on iron, steel, silver or gold mix together 1 oz. muriatic acid and ½ oz. nitric acid and use as follows:

Cover the place on which you wish to write with melted beeswax; when the beeswax is cold write the name or words plainly with a file point or an etching needle, carrying it through the wax and cleaning all the wax out of the letter. Then apply the mixed acids with a feather, carefully filling each letter. Let the acid remain for from one to ten minutes, according to the appearance desired; then put on some water, which will dilute the acid and stop the process. Either of the acids separately would cut iron or steel, but it requires the mixture to take hold of gold or silver. After the acids are washed off, it is well to apply a little oil.—Contributed by Howard H. Iszard, Cuyahoga Falls, Ohio.

IMPROVEMENT IN PORTABLE SCAF=FOLD BRACKETS

In "Shop Notes" for June, 1905, the portable scaffold bracket, shown in Fig. 1, was de-

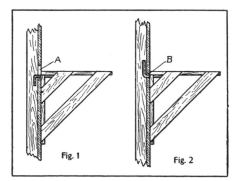

Improved Scaffold Bracket

scribed. I have found this form of bracket to be very useful and handy, but think it can be improved by turning the hook up (Fig. 2) instead of down. By so doing a longer hook may be used and the hole in the sheathing can be made much smaller than when the hook turns down. To remove the bracket it is only necessary to raise the outer end and draw the hook out of the hole, but the hook cannot come out when the bracket is loaded. —Contributed by Arthur Gray, Clifton, Ill.

TO PUT A WICK IN A TORCH

Unwind enough of a ball of wick, A, to go through the torch and push it in at B. Raise the torch to your mouth and give one hard

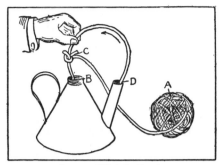

Putting Wick in Torch

blow, which will send the wick out at D. Tie it at C, making a circle about 14 in. in diameter. Then draw back from B until the mouth, D, is as full as wanted. Cut the wick off at D and push the rest in at B. This should not be done with oil above the wick pieces.—Contributed by Albert N. Crawford, 8 Lautner St., Allegheny, Pa.

PREVENTING CINDERS WHILE BURNING SAWDUST

In the power house of the Oregon Consolidated Ry. Co., where sawdust is used for fuel, the sparks and cinders emitted from the stacks have been so dangerous and objectionable that a cinder separating plant has been installed. This has not only relieved the residents and manufacturers within a half-mile radius, but has considerably increased the efficiency of the boilers.

The installation was the result of numerous complaints, due to cinders accumulating on sidewalks, porches, drying clothes, etc. A lumber company, which adjoins the power

No Cinders in this Smoke

house, has had thousands of dollars' worth of lumber refused by inspectors on account of being blackened by falling cinders.

The accompanying illustration shows how the separator is applied. The large breeching, or smoke box, over the boilers connects to an immense draft fan, which discharges into the separator at the right. This separator works exactly like the ordinary dust separator, seen in nearly all large woodworking factories. As the smoke and cinders enter they receive a whirling motion, and the cinders, being heavier, gradually work down in a spiral path to the bottom of the separator, where they are automatically conveyed to the boilers to be consumed.

The cut shows only one section of the plant, the entire equipment, as stated in the Street Railway Journal, costing about $19,-000. The smoke coming from the separators has been carefully examined by powerful field glasses without revealing the slightest vestige of cinders. This, and the increased efficiency, make the cinder separating plant worthy of consideration for other localities where similar conditions exist.

PORTABLE ELECTRIC ALARM

In rigging up an alarm for a sound sleeper, as described in our April number, Geo. Albach, 95 West Twenty-first street, Bayonne,

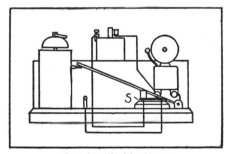

Portable Electric Alarm

N. J., made some improvements. He mounted the device on a board 12 in. by 7 in. by ¾ in., having beveled off the upper edge. At the back he nailed a piece 5 in. high and of the same length as the board. The bell he fastened to this back piece, and the battery was placed on a shelf on the rear side of the back piece. He also added a switch, S, which he fastened in the empty corner of the board, making it convenient to stop the bell. The apparatus can be placed near the bed at night and stowed away during the day.

DEVICE FOR CARRYING STEAM FROM KETTLE

"In my candy-boiling department I have used a device for carrying steam from the kettle all winter," writes A. F. Houser, 114 S. James St., Hamilton, Ont., "and find it a great convenience."

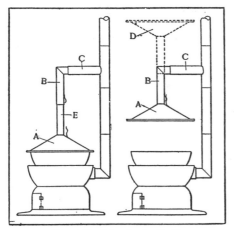

Steam Hood for Candy Kettle

Referring to the illustrations, A is a cover with a pipe, E, attached, which pipe telescopes into B and, when raised, can be fastened with a hinged clasp to the bottom of B; B is an elbow which telescopes into C the proper distance to bring the cover over the kettle; C is a short length of pipe connected to a length of stovepipe.

The cover, A, with pipe, E, attached can be entirely detached from B, or telescoped into B and attached to it by means of the spring catch, or swung up out of the way when not in use, as at D, Fig. 2. The device is made of galvanized iron and riveted.

FORMULA FOR MANUFACTURING YEAST

Boil together for one-half hour, in a copper kettle, 40 gals. of water and 2 lbs. of ground hops; pass over refrigerator to cool to a temperature of 160° F.; pass the liquor from the refrigerator to a stout tub; add 1½ bu. (about 63 lbs.) crushed malt and stir the mixture thoroughly. Allow the mash to stand at that temperature for 1½ hours, then filter from the grains and cool to 70° F. The passage over the refrigerator serves to aerate the wort. At this point allow spontaneous fermentation to set in.

The yeast can be used in 24 hours, but is better if allowed to stand two days. Keep the fermenting tubs and other vessels clean by scalding from time to time with live steam. Said to give excellent results.

HOW TO MAKE AN ELECTRIC-KEROSENE LAMP LIGHTER

A device for lighting a ruby lamp is here shown, in which a spark from a jump-spark coil vaporizes the oil and ignites it. The ruby lamp, A, is mounted on a board, B, somewhat larger than the base of the lamp. Two binding posts, C and D, are placed on the board and connected to the secondary of the jump spark coil, E. A wire is fastened to binding post, D, and soldered to the lamp at F. The wire, G, is enclosed in a piece of rubber tubing, such as is used for insulating in automobiles, and the extremity so located that it will nearly touch the wick.

The spark from the vibrator would spoil the plate if the jump spark coil were put in the dark room, so it should be put outside, or placed in a box, in such a way that no light will fall on the plate. A ⅜-in. spark is about right and about six dry batteries should be used with the coil.

This device will also light an ordinary kerosene lamp and might be useful when

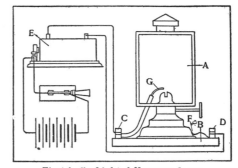

Electrically-Lighted Kerosene Lamp

the lamp is in a hall or some place where it is hard to get at.—Contributed by Chas. Buettger, R. R. 8.

TO MAKE A CRACKED GONG SOUND

The sound may be restored to a cracked gong by sawing down the crack with a hacksaw so that the two edges do not touch. The gong will sound as well as when new.—Contributed by E. Okerlund, San Francisco, Cal.

HOME=MADE POLARITY INDICATOR

To make a polarity indicator for batteries, all that is required is some sulphuric acid, two thumb bolts and nuts, some copper wire and a block of wood 4 in. long, 2 in. wide and ¾ in. thick. In the center of the block of wood chisel a hole 1 in. square and ½ in. deep to hold the bottle containing

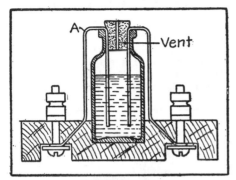

Polarity Indicator

the acid solution. On the opposite side of the block cut two ½-in. grooves ½ in. from the sides. In the center of each of three grooves bore a ¼-in. hole for the thumb nuts. From these holes drill holes to the space in the middle, as shown by the sketch. Set the bottle in the hole prepared for it, and run wires, A, to it from each thumb-screw, as shown. Fill the bottle with a solution of 1 part sulphuric acid to 4 parts water.

When the device is connected to the battery the zinc or negative pole will give off gas. This will cause bubbles in the solution.—Contributed by G. Fry and I. Van Dalsem, 903 Vine St., San Jose, Cal.

GAUGE FOR TESTING ANGLE AND CENTER OF DRILL

This device is made of sheet steel. By holding it on both sides of the drill and

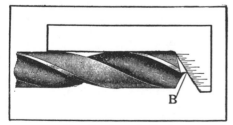

How the Gauge is Used

comparing the relative position of center to point B, one can tell whether it is accurately located. Also, if the angle of the drill coincides with the gauge, the angle is correct.—Contributed by J. Weldon, 433 Columbia St., Brooklyn, N. Y.

HOME=MADE SPEED INDICATOR

A bobbin winder from an old sewing machine, Fig. 1, will make a very good speed indicator by making a few alterations. Remove part A and C, and if possible remove the heart-shaped cam, E, from the worm wheel, D. Take off the pulley, G, and sharpen the end of the shaft, as shown in Fig. 2. Attach a small file handle, J, by means of a screw, K, and solder on the indicator, L, which may be made of sheet brass. Scratch the graduations on the worm wheel, as shown, making the total number of notches

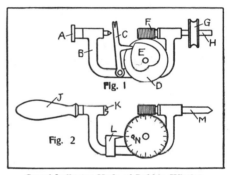

Speed Indicator Made of Bobbin Winder

equal to the number of teeth. It is well to make a center punch mark, N, to allow counting the number of revolutions of the worm wheel in taking high speeds.—Contributed by Ray Earley, New Sharon, Iowa.

HOW TO MAKE A COMBINATION PULLEY AND COUPLING

Some of the readers of Shop Notes might be interested in a problem of coupling shafting which occurred at our shop recently. I had occasion to couple two shafts of different sizes, at a point where a pulley was needed, and overcame the difficulty as follows: I setscrewed the coupling to the shaft, as shown in the sketch, and covered the set-screw heads with a piece of pipe, B, fastened with flat-head screws, C. These screws were staggered, an equal number being placed in each half of the coupling. Then I bored the spokes on an old pulley, A, to fit the pipe, and fastened it on with bolts, D, counter-

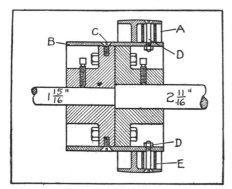

Combination Pulley and Coupling

sunk in the rim and pipe separators, E. The load on the 1 15-16-in. shaft being very light, was easily carried by the setscrews, and both the coupling and pulley are now in successful operation.—Contributed by M. E. Hood, Tuckahoe, N. Y.

HOW TO MAKE AN ASH SIFTER

The accompanying sketch shows a device which will be greatly appreciated by all who sift ashes. By its use the expensive waste of coal is prevented, without incurring the greater expense of spoiled clothing. The dust arising from the ashes is confined by a housing, A, which can be built of ¾-in. boards, or made from an old dry goods case.

An ordinary ash sifter is supported by a frame, B, which swings from the roof by the iron rods, C. These rods may be bent from old iron curtain rods or heavy galvanized telegraph wire, and are held by large screw eyes, D, in the roof and frame. Two cleats, E, nailed to the roof will distribute the weight over the entire surface.

A door, F, should be made in the front, large enough to admit the ash sifter, and another one, G, in the side should be of a sufficient size to allow removing the tub, H. The door, F, should have an opening, J, for the ash sifter handle and the door, G, ought to have a handle, K, and a spring catch, L, to hold the door up when removing the tub.

This catch may be bent out of a piece of sheet iron.

If the tub is placed on the ground it may be difficult to slide, in which case strips of wood, for tracks, should be embedded in the ground.—Contributed by Arthur W. Passage, 831 West Pierce Ave., Niagara Falls, New York.

PORTABLE SPRAY COOKER

The lime-sulphur hot sprays used by orchardists are often cooked at some central point by means of a stationary boiler, but a better device is found in the apparatus illustrated herewith.

Portable Spraying Outfit

The boiler is suspended from the back of the wagon, and the steam is carried to four barrels containing the spraying mixture. It is not necessary to buy a new boiler for this

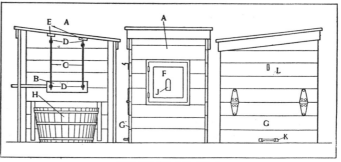

Housing for Ash Sifter

purpose, as many discarded ones would answer. A subscriber to the Rural New-Yorker used an old fire engine boiler, which he recovered from a scrap pile.

An outfit of this kind will deliver enough material to supply six or eight spraying nozzles, and the expenditure would be insignificant if divided among several members of a coöperative spraying club.

For cleansing steel articles use unslaked lime.

UNDERGROUND CROSSING FOR TOLL LINES

An underground crossing for toll lines as a method of protection against induced currents from power wires is shown in the illustration. The crossing is rather expensive, but if properly built gives good protection, says the American Telephone Journal.

An iron pipe 1½ or 3 in. in diameter, according to the wire capacity desired, is laid below the frost line from pole to pole. The usual pipe bend is made at each of the

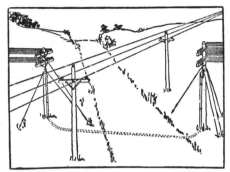

Underground Crossing for Rural Lines

poles, which are properly guyed, and at the end of the pipe, where it runs up the pole, a goose neck is used to keep out the rain. For draining the conduit of moisture, due to condensation, a hole is drilled at the lowest point of the duct over a pocket filled with crushed stone.

No. 14 twisted pair "distributing wire" used in one of these conduits has given little trouble. The wire is fused direct to the line, without fuse or spark gap protection. Where these crossings are remote from a repair man, it is better to risk losing a pair of wires at $1.47 per 100 ft. than to hire a team and send a man after every lightning storm.

SIMPLE TANK GAUGE WITH ELECTRIC ALARM

A tank gauge that is very easy to rig up and gives good service is shown in the illustration. A wooden or cork float, A, is attached to a chain, B, which runs over a small pulley, C, and then to the dial or gauge which may be placed on the side of the tank or other convenient place. The numbers on the dial read from the top downward. E

(see detail at Fig. 2) is a piece of metal which runs in grooves and moves the pointer along the dial according to the rise and fall of the liquid.

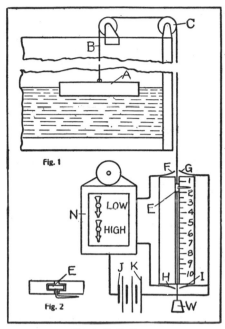

Simple Tank Gauge

The electric alarm (Fig. 1) is for calling some person when the water gets too high or too low. F, G, H, I are brass springs projecting so that the indicator, E, will close the circuit when it reaches either the top or bottom of the gauge. J, K are batteries in the circuit, and the annunciator, N, has the words high and low marked on it in their respective places.—Contributed by John M. Singer, 5915 Wabash avenue, Chicago, Ill.

GOOD CLEANSING POLISH

A good encaustic, which will clean and polish at the same time, is composed of 1 gallon soft water, 4 oz. yellow laundry soap and 1 lb. of white wax, shaved up. Boil together, stirring well, and then add 2 oz. sal soda; put the mixture in something which can be closely covered, and stir constantly until cool. If necessary dilute with water before using; lay on with a paint brush and polish off with a hard brush or cloth. Can be used on furniture, marbles, tiles and bricks. Will remove ink stains.

STANDARD SYMBOLS FOR WIRING PLANS

AS ADOPTED AND RECOMMENDED BY

THE NATIONAL ELECTRICAL CONTRACTORS ASSOCIATION OF THE UNITED STATES.

COPIES MAY BE HAD ON APPLICATION TO THE SECRETARY, UTICA, N. Y.

Ceiling Outlet; Electric only. Numeral in center indicates number of Standard 16 C. P. Incandescent Lamps.

Ceiling Outlet; Combination. $\frac{4}{2}$ indicates 4-16 C. P. Standard Incandescent Lamps and 2 Gas Burners.

Bracket Outlet; Electric only. Numeral in center indicates number of Standard 16 C. P. Incandescent Lamps.

Bracket Outlet; Combination. $\frac{4}{2}$ indicates 4-16 C. P. Standard Incandescent Lamps and 2 Gas Burners.

Wall or Baseboard Receptacle Outlet. Numeral in center indicates number of Standard 16 C. P. Incandescent Lamps.

Floor Outlet. Numeral in center indicates number of Standard 16 C. P. Incandescent Lamps.

Outlet for Outdoor Standard or Pedestal; Electric only. Numeral indicates number of Stand. 16 C. P. Incan. Lamps.

Outlet for Outdoor Standard or Pedestal; Combination. $\frac{6}{6}$ indicates 6-16 C. P. Stand. Incan. Lamps; 6 Gas Burners.

Drop Cord Outlet.

One Light Outlet, for Lamp Receptacle.

Arc Lamp Outlet.

Special Outlet, for Lighting, Heating and Power Current, as described in Specifications.

Ceiling Fan Outlet.

S^1 S. P. Switch Outlet.

S^2 D. P. Switch Outlet.

S^3 3-Way Switch Outlet.

S^4 4-Way Switch Outlet.

S^D Automatic Door Switch Outlet.

S^E Electrolier Switch Outlet.

> Show as many Symbols as there are Switches. Or in case of a very large group of Switches, indicate number of Switches by a Roman numeral, thus; S^1 XII; meaning 12 Single Pole Switches.
>
> Describe Type of Switch in Specifications, that is,
>
> Flush or Surface, Push Button or Snap,

Meter Outlet.

Distribution Panel.

Junction or Pull Box.

Motor Outlet; Numeral in center indicates Horse Power.

Motor Control Outlet.

Transformer.

———————— Main or Feeder run concealed under Floor.

———————— Main or Feeder run concealed under Floor above.

– – – – – Main or Feeder run exposed.

———————— Branch Circuit run concealed under Floor.

———————— Branch Circuit run concealed under Floor above.

– – – – – Branch Circuit run exposed.

--•----•-- Pole Line.

• Riser.

Telephone Outlet; Private Service.

Telephone Outlet; Public Service.

Bell Outlet.

Buzzer Outlet.

Push Button Outlet; Numeral indicates number of Pushes.

Annunciator; Numeral indicates number of Points.

Speaking Tube.

Watchman Clock Outlet.

Watchman Station Outlet.

Master Time Clock Outlet.

Secondary Time Clock Outlet.

Door Opener.

Special Outlet; for Signal Systems, as described in Specifications.

Battery Outlet.

———— • { Circuit for Clock, Telephone, Bell or other Service, run under Floor, concealed. Kind of Service wanted ascertained by Symbol to which line connects.

———— •• { Circuit for Clock, Telephone, Bell or other Service, run under Floor above, concealed. Kind of Service wanted ascertained by Symbol to which line connects.

SUGGESTIONS IN CONNECTION WITH STANDARD SYMBOLS FOR WIRING PLANS.

Indicate on plan, or describe in specifications, the height of all outlets, located on side walls.

It is important that ample space be allowed for the installation of mains, feeders, branches and distribution panels.

It is desirable that a key to the symbols used accompany all plans.

If mains, feeders, branches and distribution panels are shown on the plans, it is desirable that they be designated by letters or numbers.

NOTE—If other than Standard 16 C. P. Incandescent lamps are desired, Specifications should describe capacity of Lamp to be used.

BABBITTING BEARINGS

In babbitting ordinary split shaft bearings, it is a good plan to wrap the shaft with one thickness of common writing paper and then wind with string in a spiral. The paper keeps the shaft from chilling the babbitt and gives clearance enough to do away with the time-killing scraping; and the spiral groove formed by the string makes the best oil channel possible.—Contributed by E. V.

HOW TO MAKE A WATER STILL

Any water containing lime or other impurities is not good for photographic work, but the water obtained by distillation will always give good results.

The still shown in the sketch is one that is easily made and inexpensive. Obtain two thin glass bottles, A and B, and join together with a cork having a hole through the center. A quantity of water is placed in bottle A, and heat is applied, which vaporizes

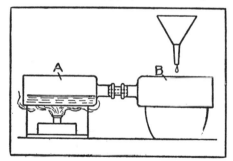

Plan of Water Still

the water and forces it in bottle B, where it is condensed.

The bottle A may be heated by means of a small gas stove, or alcohol lamp, and the other bottle may be cooled by water from a hydrant or from a funnel, with a piece of cloth in the mouth, to allow the water to drop slowly.

If a mixture of alcohol and water is placed in bottle A, the alcohol will evaporate first and condense in bottle B before much water has evaporated.—Contributed by Charles Lea, Brunswick, Mo.

TO TIN OLD SOLDERING IRONS

Some of the readers of "Shop Notes" may have trouble with old soldering irons. To

tin same, heat well and dip in pulverized sal ammoniac a moment and then rub with solder. This operation will be effective, no matter how many pit holes there are in the iron or how dirty.—Contributed by Harry Casslebury, Altoona, Pa.

AIR AS A POWER

There are other sources of energy in air besides its velocity. The energy of the heat contained in the atmosphere is sufficient to run all the power plants in the world without decreasing its temperature any appreciable amount. The problem is to maintain a difference of temperature between two

An Interesting Experiment

places, as heat produces no energy while at rest, but only when moving from one place to another.

There are many easily volatilized liquids which would boil readily at atmospheric temperatures, and thereby produce a constant pressure in any boiler, without the use of a fire, but such liquids are very hard to condense, as it requires very extreme cold to cause them to liquefy. A new source of cold might solve this problem, but all sources of cold thus far discovered require either power for its production, or chemicals which soon cease to be effective.

When dry air is confined and heated, the increase in temperature is only 1-273 of the original pressure for each degree Centigrade, but moist air expands very much more. This may be illustrated by holding a bottle upside down, under a hot water faucet, and then dipping the mouth in cold water, as shown in the sketch. A difference of temperature of only a few degrees will cause the water to half fill the bottle. It is evident from this that moist air, heated the same amount, would double its pressure. Thus, air at atmospheric pressure would increase to 15 lbs. above atmosphere, and air at 100 lbs. pressure would increase to 215 lbs. above atmosphere. If the air were heated twice as much, the pressure would be increased a corresponding amount, as the increase in pressure is directly proportional to the increase in temperature.

There are several varieties of hot air engines being made at the present time, but we are unaware of any attempt being made to utilize the increased efficiency obtained by the use of moist air.

It is doubtful if the weight of the air could be utilized for a source of power, although a device for doing this ought to be very powerful as a cube of air 31 ft. on each side weighs over a ton.

————— ◆◆◆ —————

HOW TO MAKE AND USE A PRONY BRAKE

The brake shown in Fig. 1 can be made of a piece of leather belt, B, Fig. 2, with a number of wood cleats, C, fastened as

secure, and the screw eye, F, should be used to attach the spring balance, C, the other end being attached to the ceiling as indicated.

To obtain the horsepower of an engine apply the brake, as shown in Fig. 1, and take the speed in revolutions per minute (R. P. M.) with the speed indicator, E, at the same time noting the weight in pounds (W) shown by the spring balance. Measure carefully the distance from the center of the engine shaft to the screw eye in inches (A). If the values of W, A and R. P. M. are known the horsepower may be found as follows:

$$hp. = \frac{A. \times W. \times R. P. M.}{63025}$$

For example: If A = 16 in., W = 20 lbs., and R. P. M. = 500; then, hp. = 16 × 20 × 500 ÷ 63025 = 2½ hp. The constant 63025 is obtained by multiplying 12 × 33,000 and dividing by 6.2832; 12 being the number of inches in a foot; 33,000 the number of ft. lbs. per min. for each horsepower; and 6.2832 the ratio between the radius and circumference of the flywheel.

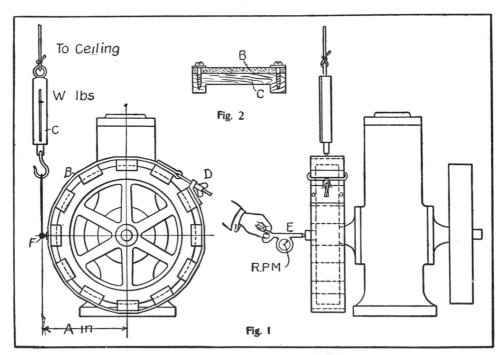

Details of Making and Using a Prony Brake

shown. A tension screw, D, Fig. 1, can be fastened by any method that will make it

To crystallize glass flow heavy alum water over it; then let it dry.

SELF=RELEASING BEAMS IN WALLS

When the ends of beams that go into a wall are cut on a slant, as illustrated, a lower insurance rate can be secured. Beams so cut will fall out easily without overturning the wall in case of fire, says the Practical Carpenter.

MAIL BOX TROLLEY FOR RURAL PATRONS

Patrons of rural routes living some distance back from the road will find a trolley for drawing the mail box to the house and sending it back again a great convenience. The illustrations show such a line, which was devised by a correspondent of the Rural New-Yorker.

At the house end of the line a stout post is set in the ground and a bicycle, with saddle and front wheel removed, is fastened with pins against the post, as shown (Fig. 1), to serve as motive power. For the main wire No. 9 is the size used, and No. 17 galvanized for the belt wire. For a short line on level ground broom wire would do.

Posts are set every 50 or 60 yds. between the house and the road ends of the line. Each of these intermediate posts has a

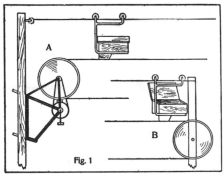

Fig. 1

Terminals of the Line

bracket (D, Fig. 2) of 2x2-in. stuff, and an iron at the top for supporting the main wire (C, Fig. 2). This iron is made of old spring-wagon tire with a half-round groove on top for the wire to rest in. The top wire is high enough above the notched guides below so the bottom of the box will not bump

when passing a bracket. The arrangement of pulleys and guides at these intermediate posts is shown at D, Fig. 2. The guides are of 1-in. hard wood, screwed to the arm of the bracket. The outside pulley is underneath the arm and 1 ft. distant from the other pulley, so that the wire cannot get tangled on windy days. A wire fence ratchet is used to keep the top wire tight. The post at the road end of the line has a wheel. An ordinary R. F. D. mail box is used, with a hardwood block one-half its length underneath it. The belt line starts at this block, runs the length of the line over the wheel on the post at the roadside, returns over the pulleys of the intermediate posts, passes around the bicycle wheel, and is fastened to the block under the box in a small hole in a piece of strap-iron fastened in the block.

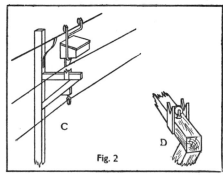

Fig. 2

One of the Intermediate Posts

The wheel at the road end can be the front wheel of the bicycle or an old sewing machine wheel, and a trough or support for the box is provided at this end to hold it firm while being opened or closed (B, Fig. 1). The device as rigged up in this instance cost about $5. The line is 250 yds. long and travels uphill 75 ft. to the road. An electric alarm to let the patron know when there is mail in the box could be added by one of a little ingenuity.

TO REMOVE A BROKEN STUD BOLT

A broken stud bolt in a casting or machine part may be removed as follows:

Drill a small hole in the broken part to be removed and use a lefthand tap. If it is a lefthand threaded stud bolt use a righthand tap to get it out. Be careful not to use too large a drill, as it would leave too thin a shell to tap in, and the expansion would cause it to bind.—Contributed by G. J. Lesperance, 425 Howland avenue, Kenosha, Wis.

PORTABLE KETTLE AND FIRE=PLACE FOR GRAVEL ROOFER

Whatever thickness of metal is used for this purpose, the construction shown in Fig. 1 is suitable. The fire pot, A A, is seamed to the bottom, B B, at C C and at its top an angle iron, D D, is riveted, as shown at a a. The elbow, E, is beaded and flanged, as shown by b c; F shows the damper in position.

The angle iron, H H, riveted, as shown, supports the grate, J J, while K shows the opening for the ash pit door, around which grooves are riveted, into which the door will slide as shown by e e. The opening for the fire door is at L and around it

When the fire pot is to be wheeled to a certain place, says the Metal Worker, the legs, D D, are raised, and afterward lowered, thus preventing the kettle from tipping. Fig. 3 shows how the slides and grooves for the doors, L and K in Fig. 1, are constructed, while A A in Fig. 3 shows the part body of the fire pot, cut out as shown from b to b. The riveted grooves are shown by B B, in which the door, C, slides, D being a handle riveted at a a.

Fig. 4 shows the construction of the grate, which can be made from band iron. The outside ring, A A, should be a trifle smaller than the inside diameter of the angle iron ring, D D, in Fig. 1, so that it can be removed when desired. Three of the grate

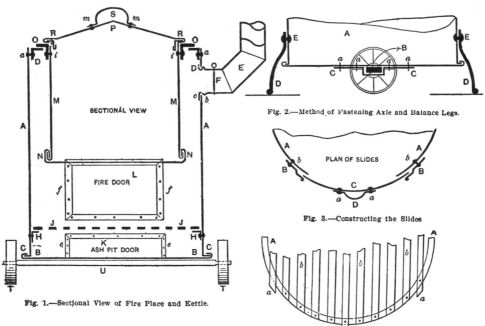

Fig. 1.—Sectional View of Fire Place and Kettle.

Fig. 2.—Method of Fastening Axle and Balance Legs.

Fig. 3.—Constructing the Slides

Fig. 4.—The Grate Construction.

grooves are riveted, as indicated at f f. The tar kettle, M M, is double seamed to the bottom at N N, on the top of which an angle, O O, is riveted, as shown by i i. The pitched cover, P, is seamed to the collar, as shown by R R. The handle, S, is riveted at m m. The wheels and axle, T U T, are fastened to the bottom of the fire pot, as shown in Fig. 2, in which A is part of the fire pot and B the section of the axle, which is fastened to the bottom by means of the angle, C C, riveting at a a a a. The balance legs are shown at D D, one being fastened on either side of the fire pot and riveted at E and E, which forms a pivot.

bars, as a a a a in Fig. 4, are to project over the ring, as shown, these projections to rest on the angle iron, H H, in Fig. 1. The balance of the grate bars, as b b b, etc., in Fig. 4, are riveted. It will be noticed that the angle iron ring at the top of the kettle in Fig. 1 rests upon the angle iron ring, D D, at the top of the fire pot. This allows the kettle to be removed for cleaning purposes. If desired the fire pot and kettle can be made square, using the same construction, which can be modified to suit.

ANOTHER DEVICE FOR GETTING ENGINES OFF CENTER

Fit a jaw over the rim of the wheel and pivot it to a handle or lever as shown. Se-

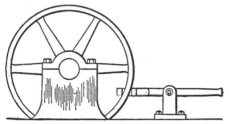

Turning Engines Off Center.

cure the handle to a block of wood, from which to get leverage. When engine is on dead center, says the Engineers' Review, place the device in front of the wheel and the jaws on the rim of the wheel and bear down on the outer end of the handle.

ROLLED A BOILER NINE MILES

A 125-hp. boiler was rolled nine miles from the railroad station to the Marine Hospital at Ft. Stanton, N. M. The process was very similar to the movement of a road roller. The roads were too soft to support a wagon with such a load, hence this unusual method of transportation was resorted to. Ryerson's Monthly says: "It was necessary to transport this boiler nine miles over the plains and mountains in order to reach its destination, and as it was found that the roads were in such condition that they would

Mules Rolling the Boiler.

not support a wagon with any considerable load, it became a very pretty problem to solve. The boiler was finally rigged up as shown in the illustration — a heavy pipe

being used as an axle and fourteen mules furnishing the motive power, the boiler being safely rolled the nine miles from the railroad to the hospital, reaching there none the worse for the rough usage to which it was necessarily subjected.

HOME=MADE IMPROVED BUFFER

A good buffing wheel can be made of a metal band, A (see sketch), drilled to receive a number of cords, B, a hardwood hub, C, and a babbitt bushing, D. If a narrow buffer is desired, one row of cords, as shown in the side view, will be sufficient, but if a wide buffer is wanted the required width can be obtained by making several rows, as shown in the section. If more than one row is used, the holes should be drilled diagonally.

The pieces of rope may be taken from sash

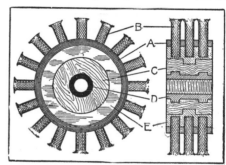

An Improved Buffer.

cord, or if the buffer is intended for very smooth work a soft, braided cotton cord should be used. It is unnecessary to ravel the ends of the cord, as they will soon ravel themselves after a little use. The cords are held in by melted rosin, E, which is poured in the cavity after the other parts are assembled and carefully centered. A little beeswax, tar or paraffine stirred into the melted rosin will make it less brittle. The bushing, D, may be made of either lead or babbitt, and is made to fit the shaft of the buffing machine.

A buffer of this kind will do the work better and quicker than any muslin buffer I have ever used.—Contributed by Stoke Richards, Santa Clara, Cal.

AQUARIUM CEMENT

A good cement for aquariums is made as follows: Mix 1 gill plaster of Paris, 1 gill litharge, 1 gill fine white sand and $\frac{1}{3}$ gill finely powdered rosin together, and add an equal quantity of boiled linseed oil and turpentine, until the consistency is about the same as putty. This cement will dry hard in a few days.

GUARD FOR AIR DUCT IN HOT AIR FURNACE

When there is a strong wind from the outside blowing into the air supply duct of a hot air furnace, the swinging damper

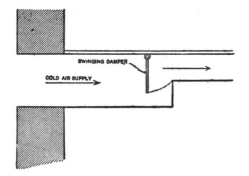

Wind Guard for Air Supply Ducts

shown in the illustration can be used to prevent the admission of too much air, says the Metal Worker. The damper is hinged at the top and swings loosely in an enlarged entrance to the air supply duct. Under excessive wind pressure the damper is blown up against the opening of the duct leading to the furnace, closing it off and preventing the cold air from entering too freely.

DEVICE FOR DRAWING CORNERS

A device more convenient than compasses for drawing round corners and fillets of various sizes is shown at Fig. 1. Radii are marked, the outside ones being made enough smaller and the inside ones enough larger to make the corners the size indicated when drawn with a pencil or inking pen. They can be of various other radii, and if the draftsman wishes to mark what the radius of his curve is, he has the figures before him.

Sheet metal, nickel-plated or celluloid is the proper material for this instrument. It should be ½ in. thick, beveled on one side and used flat side down for the pencil and up for the inking pen. Fig. 2 shows its application. Curves A and B were drawn by using the outside corners, says the American Machinist, and the others by using the inside corners.

TO FIND THE CENTER OF A CIRCLE

To find the center of a barrel-head or other circular object lay a steel square on the circle with the point touching any part of the circumference A. From the intersections, C B, of the two legs with the circumference

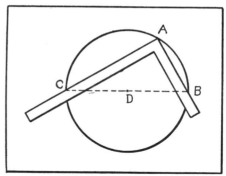

Finding the Center of a Circle

draw the line C B. Bisecting this line at D gives the required center of the circle.— Contributed by H. J. Heaton, Sidney, Iowa.

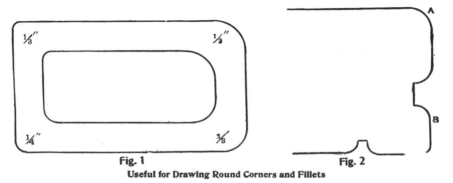

Fig. 1   Fig. 2
Useful for Drawing Round Corners and Fillets

TO COLOR COPPER ROOFS GREEN

To 5 gal. water add 1 lb. sal ammoniac, dissolve thoroughly and let stand 24 hours. Then apply the solution to the copper with a brush, covering the entire surface carefully. Let it stand for one day, says the American Artisan, then sprinkle it lightly with water, using a brush. Do not use too much water or it will run the color and streak it.

The same effect can be produced by using ½ lb. salt to 2 gal. water.

HOME=MADE LOCK=NUT STRIP

It is often handy to have a lock-nut strip to fasten wires on when testing. The diagram shows a strip that is cheaply made by using the binding posts from the carbons of old dry batteries.

Cut out a piece of ¼-in. oak, or white wood, 4 in. long and 2 in. wide, and bore a hole, A, in the center on each end to receive screws for fastening the strip down. Bore a row of holes, ½ in. apart, down one side and another row the same distance apart on the opposite side, so that they are on a line between the holes of the first row. Insert the binding posts, which should fit snugly, in these holes and lock them tightly with the small nut that was next to the carbon. Place two brass or copper washers on each post and screw on the thumb nuts. Place one wire under the bottom washer and the other between the two washers and fasten them down with the thumb nut. The strip can be made any length to suit the number of connections.

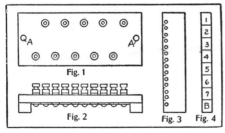

Fig. 1

Fig. 2

Fig. 3 Fig. 4

Lock=Nut and Form Strips

A form strip to go with the lock-nut strip is shown in Figs. 3 and 4. It is made of a piece of the same wood, 1 in. wide and 4 in. long. Bore holes, according to the size of wire used, ¼ in. apart, ¼ in. from the edge. Bore a hole at each end through the 1-in. way for fastening screws. Sandpaper

the face of the board and shellac it. Then with a saw cut niches ½ in. apart across the top, so as to bring two holes in each space. Number the spaces to suit the job (Fig. 4).—Contributed by H. H. Fountain, Brooklyn, N. Y.

RENEWING A RUNNING THREAD NIPPLE=-A PROBLEM IN PIPING

On testing a low-pressure boiler we had put up at Riverdale, N. Y., we found a defective nipple, N, Fig. 1, which connected the section, S, and the drum, D. The distance between S and D could not be changed,

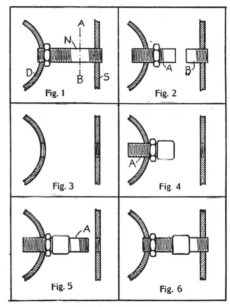

Fig. 1

Fig. 2

Fig. 3

Fig. 4

Fig. 5

Fig. 6

Problem in Piping

so we cut the nipple on the line A B, and ran the lock nut up to the end of the thread on piece A, Fig. 2. We then screwed the half A into the drum, far enough to remove the piece B. This made room enough to remove the half A, thus leaving both openings clear as in Fig. 3.

We then made a running thread nipple, A, Fig. 4, with lock nut and coupling attached, and screwed it into the drum as far as possible (Fig. 4). Then we screwed a short nipple, A, Fig. 5, into the coupling, and unscrewed the running thread nipple, thus bringing the connection into the section, as shown in Fig. 6. The lock nut was then screwed tightly against the drum, as shown, and the job was complete.—Contributed by Gus Cook, 153 W. 62nd St., New York City.

LABOR=SAVING SACK HOLDER

A handy sack holder, the device of a correspondent of the American Miller, is shown in the illustration. The materials used in its construction did not cost more than 25

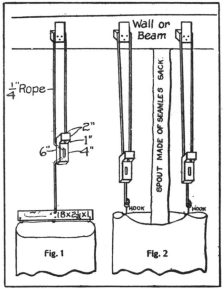

Handy Sack Holder

cents, and yet the device saves the labor of one man.

The holder can be raised or lowered to suit the height of the sack being filled, by catching the board, or lower rope, with one hand and raising or lowering the block with the other.

HOW TO RESHARPEN OLD FILES

Clean the files thoroughly, using a scratch brush and a strong solution of washing soda in hot water, then wash off the soda with hot water.

Prepare a bath of 1 part nitric acid to 4 parts water contained in an earthen vessel. Sort and grade the files according to fineness and immerse those of each grade in the bath. The finer files should be left in the bath about a minute, and the coarser cuts five or six minutes, says the Metal Worker. After the acid bath, wash the files in hot water, dry, and grease them while still warm with vaseline.

In preparing the acid bath pour the acid into the water very slowly, as the heat action is great.

HOW TO MEASURE BELT ON PULLEY

A short rule for finding the change required in the length of belt when one of the pulleys on which it runs is changed for one of different size, is as follows: Take three times the difference between the diameters of the pulleys and divide by two. The result will be the length of belt to cut out or put in.—Practical Engineer.

FATIGUE OF MATERIALS

In a former number of Popular Mechanics, a description was given of the fatigue of metals, showing that great precaution should be used in designing machinery subjected to varying loads. The necessity of observing this property of matter has been emphasized by other examples of fatigue, which have recently been brought to our notice. It has been found that watch springs often break several hours after the last winding, although the tension at the time of breaking is much less than when wound up tight.

In larger machines the same thing often occurs. Crane hooks which have, in many instances, carried 20 to 25 tons, break with a load of 10 or 15 tons, and valves which are tested to several hundred pounds hydraulic pressure, sometimes break on less than 50 lbs. For this reason the hydraulic test used on boilers should not be carried to excess.

Probably the most remarkable cases of fatigue are found in floors. The top floor of a five-story factory building, which was heavily loaded with paper, fell in the dead of night, taking the other four floors with it, and crashing down into the basement. All the machinery in the building was in operation the day previous to the disaster, and the heavy jarring and rapid vibration would be expected to determine the time of falling, but the jarring and vibration evidently ceased slightly before the stress in the material reached the yielding point. Another still more remarkable case occurred in France a few years ago. In this instance, a ball room floor which had been crowded with dancers the entire evening, gave way with a sudden crash, after all the people had left and the only load was its own weight.

SHOP NOTES

TO SET A BELT SHIFTER

Anyone who has had trouble with a belt sliding over to the wrong pulley will appreciate the following device: The shifting mechanism is the same as an ordinary belt shifter with the exception of the lever, which has a spring at the upper end, as shown in

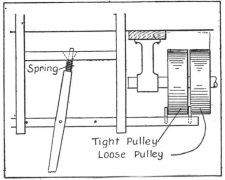

Spring

Tight Pulley
Loose Pulley

Belt Shifter

the cut. This spring, which is in compression, forces the shifter to the extreme position in either direction and holds it there.—Contributed by C. E. Holcombe, 2912 Edina Blvd., Zion City, Ill.

STARTING SCREWS IN CLEANOUT COVERS OF TRAPS

Considerable difficulty, oftentimes, is experienced in starting the screws when removing brass cleanout covers from traps. A good way, says the Metal Worker, is to give the wrench a few sharp strokes with a hammer at the point indicated in the sketch.

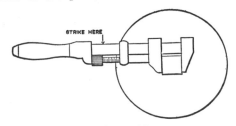

STRIKE HERE

Starting Cleanout Screws

The shock will make the brass let go and the cover can be readily unscrewed.

WIRE FOR STRINGING WATCH PARTS

A very simple and convenient device for watch repairers is shown in the sketch herewith, and is used for stringing the parts of a watch during the process of cleaning. It

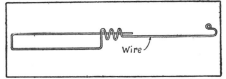

Wire

Wire Stringer for Watch Parts

can be easily made by any repairer, says a correspondent of the Keystone, and will soon pay for the time required to make it.

ADJUSTABLE RING FASTENING FOR A ROPE

An adjustable rope fastening, such as is shown in the sketch, will be found very effective for guy-rope fastenings, derrick fastenings, jury-mast knots, temporary mast

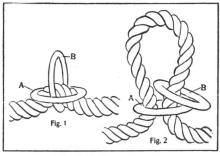

B

A

Fig. 1

B

A

Fig. 2

Adjustable Rope Fastening

bands, and numerous other devices where ropes are used. When used on the neck ropes of horses, a snap should be fastened to the end of the rope and hooked to the ring B. The size of the noose can then be made larger or smaller by drawing the rope through ring A, as shown in Fig. 2, and moving ring B the required distance. Then when the rope is drawn back, it will leave the rings as shown in Fig. 1. The rings can be made of iron or steel, somewhat smaller than the diameter of the rope, and when a number of fastenings are to be placed on one piece of rope, the rings, A, should be made oval-shaped so that they may be passed over the others. When only one fastening is required both rings may be made round.—Contributed by Harry Hall, Brooklyn, Iowa.

MAGNET FOR A BROOM HANDLE

Shop brooms equipped with the following device will be very useful for recovering brads, small screws, and other articles from the shavings. The broom handle is slotted a short distance and a magnet is held in

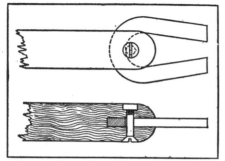

Magnet Attachment for Broom Handle

the slot by a $\frac{3}{16}$-in. stove bolt, as shown in the sketch. I use this device every time I sweep up, and usually find large quantities of brads, staples, and small screws. I upset a box of brads once and they fell in a lot of shavings and dust, but were quickly separated with the magnet.—Contributed by Edwin Howland, Baltimore, Md.

CABLE DRUM CARRIAGE

This device is used for holding the large spools, upon which is wound the lead-covered cable used in electrical work. The handling of these reels of cable, which has always been very difficult, owing to their great

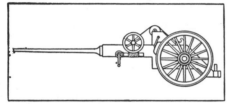

Cable Drum Carriage

weight, can be done by one man when using this device. With it the cable can be unwound either backwards or forwards and the drums can be easily raised by means of the powerful worm gear.

With the exception of the shafts and wheels the apparatus is built entirely of steel and is designed to carry varying sizes and weights of drums.

IMITATION ROSEWOOD STAIN

Put 1½ lb. logwood chips in a gallon of water and boil until reduced in volume to 2 qt. Apply boiling hot, says the Master Painter, and if several coats are necessary, let each coat dry before applying the next. Grain the finished surface with a camel's hair pencil dipped in logwood infusion containing the sulphates of iron and copper.

HOW TO SHEAR WIRE IN A LATHE

Instead of having a shaper rigged for shearing, this work may be done on the lathe, says the American Machinist.

Swing the mandrel, A (see sketch), which has a circular shear, B (made of tempered tool steel), on it, between the centers. Fasten a tool-steel piece, C (drilled for the wire, E, to be sheared and for the stop, D,

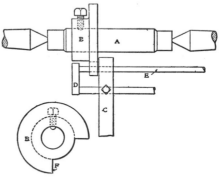

Shearing in a Lathe

which determines the length of the pieces to be cut), in the tool-post.

Operate as follows: Start the lathe, enter wire, E, in the hole in C, and press toward stop, D; when opening, B, is opposite the hole in C, press the wire up against D, and cutting edge F will shear it off. The piece C can have a series of holes in it to suit different sized wires. The circular shear, B, will last for a long time as there is plenty of stock for grinding.

A NEW METHOD OF TURBINE CONTROL

In a paper read before the American Institute of Electrical Engineers, Mr. Lamar Lyndon describes a form of governor bypass shown in the sketch. It has been found that when the supply of a turbine is suddenly checked, the momentum of the mov-

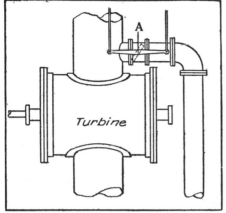

Turbine Governor

ing column of water causes an enormous increase in pressure, which would probably burst the pipe if it were not for the relief valves, which open and thus allow part of the water to escape.

In the new method the relief valves are replaced by the compensating valve, A, which operates in connection with the governor. This arrangement prevents the oscillatory movement of the governor, and gives a more uniform speed in the turbine.

HANGER FOR BLUEPRINTS

In hanging blueprints on the line to dry, they are apt to be torn or hung so that they dry unevenly. The hanger illustrated eliminates this difficulty. The blueprint is clipped with the hanger while in the water, says a writer in the American Machinist, and the whole thing is then lifted out easily.

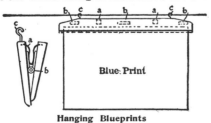

Hanging Blueprints

HOW TO LEVEL AN OILSTONE

For use in properly truing up oilstones provide a block of cast iron 1½ in. thick, 9 in. wide and 12 in. long, with a projecting ledge ½ in. wide and ½ in. high on one side, this to keep the block from slipping when on the bench. Plane the block up true on both sides and the three edges, says the Patternmaker, and place on the bench convenient to sink water; also provide coarse and fine emery powder.

To true up an oilstone or slip, place a small quantity of the coarse emery powder in the middle of the block, pour on a little water and rub the oilstone back and forth until its surface is level; then repeat the operation, using fine emery powder with water. To true the round side of a stone, and preserve its original radius, turn the stone while rubbing.

This method will entirely remove all the glaze, so objectionable in oilstones, and leave a nice surface similar to that obtained by grinding.

PUMPING TO A 100-FOOT ELEVATION

With two piston type steam pumps for tank service, either of them able to discharge sufficient water to a 50-ft. elevation with a nominal lift of, say, 10 to 15 ft., it is possible to force water 100 ft. vertically by the following method:

Connect the suction of one of the pumps to the water supply and the discharge to a receiver capable of holding the required pressure, in this case 21.7 lb. Connect the suction of the second pump to this receiver also and connect the discharge to the main that carries the water to the 100-ft. elevation. To steady the action of the pumps, says a correspondent of the Engineer's Review, the receiver must be fitted with a good-sized air chamber.

In operating keep the steam valve on the first pump open full and control the speed with the steam valve on the second pump. The second pump not having any lift will be able to overcome the increase of friction in the discharge main. Any boiler will do nicely for a receiver, but it would be better not to use too large a receiver.

This scheme will work on rotary pumps as well, but not on plunger pumps. The two-pump scheme can be worked very nicely for fire service at a distance and in a great many other ways as well.

BENDING AN OIL CAN SPOUT

To make a bend in a spout for an oil can or a machine oiler proceed as follows:

Form the straight spout in the regular way over the blowhorn stake and solder the seam. Plug the small end of the spout with a piece of wood and pour melted resin into the spout until it reaches the point where the bend is to be made. Let the resin cool till solid, then make the bend over the round stake or mandrel to the desired form without a buckle.

Heat the spout gradually over an oil torch, says a writer in the American Artisan, until the resin again melts and runs out.

A NEW WAY TO BEND TUBES

The principal difficulty in bending tubes is the tendency to buckle and wrinkle. This has been overcome in some instances, by pouring melted resin into the tube before bending, and while this method prevents the tube from wrinkling in long radius bends, it has been found unsuitable for making sharp bends or for making bends in which the exact diameter of the tube is to be maintained. The tube is also slightly flattened at the bend, and is therefore not perfectly round.

It being required to bend a number of brass tubes through 90° without any wrinkles, creases, or change in section, a correspondent of the American Machinist made use of the "fluid punch" principle. The tubes were forced through a die, as shown in the sketch, and a water pressure of 6,000 lb. per sq. in. applied to the inside of the tube. The tube being closed at the end was forced through the die by the pressure of the water, and as the diameter of the die all around the bend was the same as the tube, there was no place for the metal to go except in the desired direction. The diameter could not be increased because the walls of the die prevented this, and it could not be decreased at any point on account of the high pressure within.

In using this device the end, A, became rounded as a result of the pressure, and was afterwards cut off. If the die is supplied with a liberal amount of oil it will last a long time and do good work.

TO REPLACE A BROKEN CASTING

When a cast-iron part of a stove or other article is broken the following method is usually the cheapest way to replace it: Take the broken casting to a foundry and have a new casting made, using the original as a pattern. The molder can easily place the broken parts together so that the duplicate casting will be perfect unless it is very complicated.

The duplicate casting will be a little smaller than the original as cast iron shrinks about ⅛ in. in a foot in cooling. If the shrinkage should be an objection it may be partially overcome by annealing, as suggested by a correspondent of Machinery. To anneal the casting, heat it in a slow charcoal fire to a dull red heat, and then cover it over about 2 in. with fine charcoal. Sprinkle several inches of dry ashes on top and allow to cool slowly. This will permanently expand the casting which will then be very nearly the size of the original.

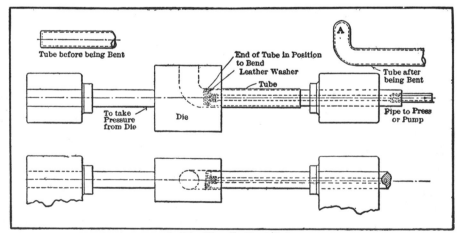

A New Way To Bend Tubes

CUTTING A KEYWAY WITHOUT A MACHINE

A keyway can be cut in a pulley, gear, or other piece of machinery without the use of a planer or slotting machine by the tools shown in the sketch, and a hammer. The cylinder, A, is made of hard wood and turned up to fit the bore of the pulley. The groove, B, is the same width as the

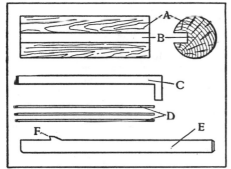

Home-Made Keyseating Tools

keyway required, and deep enough to receive the iron piece, C, and the steel chisel, E. The piece C has the end bent over as shown to prevent it from sliding out of the groove. The shims, D, can be made of galvanized iron, thin strips of hard wood, or almost any material obtainable.

To use these tools put the cylinder in the bore of the pulley and put piece C in the bottom of the groove. Drive the chisel through the bore and then shim up with the strips, D, driving the chisel clear through each time.

About six shims will be required for making most keyways, but it is well to have more as the depth of the groove, B, will not then have to be an exact dimension.

TO KEEP PLASTER OF PARIS FROM HARDENING QUICKLY

In the May number G. M. Backus says: "To keep plaster of paris from hardening so quickly, use vinegar instead of water for mixing." That depends on how long you wish to keep it from hardening. After thirty years' experience with plaster of paris I find that mixed with clear vinegar it will not harden in six hours, but will work like putty.

The better way is to add one-fourth, or possibly one-half vinegar to the water. If wanted for stopping cracks in walls, one-half vinegar will give all the time required and will make a better filling than when all vinegar is used; one-fourth vinegar will give ample time and make a still better stopping.—Contributed by W. C. Bunker, D. D. S., Oregon, Ill.

HOW TO MAKE A SMALL SPLIT PULLEY

To make a small split pulley up to 10 in. in diameter, the following method is excellent, says a writer in the Wood-Worker:

Take two pieces of firm stock, A A, as long as the desired diameter of the pulley, plus a little to work off, and as wide as the desired face. Join them up and make a light saw mark across the center, as in making a wooden box, then bolt them together with a piece of heavy cardboard or very thin wood, a a, Fig. 1, between. This cardboard or wood should be cut through at o, so that there will be a hole there for the worm of the bit to follow.

Having bolted the pieces together, bore a hole of the size of the shaft. Now take two pieces, B B, of the right thickness to complete the circle, saw roughly to size, fit them over the bolt heads and nuts, and screw on, being sure to countersink the screw heads sufficiently to allow for the turning. Mark piece B, which covers the nuts, so that the pulley may be taken apart by removing that piece only.

Having built up the rough pulley in this way, take off the piece B, remove the nuts

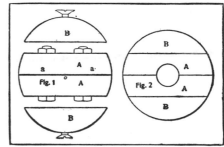

Small Split Pulley

from the bolts, take apart the pieces A A, remove the thin pieces—you have no further use for them—and having made a wood mandrel of exactly the size of the shaft, clamp your pulley on it, and turn as desired. The pieces A A need not be of especially hard wood; white pine has been used with perfect success, and they are doubtless the better for being thin enough so that when the bolts are drawn up they will have a slight tendency to spring, thus bringing the end grain to bear on the shaft and clamping it tighter than if they were rigid.

◆ ◆ ◆

PROBLEM IN ARRANGING PULLEYS

In the ordinary method of using two single-block pulleys, the pulling force is only doubled, but by arranging the pulleys and rope, as shown in the sketch, the force is increased to four times that of the power

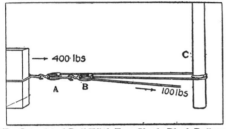

To Get a 4 to 1 Pull With Two Single Block Pulleys

applied to the end of the rope. The pulleys A and B are connected, as shown, and the rope is then given one turn around a post, tree or other object, C.

When the pulley B reaches the post C, loosen the rope and slide pulley B back to pulley A, which will have traveled half the distance traveled by pulley B.—Contributed by A. D. Newlin, Dunlap, Cal.

◆ ◆ ◆

A MACHINIST'S TAPER GAUGE

The sketch shows a taper gauge made by a correspondent of the American Machinist, and found useful for measuring the taper of lathe centers and other tapered work. The principle used is the same as that found in the taper attachments of a lathe. The lower jaw slides up or down to adjust the work; the upper one swings on a stiff joint, C, to adjust the taper; both jaws are locked with thumbscrews.

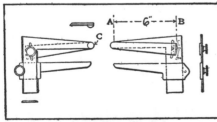

Useful Taper Gauge

As it is half a foot from A to B, the graduation is made one-half size, so that a distance of ½ in. on the scale should read 1 in., which gives the taper in 1 ft.

◆ ◆ ◆

SUPPORTING LONG LINES OF PIPE

Often it is not desirable to support long lines of heavy piping with trestle or bridge work. A correspondent of the Metal Worker describes his method in such case.

Three lengths of 6-in. iron pipe, each about 14 ft. long, were to be used in crossing a street, leaving an unobstructed clearance of 15 ft. The pipes were arranged to rise in a vertical line above each sidewalk and near the riser were placed two 10x10-in. posts to support the pipe line and the weight of water in it. The three lengths of pipe were joined together with flanges, giving the abutting ends maximum bearing surface and assisting materially in keeping the line rigid.

A block of wood was placed toward each end of the line and over these were passed

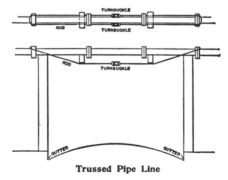

Trussed Pipe Line

two ½-in. round iron rods, bearing underneath two other blocks 6 by 8 in. in size, placed as shown. The rods were screwed together by turnbuckles. The size of the rods is determined by the length of the span and the bends they are to be given.

◆ ◆ ◆

TO CUT INDIA RUBBER

Those who have had to cut heavy gaskets or other rubber articles have found that substance an unpleasant material to work. The cut can be made neat and clean, says a correspondent of Machinery, if the knife be kept wet; and if conditions permit, this can be best effected by doing the cutting under water, as good housewives know to do when peeling onions. Potash water is better than plain.

BORING A HOLE IN A CEILING

A man who wanted to bore a hole through the ceiling in his house, accomplished the task without getting any plaster or chips on the carpet, though his wife had told him he surely would, says American Machinist. He thrust the bit through the bottom of a pasteboard box, mounted a stepladder and bored the hole, catching all the litter in the box.

◆◆◆

T=SQUARE ATTACHMENT

The device shown in the sketch will keep the T-square true at all times, and saves many movements of the left hand when working near the end of the blade with a triangle. A piece of angle brass, A, is screwed to the drawing board near the left-hand edge on the under side. A piece of sheet brass, B, is bent, as shown, and screwed to the head of the T-square. A steel

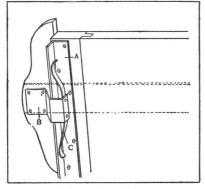

T=Square Attachment

spring, C, is fastened to B and slides on the brass angle, A, thus keeping the square true at all times. The sketch shows a view of the under side of the drawing board.—Contributed by A. L. T., Lansing, Mich.

◆◆◆

CHALK IN THE SHOP

A good way to keep a file from filling up with the metal being filed is to rub it with chalk; especially is this good, says Wood Craft, in reducing a shaft by means of a file.

Chalk makes a good oil extractor for old belts, also. Rub the chalk into the belt thoroughly, then pack the belt in chalk and let stand for a day or two. The capillary action induced will draw the oil from the belt into the chalk, and enough will be removed to make the belt fit for service.

EASILY MADE TRAMMEL POINTS

A trammel point in which no fine adjustment is required, can be made from pipe fittings and a steel rod, as shown in the sketch. The device can be made with either one traveling point, A, and one stationary

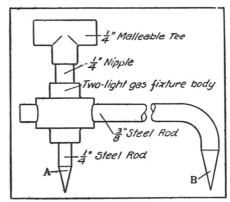

Trammel Points

point, B, or with two traveling points, as may be desired.

In making the traveling point a two-light gas fixture body is drilled to receive the ⅜-in. rod, and tapped for the steel point, as shown. The ¼-in. nipple acts like a set-screw, and the ¼-in. malleable tee serves as a handle. The ⅜-in. steel rod can be made any length desired and can be bent either hot or cold.—Contributed by Geo. A. Madison, Baltimore, Md.

◆◆◆

KINK FOR TELEGRAPH LINE

A friend and I use the accompanying kink on our telegraph line, doing away with the dirt and cleaning of gravity battery; we use dry cells instead. A A are two-point switches; keep the switches on left-hand point when not in use. When B calls C simply put switch on right-hand point

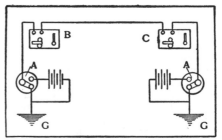

Wiring Kink for Telegraph

and call as usual. In connecting up the battery, observe that the positive pole is connected to switch at one station, while the negative pole is connected to the switch at the opposite station, giving a chance to use both batteries, if desired.—Contributed by F. L. Wheeler, Cliftondale, Mass.

LAYING A FIREROOM FLOOR

The fireroom floor should be planned not only to give good wearing value, but for comfort as well. The following plans, with modifications to suit the individual needs, is excellent:

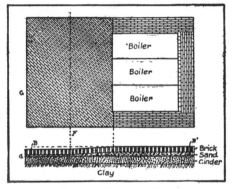

Laying a Fireroom Floor

First provide a supply of material: bricks, cinders, sand and cement, then proceed to excavate the part of the fireroom where the bricks are to be laid to a depth of at least 15 in. below the door sill. In this excavation lay a course of cinders 8 in. deep (see sketch); the cinders should be slightly wet and tamped in place thoroughly with tamping tools. Follow the cinders with a layer of coarse, sharp sand 4 in. deep at B' and 2 in. deep at B. In part of the fireroom the brick should be laid diagonally, but as there is considerable waste in making broken joints, they may be put in straight at the sides of the floor and the rear of the boiler.

In front of the boilers the floor should slope slightly so that water from the ashpit which comes out with the ashes when the fireman is cleaning fires will not form small pools which do not conduce to comfort. The heaviest work of the fireroom comes on the space between the boiler fronts and the dotted lines, FF, therefore the brick should be thoroughly grouted in there. To do this, mix up clear Portland cement with water,

very thin and pour in all the joints. When the joints are full to overflowing, spread the cement all over the space with a coarse broom. Cover that portion of the floor from the dotted lines FF to the outer wall at G with very fine sand, tamping thoroughly; then when all the joints are filled, sweep off the sand. Vitrified brick, which is very hard, should be used for laying the floor. A correspondent of the Practical Engineer says that a floor laid in this way will give excellent satisfaction and last a great while.

CEMENT BLOCKS CURED BY STEAM

Cement blocks or bricks made by the dry process may be cured by steam, says Municipal Engineering. Where the block plant is operated by steam, the exhaust steam can be used for curing and the extra cost is very small. It is necessary to use a closed shed for storing the green blocks until they are ready to be removed to the curing yard. This is less convenient than the open shed, but if cars for handling the blocks and holding them while in the steam were provided, there would be no difficulty in this respect.

SCREWDRIVER THAT HOLDS THE SCREWS

For very small screws the screwdriver illustrated is convenient, especially, says American Machinist, for putting screws in place in the interior of typewriters, adding machines and the like.

The side view, Fig. 1, shows two prongs on which a slight pressure is exerted when a screw is to be held; as soon as the pressure is removed the prongs spring back gripping the screw firmly. The handle of the rod is knurled to afford a good grip for

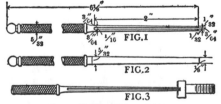

Screw-Holding Screwdriver

the fingers in turning. Spring steel rod is the material used for this device. The ends are made quite thin in order to have the spring as sensitive as possible. The method of using the driver is shown at Fig. 3.

RECIPE FOR MARINE GLUE

One part of pure india rubber dissolved in naphtha. When melted add 2 parts of shellac. Melt until mixed. Pour out on tin until cold. Melt and use with a brush at water-bath heat.

Or take a handful of quicklime and 4 oz. linseed oil. Boil, and pour out on a plate until hard. Melt and use.

Or take 1 lb. of common glue—not fish glue—in 2 qt. of skim milk. Soak and boil.

All these are good.

HOW TO MAKE A CUTTING SHEAR

A very handy cutting shear can be made at little expense and requires little more than a couple of hours' labor, says a correspondent of the American Blacksmith.

Make the stand or bench of 4x6-in. oak lumber, similar in construction to an ordinary work truss, and 4 ft. long. Secure two cutter-bars from an old reaper and bend the end of one up and the end of the other down and rivet the two bent ends together. Make the lever or handle of ½-in. stock 4 ft. long. Split one end of this piece so as to evenly distribute the strain on the rivet by which the lever is hinged to the lower blade or jaw About 5 in. from the split end drill another hole. Cut two pieces of stock, 1 by ½ by 6 in. long and drill a hole in each end of both pieces and rivet one on each side of the upper blade or jaw and connect them in turn to the lever or handle.

Fasten the lower jaw to the bench or stand with two or four brackets, one or two, as the case may be, on each side of the jaw and bolt firmly to the wood base.

Forge a hook on the end of a piece of ½-in. round stock, run the straight end down through the bench, hook the other end over the top edge of the lower jaw and bolt

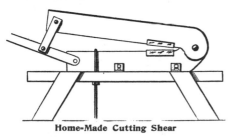

Home-Made Cutting Shear

the lower end firmly to the floor, thus holding the shear rigid. This tool can be used to cut flat stock ¼ by 3-in. or ½-in. round rods.

COMBINATION TELEGRAPH AND TELEPHONE LINE

The accompanying diagram shows a system which I recently installed in Kansas for simultaneous telegraphy and telephony and which is giving as good results as could be had were they entirely separate. On account of its simplicity it can be made by

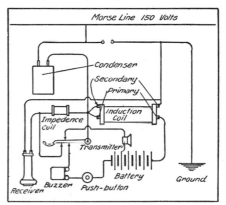

Wiring for Combination Telegraph and Telephone Line

anyone for less than the cost of any standard telephone made.

A word explaining its operation may prove useful. When receiver is on the hook in its normal position, the pushing of the button completes the circuit of six cells through an ordinary buzzer, primary of induction coil back to the battery, thus giving an interrupted direct current through this circuit and generating an induced alternating current in the secondary of the induction coil which passes out over the line, actuating the diaphragms of all receivers and vibrating them in unison with the buzzer of the ringing telephone. Receivers in this way act as "howlers" in addition to their usual function.

The condenser of course prevents the Morse current from reaching or working through the telephone to ground. The impedence, or retarding coil, may be made by using one of the coils out of an ordinary Morse relay (150 ohms), as its resistance is 75 ohms. Where Morse sets come between telephones on the line, both key and relay of the set should be completely bridged across with a condenser of small capacity. Where it is possible to use two telegraph wires and make a metallic circuit, a 1 micro-farad condenser on each side of telephone will serve the purpose of the 2 micro-farad condenser shown in diagram.—Contributed by C. V. Patterson, Independence, Kan.

DEVICE FOR RIPPING LONG STOCK

Long stock for moldings, etc., is easily ripped when a device like the one illustrated is used, says a correspondent of the Wood-Worker.

In the sketch, A is a plan view of the

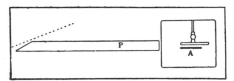

For Ripping Long Stock

saw table and P is the top of a bench, or trestle, for the stuff to run out on. This top, P, may be independent of the saw table, and made with four legs adjustable to height, if the saw table is adjustable, or it may be secured to the saw table at the one end and have a leg at the other. The entire efficiency of the device lies in having it a little over half the length of the longest stock to be worked, say 10 ft. long for 16-ft. stuff, and having the outer end cut on a long bevel, as shown. A strip being ripped off, it will lie on the table till the next pushes it along; then when the center passes the end of the bench, it will tip and slide off the bevel end, falling to the floor in the position indicated by the dotted line. With a device of this kind one man can rip molding stock very nearly as fast as two could do it without.

ANVIL MADE OF STEEL RAIL

The amateur blacksmith can make himself a very satisfactory anvil of a piece of steel rail—often to be found at the junk shop. A in the sketch shows the rail; BB, two blocks of wood just the length of the rail, used to prop it; C, two bolts; DD, four long screws, and EE, two pieces of angle iron of the same length as the piece of rail. The Model Engineer, London, says this makes a strong and useful anvil.

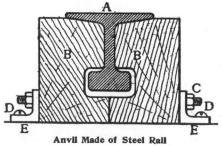

Anvil Made of Steel Rail

SUPPORTING POLES IN SWAMPY GROUND

In setting telephone poles in swampy land where the mud is too soft and deep to give a solid bottom, a cheap and easy method of supporting them is shown at Fig. 2. Bolt to the foot of the pole two pieces of creosoted pine planking, crossing at right angles. Reinforce the pole, if necessary, by putting in a push and brace, with planks bolted at the foot the same as at the base of the pole. Where the line will be exposed to strong winds fill a hole around the base of the pole with concrete, says the American Telephone Journal.

Where the ground is too soft for this

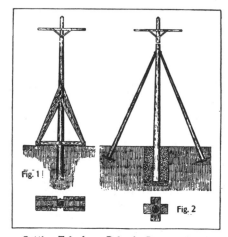

Setting Telephone Poles in Swampy Land

method to be successful, plant the pole and bolt to it just above the ground and at right angles to the line, two pieces of planking about 10 ft. long (Fig. 1). Nail short pieces of planking 3 ft. long to these 10-ft. planks and at right angles to them. Then on each side of the pole fasten two pieces of planking to extend from a point on the pole about 5 ft. above the ground to the ends of the 10-ft. planks.

TO CUT HARD RUBBER

Hard rubber in sheets is very difficult to cut under ordinary conditions, but by placing in hot water it becomes soft like a piece of leather and may then be easily cut in any shape desired by using ordinary shears. When it begins to cut hard dip in water again and continue until the cutting is done. Then lay on a flat surface and allow it to remain there until cold.

ETCHING ON BRASS OR STEEL

In the usual method of etching on tools or instruments of any kind, the article is covered with melted paraffin and then marked with the name, monogram or other inscription, by means of a pin or scriber of some kind. In a new method, described by a correspondent of Machinery, a rubber stamp is used in place of a scriber, and asphaltum varnish is used as a "resist" in place of paraffin. If the stamp has a fancy border it will add greatly to the appearance. The varnish is used on the stamp in place of ink and the impression is then made on the article to be etched. When the varnish has dried, apply the acid, which will eat into the metal at the exposed places and leave the letters in relief.

The following acids for etching will be found to give good results:

IRON AND SOFT STEEL.—Nitric acid, 1 part; water, 4 parts.

HARD STEEL.—Nitric acid, 2 parts; acetic acid, 1 part.

DEEP ETCHING.—Hydrochloric acid, 10 parts; chlorate of potash, 2 parts; water, 88 parts.

ETCHING BRONZE.—Nitric acid, 100 parts; muriatic acid, 5 parts.

BRASS.—Nitric acid, 16 parts; water, 160 parts. Dissolve 6 parts potassium chlorate in 100 parts of water, then mix the two solutions and apply.

BOILER FOR HEATING GLUE SIZING

For this device use No. 24 galvanized iron, making the boiler 13 by 30 in. and 13 in. deep. Double seam the bottom like a washboiler and pane the top on and solder it. Make the three pitchers about 9 in. at the top, 5 in. at the bottom and 14 in. deep, and fit them into holes in the top of the boiler so

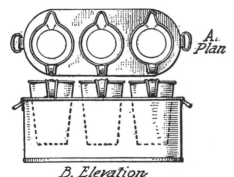

Boiler for Heating Glue Sizing.

that the bottoms of the pitchers are 2 or 3 in. above the bottom of the boiler. The pitchers should have a large solid lip like camp coffee pots, says the American Artisan, so that the glue will not clog when pouring. Wire the handles heavily and place them so as to just rest on the top plate of the boiler.

HOW TO MAKE AN ADJUSTABLE DRAWING TABLE

An adjustable table, which can be used for either drawing, reading or writing, can be made as shown in the sketch. The ¾-in.

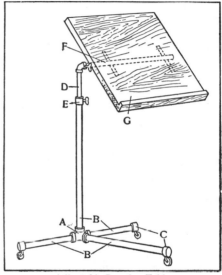

Adjustable Drawing Table.

side outlet tee, A, unites the four ¾-in. pipes, B B, and the three caps, C, are drilled to receive castors, as shown. The cap, E, is drilled for the 13-16-in. rod, D, and tapped for a thumb screw. The ½-in. pipe, F, holds the board, G, and if necessary should have holes drilled and rods passed through, to prevent board from twisting. A narrow strip of wood, screwed on at the lower edge of the board, G, will prevent the drawing board or other article from sliding off.— Contributed by Subscriber, N. H.

EXAMINING PRINTS WHILE DEVEL= OPING

During the development of a print do not take it out of the solution to examine it. It is entirely unnecessary and is liable to result in stains and discolored lights.—Photographic Times.

THE SLIDE RULE A COMPLETE WIRE TABLE

By S. H. Graf, Corvallis, Ore.

Since the slide rule is now recognized as a necessary adjunct to the practical engineer's equipment, the following directions for readily finding the properties of copper wire, as given in the common wire table, will perhaps be appreciated by those engaged or interested in electrical work:

In the October, 1905, issue of the Electric Club Journal there appeared an article giving a method for finding the resistance per thousand feet of any size of copper wire. This article led to further study of the subject and brought about the discovery of methods for finding the other equally important properties recorded in the wire table. In order to make the list here complete, and owing to the fact that the method for finding the number of feet per pound is based on the rule given in the article spoken of, it will be well to give in brief this rule.

To find the resistance in ohms per thousand feet (at 20° C.) of a given size of wire, draw out the slide until the right hand index on the under side of the rule is at the units figure of the given number on the equally divided or logarithmic L scale; that is, for No. 18 place the index on 8; for No. 9 place it on 9, etc., and multiply result by 10. Example: Required ohms No. 18 wire (1,000 ft.). Set slide (holding rule upside down) at 8 on the logarithmic L scale, then (holding rule right side up) read on scale D the number .632. Multiplying by 10 gives 6.32 ohms for the resistance of 1,000 ft. of No. 18 wire. The exact resistance as given in the tables is 6.35 ohms, the difference being less than one-half of 1%.

In order to know where to place the decimal point, it will be necessary to remember the following:

The resistance of No.	0 wire is	.1 ohm per 1,000 ft.
" " "	10	" 1 " " 1,000 ft.
" " "	20	" 10 " " 1,000 ft.
" " "	30	" 100 " " 1,000 ft.
" " "	40	" 1000 " " 1,000 ft.

Sizes between those given have proportionate resistance, and if the order is observed it will take but a minute to memorize the little table above.

To find the number of feet per pound, simply multiply the number of ohms per thousand feet, as found above, by the constant 10 π [or 31.4 approx. (10 π=10×3.1416

=31.4)]. The following shows where to place the decimal point:

No. 000000............	1 ft. per pound
No. 5................	10 ft. per pound
No. 15................	100 ft. per pound
No. 25................	1000 ft. per pound etc.

The rule for finding the diameter in inches of any size wire is not quite as simple as the above, yet it can be mastered with very little effort.

The diameters of the wires, Nos. 2, 6, 10, 14, 18, 22, 26, 30, 34 and 38, may be found directly by placing the right under index on the units figure of the number as before and reading the result over the left hand index of the slide on the A-scale. For wires larger than No. 11 place a decimal point before the value read: as for No. 2 we have .258; for wires larger than No. 31 but smaller than No. 10 place a decimal point and one zero before the significant part of the result; and for wires smaller than No. 30 place a decimal point and two zeros before the answer.

The diameters of the sizes not given in the series must be found by interpolation. This may be done very readily on the slide rule. For example, suppose we wish to find the diameter of No. 15, B. and S.: Place the right under index on 4 (for 14), then, as No. 15 has a smaller diameter than No. 14, move the slide back or to the left one-fourth of a whole division and read over left top index of slide as before; the result is .057. The same result could have been obtained by setting the index on 8 (for 18) and moving the slide to the right three-fourths of a division. Try it.

To find the diameters in millimeters, multiply the results obtained by the last method by 25.4. This merely reduces inches to millimeters.

To find the area in circular mils, square the diameters in inches and multiply by 1,000,000.

The other measures, such as feet per ohm, ohms per pound, etc., are so simple that anyone familiar with the manipulation of the slide rule can find them from what has been given, without further directions.

The mastery of these few simple rules, a task of less than an hour, is equivalent to memorizing more than four hundred three- or four-place numbers, a practically impossible task. Also, as will be evident, the rules are not limited to copper wire alone, for the resistances of wire made of any given metal may be found by multiplying the resistance of a copper wire having the same cross section area by the specific resistance of the given metal as compared to copper.

The results obtained by means of the slide rule in the manner described are very nearly correct for the larger sizes of wire, and the error is in no case greater than 3 per cent. This gives as great a degree of accuracy as is ordinarily required. In case it is required to know the number of feet per pound more accurately than the rule already given will permit, multiply the number of ohms per thousand feet by the following instead of by 31.4 for all sizes:

For sizes up to   No. 10 multiply by 31.4.
For sizes from No. 11 to No. 20 multiply by 32.0.
For sizes from No. 21 to No. 30 multiply by 32.6.
For sizes from No. 31 to No. 40 multiply by 33.2.

The constant is seen to increase by .6 each tenth size.

To conclude, it might be added that these rules are really practical, and will, when mastered, be found of great advantage, as those engaged in any branch of electrical work will readily realize.

A NEW METHOD OF BALANCING ENGINES

Many attempts have been made to balance reciprocating engines, so that no vibration would be produced, but none, so far, has been successful.

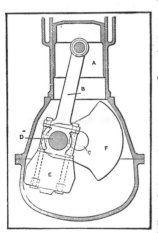

A new method has recently been patented, which consists principally of a cast-iron weight, E (see cut), so proportioned that the center of gravity of the weight and connecting rod combined is located at the center of the crank. The counterweight, F, is of sufficient size to just balance the weight of the connecting rod and attachment, so that the center of gravity of all revolving parts is at the center of the main shaft, C. This device, if effective, would be invaluable for all gas engines and high-speed steam engines, as the vibration of these engines is always a great objection.

DURABLE WOODEN DAM

A good type of wooden dam and one that when well constructed of sound material will last upwards of a half century is shown

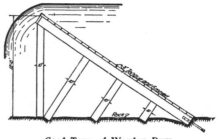

Good Type of Wooden Dam

in the illustration, taken from the American Miller.

The dam has a plank face supported by stringers, the latter being held by supports carried to the rock. Ice is about the only thing that can damage such a structure.

SIMPLE ELECTRIC HEATER

A good electric heater is made as illustrated. A and B are two porcelain disks. Through a hole in the center of these run an iron rod having bolt threads at the ends. Hold the bolt firmly, says Practical Machinist, by a ½-in. iron pipe covering it and forming a butt at each end.

Use German silver wire for the coils; its resistance is 13.91 ohms and by sending a current of electricity through the coils, three times as much heat is generated as with galvanized iron coils; it requires more current to heat the German silver coils, however. Nos. 13 and 15 or Nos. 12 and 14 wire is suitable.

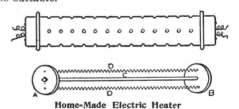

Home-Made Electric Heater

Thread both ends of a suitable length of 1¼-in. loricated conduit pipe to fit 1¼-in. caps and drill ¾-in. holes, 2 in. apart, around the circumference of the pipe for its full length. Fit this over the heater passing the feed wires to heater through ¼-in. holes in the caps.

HOW TO MAKE AN INVISIBLE PATCH IN TRACING CLOTH

A method of making invisible patches in tracing cloth, the discovery of a correspondent of the American Machinist, is as follows: The portion to be cut out is laid on a piece of plain tracing cloth, and both pieces are cut at the same time with a sharp knife. This makes a patch the exact shape of the hole. The patch is then placed in the hole, and the edges coated with liquid court-plaster. The butt joint thus formed is flexible, tough, and so transparent that the patch is practically invisible in the blueprint.

USEFUL DEVICE FOR MAKING SYM= METRICAL DESIGNS

In making mechanical or artistic designs it frequently happens that right- and left-hand views are required of the same figure.

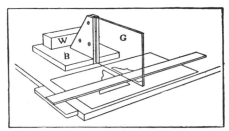

For Reversing Figures

A mechanical drawing having this requirement, usually necessitates considerable time for duplicating all the dimensions, and a freehand drawing gives even more trouble, as it is almost impossible to make two figures symmetrical by using the eye alone as a guide.

The apparatus shown in the sketch can be made by almost anyone and enables a person to make a symmetrical duplicate of either mechanical or freehand designs, without taking a single measurement. The piece of glass, G, is held by the wooden base, B, so that the lower edge of the glass is about ⅛ in. from the drawing board. This allows room for the paper and T-square blade underneath. A heavy weight, W, prevents the apparatus from tipping forward. The glass should be firmly fastened to the base and if a large piece is used a quantity of bicycle rim cement should be used to fasten it in the groove. If desired, holes may be drilled in the glass to receive screws. In drilling glass use an ordinary twist drill

and keep the point moist with turpentine. In mounting the glass be sure that the surface is exactly perpendicular with the base; otherwise the two figures will not be symmetrical.

In operation the lower edge of the glass is placed directly over the axis of symmetry, and the reflection in the glass will then reverse any figure on the paper underneath making it appear reversed on the opposite side of the glass. The glass being transparent enables the operator to look through and trace the reversed image without any difficulty.

OIL FINISH FOR WOOD

A good, durable finish for wood can be obtained by soaking the article in linseed oil for a week and then rubbing with an oil-soaked cloth a few minutes each day for about two weeks. This solidifies and preserves the work, says a correspondent of Machinery, and gives a much more durable finish than French polishing.

PORTABLE BONFIRES FOR BURN= ING BRUSH

An Oregon orchardist who found it required a great deal of time and labor to haul away his orchard prunings, rigged up a portable brush burner which is drawn by horses down the rows of trees and consumes the brush as fast as it is thrown in.

He made a frame or running gear of four poles about 6 in. in diameter, using two 7-ft. ones for axletrees and bolting the other two (10. ft. poles) on top of these near the ends to form a rectangle. To the under side of one he fastened a round iron rod and used the projecting ends as spindles for two old farm implement wheels 1 ft. in diameter. The wheels were held in place by 8-in. pins put through holes made in the

Bonfire Wagon

ends of the spindles. The burner proper, says the Rural New-Yorker, was a huge iron basket or crate 6 by 10 ft. on the bottom and 2 ft. deep, made of old wagon tires riveted together. The meshes of this crate were nearly a foot in diameter but close enough to hold the brush. To keep the coals of fire from falling through, the bottom was covered with old sheet iron scraps. At the front end to which the team was hitched the crate was sided up with sheet iron to screen the horses from the heat, and chain or iron rods extended 10 ft. forward to give the team plenty of space between it and the fire.

As this vehicle passed through the orchard the brush was piled on the fire kindled in it and immediately consumed. Not enough brush was burned at a time to hurt the trees.

KEY=SEATING WITH THE DRILL PRESS

In cutting key seats through long hubs the drill press can be used to an advantage; for rapid work the lever should be used.

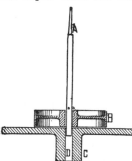

Referring to the sketch: A is a bar with the cutter the required width; B is a pulley bolted to the drill faceplate; C-D is the hole through the faceplate for which bushings can be made to fit any size bar. After each stroke of the lever, tap the work, B, with a hammer, which will move it enough for another cut.

This does better work than can be done with a hammer and chisel and is a time-saving device. For tapered key seats tip the work by means of a piece under one side.— Contributed by Paul S. Baker, Muscatine, Ia.

A GLASS HONE

Take a piece of plate glass, 2 in. by 6 in., the usual size of a hone, and rub the surface thoroughly with a similar piece of glass with emery flour (the finest powder of emery) and water until the surface is evenly ground, then wash the surface with water. Hone the razor in the usual way from heel to point, using a lather made by rubbing the surface of the hone with an ordinary slate pencil and water. The lather should be of the consistency of thick cream. Follow

this by stropping in the ordinary way. The surface of the hone will become smooth in course of time, but can be reground as before. Try it.—Contributed by Dr. W. H. Mayfield, 722 First St., Louisville, Ky.

HOW TO MAKE A SMALL GASO= LINE BURNER

I have found a small gasoline burner, like the one illustrated, very useful for melting babbitt and lead. An old coffee flask, A, is soldered to a piece of ⅛-in. pipe, B, about 2 ft. long. This is screwed into a ⅛-in. elbow, C, which holds a ⅛-in. by 3-in. nipple, D. A ⅛-in. coupling, E, connects this to a ⅛-in. needle valve, F, which holds a piece of ⅛-in. pipe, G, 10 in. long, bent as shown, and covered at the end by a ⅛-in. cap, H, with a $\frac{1}{32}$-in. hole drilled through the upper side.

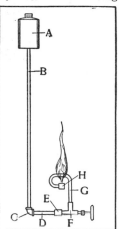

In making this device be sure to have all the joints screwed up tight, and a good soldered joint between the flask and vertical pipe, as a small leak might result in an explosion.—Contributed by A. Laughlin, Winona, Minn.

TIGHTENING BRISTLES IN PAINT BRUSHES

Any person who uses a paint brush has suffered annoyance from the brush losing bristles. A good remedy is to stand the brush, handle down (in a vise, if convenient), separate the bristles with a knife blade and pour in a small quantity of shellac varnish, just enough to saturate the bristles at the base only. Leave the brush in that position until dry.—Contributed by Andrew Whiton, 9 Kinsley St., Hartford, Conn.

Rust spots on marble may be removed by applying a mixture of 1 part nitric acid and 25 parts water, then rinsing it off with 3 parts water and 1 part ammonia.

HOW TO MAKE A SLIGHT BEND IN LARGE PIPE

In installing an 8-in. main pipe to lead from a boiler and swing by two easy bends to a higher level, it was found necessary to

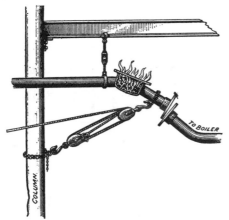

Making Slight Bends in Large Pipes

bend the pipe a trifle more than had been expected, in order to bring the ends together for bolting through the flanges.

The pipe was anchored securely and fastened overhead with a hanger, which in turn was fastened to a strong beam. A basket of charcoal was then placed at the joint and a fire started. The basket was made of sheet iron with holes in the bottom to induce a draft and was supported on the pipe by pieces of small-size wrought-iron pipe. The heat of the fire softened the metal sufficiently, says the Metal Worker, to permit the joint to be drawn up by means of a block and fall. The chain, as is absolutely necessary, was fastened to some strong object, in this case a column.

LAWN ROLLER MADE OF KITCHEN BOILER

A good lawn roller can be made of an old kitchen boiler. If the boiler is too long, cut it to the desired length. Run a piece of pipe through the center lengthwise, allowing it to protrude about 6 in. Then fill the boiler with concrete and if it has been cut short, block up the end. Then attach a handle to the pipe ends.

A roller 3 ft. long and 1 ft. in diameter is made of a piece of heavy galvanized iron 36 in. wide and 40 in. long. Roll it so as to make a 2-in. lap and rivet. Block in one end, put a pipe through, fill with concrete,

and block up the other end. When the concrete hardens you have a good, heavy, durable lawn roller at little expense.—Contributed by W. S. Barrows, 628 Dover Court Road, Toronto, Canada.

OILER FOR WORKBENCH USE

Take a can about 2½ or 3 in. in diameter and cut it off smoothly about 1½ in. from the bottom. Cut a strip of old ingrain carpet, felt or other suitable material, about 2 in. wide, and roll up enough of it to fill the can tight. Saturate with oil and you have a handy oiler to keep on the workbench for oiling saws, etc.—Contributed by P. P. Simmons, La Jolla, Cal.

FINDING SHORT CIRCUITS

To find a short circuit in a lighting system, screw in a plug on one side of the cutout and an Edison base lamp on the other side and turn off at the socket all the lamps on that circuit. The pilot lamp will remain lighted until the short circuit is found. When the pilot lamp goes out it shows that the circuit is clear.

An open circuit may be found by the same method: have the lamps all turned on at the socket and the pilot lamp will light up when the circuit is closed through the load. This method is also useful in finding a ground that blows the fuse. The system can only be used with Edison cut-outs. It requires no special apparatus and the necessary materials are at hand on any job.—Contributed by A. T. Senecal, Watertown, Ill.

HOW TO MAKE QUARTER=ROUND MOLDING

The sketch at the top shows how to run quarter-round mold, four to eight at a time, on a 14-in. machine. Let top head cut en-

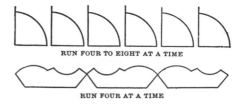

RUN FOUR TO EIGHT AT A TIME

RUN FOUR AT A TIME

tirely through on thin stock, says the Wood-Worker, and on thick stock nearly through, the bottom head finishing the cut. Crown mold is run four at a time and practically the same way.

TESTING CONDENSER WATER PIPES FOR ANIMAL INCRUSTATION

An electric station at Galveston, Texas, takes salt water for condensing purposes from a bay through a 10-in. iron pipe about 3,700 ft. long. Screens, strainers and other precautions are used at the intake end, but despite this, a large amount of oyster and barnacle spawn and spats is drawn up by the suction and these attach themselves to the inside of the pipe and build their shells. In time this incrustation would reduce the carrying capacity of the pipe, if it were not carefully watched and removed when necessary. The Street Railway Journal describes the method of determining the inside diameter of the pipe.

Copper balls of different sizes and having very thin shells, so that they will crush easily, are used in the tests. These balls are inserted at the intake end of the pipe and allowed to be drawn up by the force of the water. The test begins with balls 2 in. in diameter, followed by 2½-in. balls, and increasing sizes. Each ball as it comes up is carefully examined for scratches and when these begin to appear the largest ball passed through is taken as the minimum size of the opening of the pipe. When other balls are not obtainable, copper balls are borrowed from steam and water traps in the power house and replaced after the tests.

One of the means employed to kill the crustation-forming spats is by feeding creosote, by means of an injector lubricator, drop by drop into the condensing water at a point just inside the intake end. This kills the spats before they form their shells.

TO REDUCE THE SIZE OF A HOLE IN IRON OR STEEL

When a hole has been bored out too large by mistake, if the shape of the piece will allow, the following method may be used to reduce the size of the hole, says a correspondent of Machinery:

Heat the piece red hot, and dip in water up to the center of the hole. Half of the metal around the hole will become cold and shrink. The other half, that is still red, will shrink while hot, being pulled together by the cold part, and when it gets cold will shrink still more, becoming smaller than the original size. Heat the piece again and dip the other half in water. Repeat this operation, dipping each end alternately, until the size of the hole has been reduced enough to allow a nice cut to be taken to bore it to the right dimension.

A BED=TABLE MADE FROM PIPE FITTINGS

A bed-table will be found a most convenient article for the sick room, or for those who wish to read in bed. The table may be made to hold the book or dishes, as

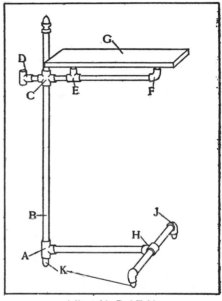

Adjustable Bed Table

the case may be, in any desired position without the slightest effort on the part of the patient or reader.

In the sketch, which shows the assembled table, A and H are ½-in. tees; B is a ½-in. pipe; C is a ¾x⅜-in. cross; D is a ⅜-in. tee used as a handle to tighten the short nipple, L, which acts like a set screw; E is a ⅜-in. tee; F is a ⅜-in elbow, and K, knobs of hard wood driven into the fittings, as shown.—Contributed by H. N. Barth, Chicago.

FOR CLEANING OLD BRASS

A good formula for cleaning old brass is as follows: Take 1 oz. of oxalic acid, 6 oz. rottenstone, ½ oz. gum arabic, all in powder; 1 oz. sweet oil, and sufficient water to make a paste. Apply a small portion, and rub dry with a piece of flannel or soft leather.

HINTS ON LATHE WORK

DRILLING IN THE LATHE.—In boring holes in work held in the chuck it often happens that the hole must go through solid stock. In this case it is desirable to take out most of the stock to be removed with a drill held in a chuck, or other suitable holder, fitting the tail stock. It is the general practice to make a countersink in the work with a tool held in the tool-post (called a centering tool) to insure the drill

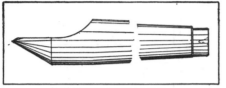

Half Center for the Lathe

starting and keeping in the center of the work. This involves accurate grinding and setting of the tool, and, except in certain cases, is unnecessary. A very quick and accurate method of centering the drill in the work is to face the work off square, not making any countersink at all; place the drill in the chuck or holder with the point as near the center of the work as convenient; select any lathe tool that is fairly square across the back end and clamp it in the tool post so that the square end nicely clears the work and is in such position that when pushed forward by the cross feed-screw it will bear against the lip of the drill; start the lathe and feed the drill in a little, then push the tool against the lip of the drill until the drill appears to be central; back the tool away from the drill and if it is central, proceed to drill the hole; if not, repeat the operation. After a little practice one will generally be able to center the drill the first time. The method only holds good, however, until the drill begins to cut full size, unless the drill is very small or the work projects so far from the chuck that it will spring.

A HANDY CENTER FOR THE LATHE. --A very handy center for facing the ends of work held between the centers is shown in the accompanying sketch. It can be made in the same way that an ordinary lathe center is made, or an old center may be cut or ground away in the manner shown. To use it, place it in the tail stock with the part cut away toward the front side of the lathe. This center will allow you to use most any kind of a facing tool and leave a

clean end with no fin or ridge at the center to be taken off afterward.

A RAPID WAY TO CUT THREADS IN THE LATHE.—(This method applies to lathes with a compound rest only.) To cut an ordinary V-thread of 60° angle, loosen the compound rest and swing it around 30° and clamp it fast; clamp an ordinary threading tool in the tool-post at right angles to the work to be threaded; if a stop is available, push the tool up to the work with the cross feed-screw and set the stop so that it can go no farther; proceed to cut the thread in the usual manner, only do not move the stop, but feed for each cut with the compound rest screw. As the compound rest is at an angle equal to one side of the thread, the tool will cut on one side and not on the other and still preserve the shape of the thread. As the tool only cuts on one side, the tendency to dig in and tear is relieved and a fairly heavy cut can be taken. When the thread is well roughed out, a few light cuts may be taken over it, feeding with the cross feed-screw, thus giving a good finish to both sides of the thread. In cutting threads of a coarse pitch it is well to use two tools, the first one with a little top rake away from the cutting side, the other ground in the usual manner for finishing the thread.

The writer does not claim that the methods of doing the work described are original, but that they are not as generally known to lathe hands as they should be.—Contributed by "Tap."

RENEWING SCREWDRIVER EDGE

When the point of a screwdriver is worn away so that it jumps the nick in the screw, the edge can be renewed as follows:

Hold the screwdriver in the vise with the bevel of the point lying horizontal and projecting above the surface of the vise jaws; then use a medium flat file on it, giving a forward thrust only, and keeping a horizontal position throughout, directs the British Optical Journal. Turn the driver over and repeat the operation until the edge becomes very thin. Then file it down to a perfectly straight margin and regulate its width for the size required. This method is more satisfactory than truing up the point on a grindstone.

A great difficulty in the production of power from peat gas is the rapid formation of tar. This has to be separated and constitutes a serious loss of heat.—The Engineer.

SHOP NOTES

ONE=MAN HOIST AND AUTOMATIC DUMP

By H. E. Bowcher, Dawson, Y. T.

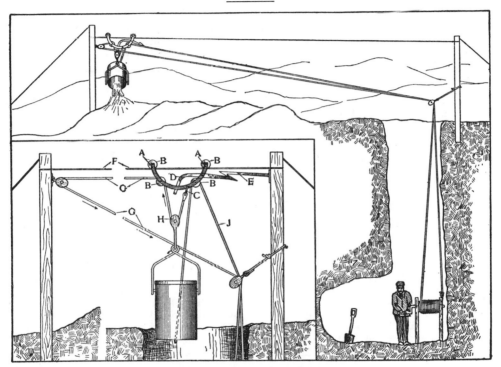

Details and General View of Hoist

Having had considerable experience as a prospector, and not finding a suitable prospector's device for excavating, I decided to make one, and constructed the apparatus about to be described. This device enables one person to sink a shaft of practically any depth and hoist the dirt from the shaft and take it away and dump it at a distant pile, without having to come out of the shaft to operate it, as the windlass is located down the shaft. The device weighs but 15 lb., and can be carried readily in the prospector's pack.

The trolley frame, A A, is made of flat iron or steel, 1/8 in. thick by 1 1/2 in. wide. When bent to shape as shown, the ends, A A, are about 20 in. apart.

Six holes are drilled in the frame; four to receive the grooved wheels, B B B B; one for the ring, C, and one for the trigger, D. This trigger catches on the hook, E, and locks the trolley in place, until the pulley, H, strikes the trigger, thus releasing the trolley and allowing it to travel along the steel wire cable, F.

The rope, G, is connected to the windlass and moves in the direction indicated by the arrow when the windlass is being wound up. This movement of the rope, G, has a tendency to raise the bucket and move the trolley on the cable at the same time, but as the trolley is locked at E, it will not move until the pulley, H, strikes the trigger. The bucket by that time having left the shaft is ready for its trip to the dumping pile.

A second rope, J, is fastened to the bottom of the bucket at one end, the other end being secured to any fixed object in the bottom of the shaft. This rope is fastened at such a length, that the bucket on reaching the dumping pile will be turned over, the rope having traveled its entire length. The trolley cable being slightly elevated at the dumping end causes the bucket to return to the shaft by gravity.

When ready to hoist, the operator starts the windlass at the bottom of the shaft, which causes the bucket to ascend until the pulley, H, strikes the trigger. The trigger is then released from the hook, E, and the traveler moves with the bucket to the dumping pile, where it is dumped by the rope, J, as stated above. The traveler then returns to the shaft, by gravity, and is locked in position by the hook, E. The bucket then descends the shaft ready for the next cargo.

I had this device in successful operation for many years in Australia and am using it at present in the Klondike.

HOW TO MAKE A SIMPLE SPRING WINDER

A good spring winder, suitable for use in a lathe, can be made by bending a piece of stiff wire to the shape shown at A in the sketch, and in detail at D. The wire, B, of which the spring is to be made should be smaller than the wire used for the winder, as the pitch (distance between coils) of the spring is determined by that of the winder.

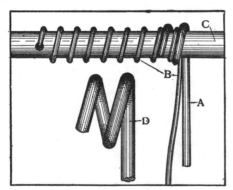

Simple Spring Winder

If the wire of which the spring is to be made is very heavy, the winder should be made of a flat strip of steel, in place of

wire, as this is more easily bent to the required shape and is more rigid. The arbor, C, determines the inside diameter of the spring, and should always be used in connection with this winder.—Contributed by L. G. Harren, 14 Barnett St., New Haven, Conn.

HOW TO MEND A BROKEN DRIVING PULLEY

All the spokes on a driving pulley from a 40-hp. engine were broken at the hub as shown in the sketch at A. The pulley was mended by a correspondent of the American Blacksmith as follows:

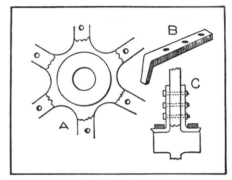

Mending a Pulley

Two pieces like B were made and bolted on the foot to run out over the hub and ⅛ in. off, as shown at C. These were used on each spoke and when all the pieces were on, two rings 1½ in. square (shown in section at C) were driven on hot and allowed to shrink on the feet, thus drawing the spokes down tight. The engine has been used a long while since the repair was made and the job still holds good.

TO FIND CENTER OF SQUARE OR OBLONG CEILING

Rub the line with chalk or charcoal and stretch it across the ceiling from diagonal corners. Two persons will be required to do it. The point where the two lines cross each other, says the Master Painter, will be the center.

If there is a deep chimney breast abutting out into the room stretch the lines from corners made by drawing a line across the breast, and not from the true room corners. This in order that the center may not appear too close to the breast.

TO DUSTPROOF A WATCH

During long automobile tours, fine dust and grit is sure to clog the works of one's watch, sometimes causing it to stop just when most needed. To prevent this, says the Automobile, cut a match chisel-shaped at one end and with it apply a thin coat of vaseline all about the seat of the case where the lid fits. Treat the back and front lids both in the same manner. This will make the watch dustproof and waterproof.

◆ ◆ ◆

EXTENSION CALL BELL FOR A TELEPHONE

In many shops, where the telephone is in the office and the proprietor spends a great part of the time in the shop, the telephone often rings repeatedly without being answered, as there is nobody within hearing distance. In many cases of this kind an extension call bell, such as is shown in the sketch, could be used to advantage.

The telephone bell, A, is fitted with a piece of hard rubber, B, having a metal contact, C, which is placed so that the hammer will strike it and make contact. Part of the gong may be cut away to do this, or if necessary, the whole gong may be removed. The other gong is connected to one side of the battery, and the other side connects to an electric bell, D, which can be placed in any desired location. If the bell does not work well, short circuit the interrupter. This will not prevent it from vibrating, as the current is intermittent, being

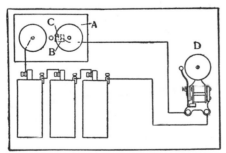

Extension Call Bell

interrupted at C, and if the interruptions at C and D are not in unison the result will not be good.

I have one of these bells in use at the present time and find it a great convenience. —Contributed by Frank H. Kimball, Ballston Spa, New York.

A HANDY TIN CENTER FOR MACHINISTS

In locating the centers of castings, such as the flange shown at A in the sketch, most machinists use a piece of wood, B, and find the center by means of a compass or calipers. The center is then marked on the wood, and the drilling or other work to be done is laid out from the point thus

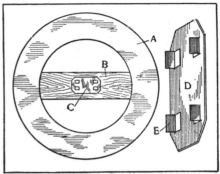

Machinist's Tin Center

located. A piece of tin plate nailed to the wood makes a better working surface than the wood alone, but most machinists dislike the trouble of finding the nails and fastening the tin to the wood.

To obviate the use of nails, and to provide a tin center which can be easily and quickly applied, J. G. Campbell, 404 N. E. Border St., Cleburne, Texas, devised the center shown at C in the sketch, and in detail at D. This center, which can be made in one operation with a blanking and forming die, is made of medium heavy tin plate, and is provided with four tongues, shown at E, which take the place of nails. To fasten it to the wood, simply lay it on the desired location and strike two or three blows with the hammer.

◆ ◆ ◆

HOW TO FROST GLASS

Glass cutters' sand and water, or even clean, washed sea sand rubbed on with a smooth block of marble will produce a frosted appearance on glass, says the Master Painter. Finish with emery for a fine appearance.

A fair imitation of frost may be produced by a hot solution of Epsom salts and gum arabic water. Apply warm. Strong alum water gives the same effect, but with neither of these last is the result durable.

ADJUSTABLE TIGHTENER FOR ELEVATOR BELTS

A tightener for elevator belts is shown in the illustration. A and B represent upper and lower ends of elevator belt; C and D are hooks made of $\frac{5}{16}$-in. spring steel, bent in round ring 2 in. in diameter, to receive lug of awning pulley; E, ½-in. hook at top to hook in cup bolt holes, from which cup has been removed. The pulleys are common awning pulleys, one double and one single. As it is impossible to get an awning pulley with becket, F, a screw-eye can be tapped into the end of the single block. A common sash cord is the best and strong enough to bend any head shaft. To hold the belt after it has been tightened, and while the splice bolts are being put in, pass the pall or pulling end 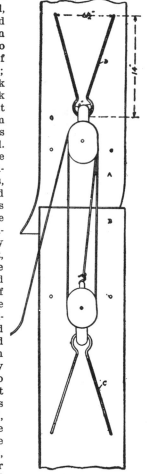 through under the other strand, as per dotted line, G, and pull it up tight against the pulley. No other knot is necessary, says the American Miller. The spring steel hooks are readily adjustable to any width of belt.

＊＊＊

The town of Ringwood, Okla., has established a municipal cyclone refuge—a large centrally located cave or cellar—and has appointed a cyclone crier to arouse the people on the approach of a storm.

TO CLEAR SEDIMENT FROM ENGINE PUMPS

Sometimes a quantity of the sand used in the foundry in making the castings remains in the water jackets of cylinders and, becoming loosened by the circulation of the water, finds its way into the pump when it is fitted low and close to the motor, to the disconcertion of the motorist who is his own chauffeur. With centrifugal pumps, this sand tends to wear away the pump vanes, says the Automobile, and in a new car it is advisable to occasionally disconnect the pump and clear it of sediment.

Many rotary pumps set up end thrust which forces the vanes up against one side of the pump and in time wears them down, until the pump leaks and fails to circulate the water. A simple temporary remedy is to solder a strip such as a short length of wire, along each of the worn vanes, but a permanent cure can only be effected by putting in a new thrust bearing.

＊＊＊

RECIPE FOR FRENCH PUTTY

Boil in raw oil about half the weight of umber, says the Master Painter; then slowly add dry white lead and whiting. Mix the mass thoroughly.

＊＊＊

OLD HACKSAW BLADE FOR CUT-OFF TOOL

For cutting up brass tubing the tool here shown will be found very useful. A thin piece of steel, A, is ground to the shape shown in the sketch, and firmly clamped between two pieces of 1x¼-in. steel, B, if the hole in the tool-rest of the lathe is large enough to admit that size; if not, use 1x$\frac{3}{16}$ in., or some size that will suit the dimen-

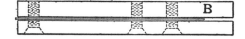
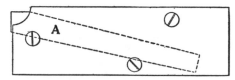

Cutting Off Tool for Brass Tubing

sions of the tool-rest. A correspondent of Machinery used an old hacksaw blade for the part, A, and found that it worked perfectly.

HOW TO MAKE A SWIVEL HOOK

A good swivel hook may be made by the following directions, which are given by a correspondent of the Blacksmith and Wheelwright: It is all constructed of Swedish iron. Fig. 1 shows the piece of iron which has been cut down at each end to one-half round as shown. Then turn the ends up, and punch a ⅝-in. hole. Turn the top end over the horn of an anvil, as shown in Fig. 2, and hammer until the top is beveled or countersunk so as to make it 1 1⁄16 or 1½ in. across the top. At the bottom where the hook goes up through it should be ¾ in. This leaves it as shown in Fig. 3. Then the hook should be made of 1-in. square iron, as shown in Fig. 4. Use a collar of 5⁄16-in. round iron welded on as shown at A, and have the shank rounded down to ¾ in. Heat the shank well and place it in the vise.

Put the swivel on and pound the shank down level with the top of the swivel as seen at B. Then heat and turn the swivel around so that it may move freely. Weld the two shanks together as shown at C.

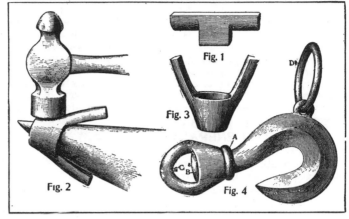

Making a Swivel Hook

Finally put on a 3- or 4-in. hinge to handle the hook by when attached to the whiffle tree, as shown at D, and you have a complete swivel hook.

◆ ◆ ◆

SUNSTROKE==INDICATIONS==TREATMENT

There are two forms of sunstroke. The mildest is that known as heat exhaustion. This manifests itself in the case of people who are overcome by heat without being actually sunstruck. In this form the skin is pale, cold and clammy, and the pulse feeble. While death sometimes results, the patients under good treatment will usually recover. Persons affected in this way should be removed to a shady spot and have their heads and chests dashed with cold water. Spirits of ammonia (hartshorn) should be applied to the nostrils, and sometimes it is necessary to administer small quantities of stimulants.

Heat stroke or insolation is the serious form of this trouble, and the one to be most closely guarded against. In cases of real insolation the face becomes purplish, eyes bloodshot, veins swollen and corded and the skin dry and burning hot to the touch. It is not always fatal, but many of those whose lives are saved are ever afterward invalids, with brain power more or less impaired. The effect of the sun's heat seems to be most marked on the brain and spinal marrow. When real insolation occurs the brain becomes so heated that the human "heat center," controlling the production of bodily heat, is affected and the temperature rises from the healthy mark of 98½ as high as 110 or over, and often keeps on rising for some time after death. The "heat center" lies at the back of the head and should be protected from the direct rays of the sun.

Insolation is so dangerous that a physician should be called as soon as possible. While waiting the doctors' arrival much good can be done and life often saved by applications of ice to the head and spinal column. It is best broken in small pieces and placed in cloth or rubber bags, but when these are not to be had, ice can be placed directly about the head and neck.

Workmen and others exposed to the direct rays of the sun should have their heads well protected and should wear woolen next to the skin. A very useful precaution is a pad of cotton batting or flannel sewed along the back of the undergarment so as to cover and protect the spine.

It is well to bear in mind the old rules: Keep cool as to temper and your body will not get so hot; avoid all alcoholic drinks; eat less than usual and more simply; walk on the shady side of the street; avoid over-exertion; let the air circulate freely about the head, either by frequent removal of the hat or by wearing a perforated head cover-ing.

Insolation is more far-reaching and dan-gerous in its effects than most people know of; therefore a doctor should be called at once to any one with the symptoms above described as indicating heat stroke or true insolation.—Bulletin of Chicago Health De-partment.

RECHARGING DRY BATTERIES WITH GENERATOR

Having heard that dry batteries could be recharged by sending a current through them, in a direction opposite to that given

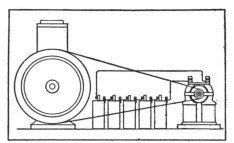

Recharging Dry Batteries

by the battery, we rigged up a small gener-ator and gas engine, as shown in the sketch, and connected the batteries in series with the motor. After running a few minutes we stopped the engine and disconnected the bat-teries, which then gave a fairly strong cur-rent. Thinking to increase the charge, we connected the batteries exactly as they were the first time and started the engine in the same direction as before, and let the outfit run several hours. On returning we found the zincs all corroded and the batteries completely run down. Desiring to learn the cause of this seemingly peculiar behavior, we connected a new lot of batteries and proceeded as before. The engine was then stopped and the belt was removed from the generator, thus allowing the current of the batteries to run the generator as a motor. We expected the generator to run in a direc-tion opposite to that used in charging, but were surprised to see it continue running in the same direction. The explanation is that the current from the batteries reversed the field, and also the armature, thus making two reverses which is the same as none at

all. Then when the generator was run again by the engine the current was reversed because the poles of the field had been changed by the batteries.

We concluded from these experiments that in charging batteries in this way it is neces-sary to either change the connections on the battery, or reverse the rotation of the en-gine each time it is started. As the engine was two-cycle it was more easily reversed than the battery connections, and in this way, the batteries were recharged without any difficulty. A stronger charge may be given to batteries in which a quantity of water has been poured in holes drilled through the top.—Contributed by A. Davis, Chicago.

FIRE ALARM FOR GRAIN ELEVA-TORS

A choke in the elevator head which stops the belt while the head pulley keeps revolv-ing is frequently the cause of fires in grain elevators, says the Grain Dealers' Journal. The pulley rubbing against the belt soon generates sufficient heat to start a blaze.

An alarm to warn the operator when the elevator head is becoming overheated has been devised. A round hole is bored in the middle of the strut board for the insertion of the device, which consists of a metal plug, shown in Fig. 1. The upper stopper of the plug fits loosely and rests against the pulley. The lower electrode, H, is firmly set while the upper electrode, G, is drawn up by a cord, J, held in place by wax. Overheating

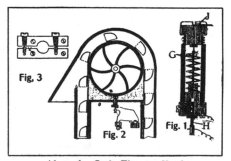

Alarm for Grain Elevator Head

of the alarm melts the wax, releases the cord, permitting the coil spring to draw the upper electrode down into contact with the electrode, H. The closing of the circuit rings a bell placed in any convenient loca-tion. Fig. 2 shows the head with alarm in place, and Fig. 3 a clamp for holding the device in position.

Frieze Design from the London Decorator

GREASE ERADICATOR FOR CLOTHING

Mix together 2 oz. oleate of ammonia and 2 oz. ammonia water; shake well and add 1 oz. ether and 5 oz. benzine. Shake well again and then add 1 oz. chloroform. Shake again, let stand a few minutes, then shake at frequent intervals until the preparation is of the consistency of cream.

AN AIR VISE

An old air brake cylinder, which had for years given good service to the S. P. Railroad, lay rusting on a scrap pile amid other discarded appliances, when, one day, C. C. Perry, of Houston, Tex., assistant foreman of the shop, conceived the idea of an air vise. He accordingly made the device shown in the sketch. An old vise, A, in which the screw had become nearly worn out, was connected to the air brake cylinder, B, in such a

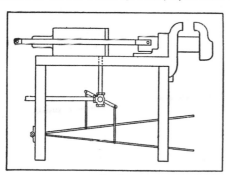

Air Vise

way that the air entering the cylinder brought the jaws of the vise together. When the air was released the spring in the cylinder would open the jaws again.

The air in this arrangement is controlled by a 3-way cock, C, which is operated by the foot levers, D. A vise arranged in this way

is not suitable for small work, as there is danger of injuring the hands, but for heavy work, which has to be changed frequently, it is a great labor-saver.

REMOVING MATCH MARKS FROM PAINT

To remove match marks from white paint, rub the spot with a cut lemon, says the Master Painter. Then to prevent a repetition of the offense apply a little vaseline and rub the spot dry with a rag. It will be difficult to strike matches there again.

POLISHES FOR BRASS

For cleaning hot brass cylinder heads and jackets, try the following recipe, which a correspondent of the Practical Engineer says works fine:

Sift coal ashes fine and mix with kerosene oil to a thick paste; add as much air-slaked lime as can be conveniently mixed with it. Apply this polish to the bright parts, rubbing hard; wipe off and polish with dry slaked lime.

Whiting and ammonia mixed to a paste is another good polish for brass. Apply and rub dry.

SAFETY CLASP FOR LAMP CHIMNEY

In carrying a hand lamp about the house, the chimney not infrequently falls off and is shattered. To prevent this, attach a wire loop to the lamp as illustrated, hinging the loop at the base of the chimney.— Contributed by T. L. Reed, La Porte City, Iowa.

SOME HINTS ON TEMPERING

One of the most essential conditions in properly hardening steel, is uniform cooling. An apparatus like that shown in Fig. 1, which was contrived by a correspondent of the Practical Machinist, will give good results for many kinds of work. The vertical inlet pipes have holes along the inner sides, which direct the stream of water to all parts of the piece to be hardened.

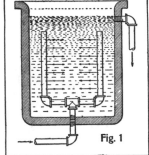

Fig. 1

In tempering a piece of steel like that shown at A, Fig. 2, it is not well to have the hardening stop at the shoulder, as there is then a great liability of cracking. Either harden beyond the shoulder, or if the smaller portion is sufficiently long, let the hardening stop short of the shoulder.

In tempering a tool such as is shown at B, Fig. 2, the best results will follow if the cutting end is not chilled until after the heavier, solid parts have contracted somewhat. If the lighter portions are chilled and contract before the heavier ones, the tendency is for the heavier parts, which are stronger than the lighter, to distort the lighter parts, making them conform to the shrinkage of the heavier, and as the steel is hard and rigid it must crack.

When hardening tools having holes it is advisable to fill the hole with fire clay in

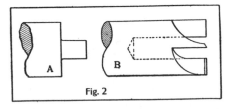

Fig. 2

order to prevent the water from entering. If the design is such that the tool is liable to crack when quenched, it should be dipped into the bath with the teeth uppermost, and the water should be warmed to reduce the liability to cracking.

Paste can be prevented from souring by adding a little pulverized bluestone.

SYSTEM OF NUMBERING FOR PARTY LINE TELEPHONE EXCHANGE

In rural districts where there are a great many party lines on the telephone exchange it is often difficult for the operator to quickly ring a certain party on a party line, because he must know the party's number and his ring also.

In an exchange with about 250 subscribers and 49 party lines, this difficulty was ingeniously overcome by a system of numbering. Take, for example, line 49: The first party on the line has one long and one short ring; his number is 491½; the next party has two rings, and his number is 492; the next has two long and one short ring and his number is 492½, etc. Suppose some one calls for No. 491½: All the operator has to do is to plug line 49 and give one long and one short ring. He has not a second's doubt, the number has told him exactly what to do. In this way an inexperienced operator can handle a party-line switchboard with ease.—Contributed by L. H. Meckstroth, New Knoxville, Ohio.

AN IMPROVED SOLDERING ACID

A very satisfactory soldering acid may be made by the use of the ordinary soldering acid for the base and introducing a certain proportion of chloride of tin and sal ammoniac. This gives an acid which is superior in every way to the old form. The method of making it is as follows.

To make one gallon of this soldering fluid take three quarts common muriatic acid and allow it to dissolve as much zinc as it will take up. This method, of course, is the usual one followed in the manufacture of ordinary soldering acid. The acid, as is well known, must be placed in an earthenware or glass vessel. The zinc may be sheet clippings or common plate spelter broken into small pieces. Place the acid in the vessel and add the zinc in small portions so as to prevent the whole from boiling over. When all the zinc has been added and the action has stopped it indicates that enough has been taken up. Care must be taken, however, to see that there is a little zinc left in the bottom, as otherwise the acid will be in excess. The idea is to have the acid take up as much zinc as it will.

After this has been done there will remain some residue in the form of a black precipitate. This is the lead which all zinc contains and which is not dissolved by the muriatic acid. This lead may be removed by filtering through a funnel in the bottom of which there is a little absorbent cotton, or the solution may be allowed to remain over night until the lead has settled and the clear solution can then be poured off. This lead precipitate is not particularly injurious to the soldering fluid, but it is better to get rid of it so that a good, clear solution may be obtained.

Now dissolve six ounces of sal-ammoniac in a pint of warm water. In another pint dissolve four ounces of chloride of tin. The chloride of tin solution will usually be cloudy, but this will not matter. Now mix the three solutions together. The solution will be slightly cloudy when the three have been mixed, and the addition of a few drops of muriatic acid will render it perfectly clear. Do not add any more acid than is necessary to do this, as the solution would then contain too much of this ingredient and the results would be injurious.

This soldering acid is used in the same manner as any solution of this kind, but it will be found that it will not spatter when the iron is applied to it. It has also been found that a poorer grade of solder may be used with it than with the usual soldering acid. From my experience I have found that a solder composed of two parts of lead and one of tin works equally as well and produces fully as strong a joint as that obtained with the customary half and half solder.—Charles H. Poland, in the Brass World.

METHOD OF BRAZING LIGHT WORK

A good method of brazing light work is illustrated. The dotted lines indicate the work—a light brass ring 2 in. in diameter, ½ in. wide and $\frac{1}{32}$ in. thick. The ring is held together in the fixture made of $\frac{5}{8}$ x $\frac{1}{8}$-in flat iron. Place a bunsen burner under

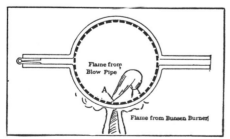

Brazing Light Work

the fixture, which will keep the work and the fixture hot, but will not melt the brazing compound. Bring the flame from a blowpipe in contact with the joint at A.

This is a clean and handy method, says a correspondent of the American Machinist, and the brass has no tendency to adhere to the iron.

HOLDING A WASTE PIPE TO FLANGE IT

When there is no helper around to hold the bath waste or other waste pipe that

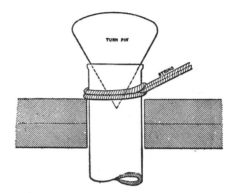

To Hold a Waste Pipe While Flanging It

must be flanged above the floor, try the following plan:

Tie a piece of strong twine around the pipe and draw it up through the hole in the floor, holding it in place by means of the twine until the turn pin is inserted as illustrated, and the pipe is sufficiently expanded to prevent its dropping down again. The pipe can be flanged over entirely as desired, says the Metal Worker, after which cut off the string.

RAISING TEMPERATURE IN DRY KILNS

In a plant where the kilns used were of the moist air type and did not have coils enough to get a high temperature with exhaust steam, they were improved by a correspondent of the Engineers' Review as follows:

A fan was installed at one side of the kiln and the hot air was drawn from the top of the kiln at the cold end and forced back over the coils and up through the lumber again. This gave good circulation and resulted in drying the lumber much quicker. The fan is driven from the line shafting of the plant, and runs only 10 hours a day. At night live steam is supplied and the circulation is set up through the duct to the fan, but only in a slow current.

A vacuum pump placed on the end of the return from the kiln coils gives a more rapid circulation of the exhaust steam and relieves the engine of about 4 lb. back pressure. With this system a temperature of 160° is maintained.

THREADING STEEL PIPE

Most of the steam, gas and water pipe, which was formerly made of wrought iron, is now being made of mild steel. Steel pipe can be made cheaper and stronger than iron pipe and has the advantage of being more ductile and homogeneous. Mr. Frank N. Speller, of the National Tube Company,

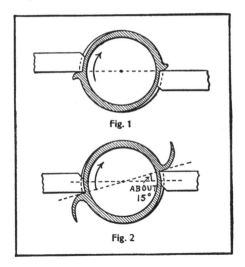

Fig. 1

Fig. 2

has prepared a paper touching upon these points, from which the following has been condensed:

Steel pipe is capable of receiving a smoother finish than iron, if the proper form of cutter is used. The old form of chaser (Fig. 1), in which the cutting edge is on the center, is not suitable for steel. Instead, the cutting edge should be advanced about 15°, as shown in Fig. 2. Many of the cutters in use at the present time are made like Fig. 1, which probably accounts for the slight prejudice against the new material. The use of the cutter shown in Fig. 2 will produce a better finish than can possibly be given to an iron pipe.

In recent tests of durability steel pipes

corroded more than iron in salt water; in fresh water the corrosion was the same for each, and in acidulated water the iron pipes corroded the most.

AN OVERHEAD SHAFT OILER

The device here shown is very useful for oiling shafting and inaccessible machines. The oil can, A, is compressed by the bell crank, B, which is moved by the connecting rod, C, and the grip lever, D. The strip of wood, E, can be any desired length and should be drilled at the end to receive the oil can as shown. The connecting rod, C, can be made of either small iron rod or heavy wire and should be made to disconnect at F, thus allowing the removal of the oil can. The other parts can all be made of wood, but if desired the cranks and brackets may be made of metal, which would allow making them much smaller.

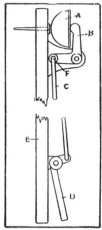

The Oiler

This device was patented about twenty years ago, but the patent has expired. It is practical, and very useful, as can be certified by a correspondent of the Wood-Worker who made several of these oilers.

TYING IRON WIRE

A method of tying iron wire which has been found an especially good joint for rural lines is shown in the illustration, from the American Telephone Journal.

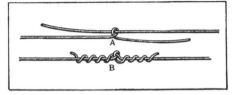

Tying Wire

Where there is danger that insecure joints may be made by inexperienced linemen, this method will be found especially satisfactory.

HOW TO MAKE A DOUBLE=CUTTING SLOTTING TOOL

Most of the tools used on planers and shapers take a cut while going in one direction, and then slide over the work on the return stroke, without accomplishing anything, but the tool shown in the sketch cuts in both directions. This tool consists of a holder, A, and a cutter, B, which is shown in detail at C and D. The cutter rests in a groove, cut in the holder, and swings from a bolt, E, which allows it to move about ¼ in., as indicated by the dotted lines. This raises the back edge, and gives the necessary clearance between the tool and the work. Each time the motion is reversed the cutter swings over to the opposite side,

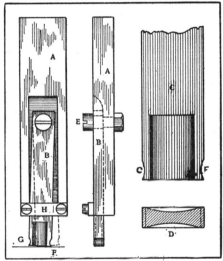

Making a Double Slotting Tool

and raises the other edge, and thus takes a cut in both directions.

When the work requires a sharp cutting edge, the cutter should be ground away on the edges, as shown at F and G, and when used for slotting, the sides should be made concave, as shown at D. In order to prevent lateral movement of the cutter, a small piece of steel is screwed across the groove in the holder, as shown at H.

We have one of these tools in our shop and use it nearly every day and have yet to find one that will do better or quicker work.—Contributed by L. G. Harren, 14 Barnett St., New Haven, Conn.

◆ ◆ ◆

Popular Mechanics' "Shop Notes for 1907" will be ready December 1, 1906.

HOW TO CUT WORM-WHEELS IN A LATHE

Some machinists will not attempt to make worm-wheels without the use of a milling machine, but a very good job can be done in a lathe, by making the simple attachment shown in the sketch. The blank

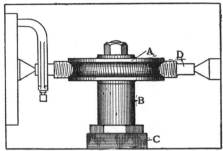

Worm Wheel Cutting Attachment

worm-wheel, A, which is to be cut, is fastened to an arbor, B, which is used in place of the tool post. The wheel is fastened in such a manner that it is free to revolve and a tap, D, is placed between the centers, and revolved by means of a dog. As the tap revolves the wheel is fed slowly against it, the pitch of the threads causing the wheel to revolve.—Contributed by Norman Baker, Hoopeston, Ill.

◆ ◆ ◆

HOW TO LAY OUT AN APPROXI= MATE ELLIPSE

An approximate ellipse can be drawn by the following method, which is used largely in laying out elliptical arches. Draw the

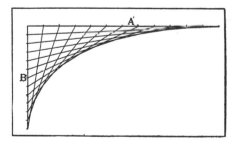

line A, equal to one-half the required length, and line B, equal to one-half the required width. Divide both lines into the same number of equal parts, and then connect the points of division as shown. This will form one quarter of the required ellipse. —Contributed by C. R. Gilkey, Sonora, Cal.

ACETYLENE AS A MOTIVE POWER FOR GAS ENGINES

By J. K. Rush, Canandaigua, N. Y.

The desirability of using acetylene for power purposes, and the great demand for a good acetylene engine for general purposes is conceded by all who have paid any attention to the rapid development of the acetylene industry in this and foreign countries within the last few years. Today acetylene is used on a large scale in all civilized countries, and in many instances where nothing else would fill the bill; it is used, not only to illuminate the homes of the well-to-do farmer and suburbanite, but even in some of the largest cities in this country it is used in competition with city gas and electricity, both for lighting homes and factories. It is not generally known that acetylene is now being extensively used for laboratory purposes where the very purest and most intense heat is desired, and it is very valuable for this purpose.

After enumerating only a few of the various places where acetylene is being used at the present time, both for illuminating and heating purposes, it can be readily seen what a wonderful field there is for the use of an acetylene engine. The farmer who lights his home, and uses acetylene to do all the cooking with an acetylene range (there are thousands in successful operation today), as well as using it for the instantaneous hot water heater in the bath room, which is heated with an acetylene heater, would much prefer to use an acetylene engine for pumping water and the various uses to which a gas engine is utilized on the farm today, than to be obliged to use some other method of accomplishing the work of a good gas engine, if it could be successfully done with acetylene manufactured on the premises, where one small machine will supply necessary gas for all of the above requirements.

Now we come to the question, "Is acetylene practical for power purposes?" In answer, it must be said that it is practical, but owing to the richness of the gas, which the analysis shows to be C_2H_2, it is not the easiest proposition in the world to figure out just how an acetylene engine should be constructed, and for that very reason, there are not as many successful acetylene engines in use as there would be if it were as easy to build an acetylene engine as one for coal gas or gasoline, but there are a few successful acetylene engines, nevertheless. It is only a few years ago that it was not possible to use acetylene for heating or cooking purposes, for the self-same reason that it is not used more in gas engines. The trouble with the use of acetylene for fuel purposes was that it is so rich in carbon that it was very difficult to mix it with the proper amount of oxygen to bring about proper combustion. But that trouble has been thoroughly overcome so far as the use of gas for fuel purposes is concerned, and today acetylene is successfully used in thousands of homes and laboratories for fuel and heating purposes.

One of the most important features of an engine to use acetylene successfully, is a perfect and very sensitive carbureter so arranged as to bring about a perfect mixture of gas and air. When this is done and all other conditions are complied with, acetylene works perfectly in an engine. Owing to the richness of the gas, a very small amount of acetylene is used and a much larger proportion of air than is the case with the use of coal gas. The writer is of the firm belief that if it were not for the fact that every manufacturer of a good gas or gasoline engine is having all he can do to fill orders for his regular line, that some of them, or more properly speaking, more of them would take an interest in the development of a good acetylene engine, and we would soon be able to get all of the acetylene engines we might desire, and have them for the various purposes for which they are so admirably adapted.

One reason why there has not been more done pertaining to the use of acetylene for engines is that only within the last three or four years have the generators been perfected to such an extent that it was possible to get acetylene of a standard quality and regular pressure. These difficulties have now all been overcome, and today there are at least six makes of generators manufactured in this country that can be depended upon to do all that their manufacturers claim for them, and are really high grade machines. But in this line as in all others there are a number of machines on the market that produce such a low grade of gas, and under such variable pressures that any mechanic who tried to do any experimenting with the use of acetylene for an engine would soon give up the job, when, as a matter of fact, it was the machine he was using that was at fault rather than the gas.

The same statement applies to acetylene

as to the use of steam, "You cannot get good results without good apparatus." You must have a good boiler and engine to get good results with the use of steam, and you must also have a good generator to get good results with the use of acetylene.

———♦ ♦ ♦———

Mold on paper may be removed by applying with a soft hair brush a solution of 1 part salicylic acid in 4 parts grain alcohol.

———♦ ♦ ♦———

TWO GOOD FORMS OF FILTERING CISTERN

To construct the cistern shown in Fig. 1, make the walls of stone, laid in hydraulic cement. For the bottom mix concrete, using 9 parts of gravel and sand to 1 of hydraulic lime, just moistened. Lay on in a mass to depth of 4 in. and pound hard. Let the lower course of flat stones of the wall (the footing) project 4 in. into the cistern to prevent cracks. Cover the top with two limestone flags, 6 in. thick, resting on the walls, with a manhole at one corner, and so cover and fit the whole with cement that insects or surface water cannot enter, except through the leader from the roof. Cover the manhole with a flagstone, cementing it at the edges, and surround it with a brick wall 1 ft. high, which cover with another flagstone, making air-tight with cement, thus leaving a foot of confined air and excluding frost. Cover the upper flagstone with a foot of earth, turf it, and then cover the whole cistern with earth.

For the filter, construct a vertical hollow cylinder, 2 ft. inside diameter, of good weather brick laid in hydraulic cement and extending from the concrete bottom to the top covering, with a 1-in. air-hole to allow

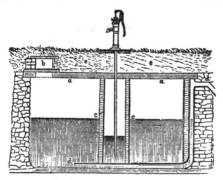

Fig. 1--Cistern for Filtering
a, a, Flags for Cover; b, Man-hole; c, c, Vertical Shaft for Filtering; d, d, Overflow; e, e, Earth.

the air to escape as the cylinder fills with water. This form of construction resists any sudden pressure of water against the exterior the same as an arch does. The water, after soaking through the 4 in. of brick, is well filtered.

Make the overflow from the cistern so as to give an escape for the filth coming from

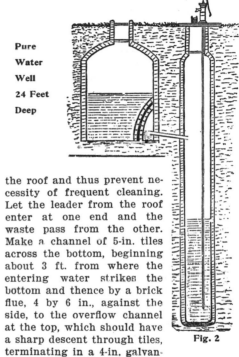

Pure Water Well 24 Feet Deep

Fig. 2

the roof and thus prevent necessity of frequent cleaning. Let the leader from the roof enter at one end and the waste pass from the other. Make a channel of 5-in. tiles across the bottom, beginning about 3 ft. from where the entering water strikes the bottom and thence by a brick flue, 4 by 6 in., against the side, to the overflow channel at the top, which should have a sharp descent through tiles, terminating in a 4-in. galvanized pipe with a self-acting valve at the bottom to be closed when no water is running. Cement well the whole channel inside the cistern.

In Fig. 2 the cistern for holding the filtered water is 24 ft. deep. Arch it with brick over the top, starting the arch 6 ft. below the surface. Make the cistern that receives the water from the roof 7 ft. deep, placing it at the side of the deeper one, and connecting the two with a pipe-tile. Make the filter of two walls of brick on edge, enclosing 2 in. of charcoal, the whole in a curve, with about 10 sq. ft. of surface, the water to pass freely through the brick. The washings from the roof and all warm rains are turned off and no waste pipe is required, says the Country Gentleman. Use a chain pump which will keep the water stirred. Bricks are used only for the arch at the top and the cement is plastered on the smooth surface of the earth.

A QUICK REPAIR FOR LEAKY PIPE

Factories, stores and other buildings, containing valuable stock, which is easily damaged by water, should be equipped with some means for stopping leaks in steam pipes, such as pinholes, as soon as discovered; otherwise the steam and rusty water coming from the pipe may cause expensive loss of property.

By having a number of clamps on hand, as shown in the sketch, a temporary repair

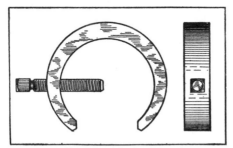

Repairing a Leaky Pipe

can be made almost instantly. These clamps can be made to take three or four different sizes of pipe, and are used in connection with small sheet steel plates and rubber gaskets. The steel plates and rubber gaskets should be about 1 in. square and about $\frac{1}{16}$-in. or $\frac{1}{8}$-in. thick. To stop a leak place the rubber on the hole; lay the piece of steel on the rubber, and apply the clamp, screwing same up tight, and having the center of the screw over the hole in the pipe. The steel pieces should be bent concave to fit the pipe, thus making a tight joint.

If desired the clamp may be left on the pipe permanently. I have two of these clamps in use which were put on over two years ago.—Contributed by O. C. Pottorff, 1310 N. 6th St., Springfield, Ill.

EXPERIMENTAL TELEPHONE LINE

In a recent issue of your magazine I noticed an article on how to make an experimental telephone, using the earth for a battery. A few days ago I built a similar line using carbon and zinc instead of water pipe for the ground and I now have a line running over to our neighbors with the very best results.

I noticed that about five o'clock p. m. each day a peculiar humming noise could be heard on placing the receiver to the ear, and later I discovered that the noise was caused by induction from the electric wires which

pass over my lines about 2 or 3 ft. above them. On experimenting with it further I found that by cutting out the ground at one end (I have a metallic circuit to use in case the other should fail) and connecting it so as to have a metallic circuit, the induction formed from the electric light lines would transmit the sounds just as well as the other.

I have a disc record phonograph which I play over the line every evening. I take the horn off and hang the receiver on a hook which holds it up against the mouth of the leather elbow. On connecting it up (with the ground circuit or metallic) the music is plainly heard at the other end.—Contributed by Stewart H. Leland, Lexington, Ill.

COMPRESSED AIR JAPANNING MACHINE

The machine about to be described is one which could probably be used to advantage in all factories where japanning is done, as by its use twice as much work can be turned out and many articles can be given a much more even coat than is possible by the dipping process, or by hand work. It is especially useful for round or cylindrical work, but can be used for japanning any article that is not too large.

A wooden hood, A (see sketch), is left

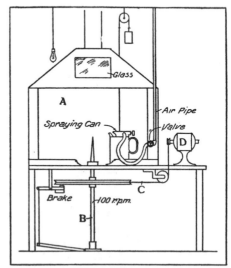

Japanning Machine

open at the front, and is provided with a pipe at the top to carry away the fumes. Four glass windows are made in the top, and one or more electric lights are arranged so as to illuminate the work. A vertical shaft, B, is revolved by means of a cord, C, which runs to an electric motor, D. The shaft is pointed at the top to receive a flat piece of wood for holding the work, nails being driven in the wood to accomplish this purpose.

As the work revolves it is given a coat of japan, by means of the spraying can, which contains the japan and is connected to an air hose, as shown. These cans can be purchased ready to use, and are provided with a special compressed air nozzle, which atomizes the japan and deposits it on the work. The japan used for this purpose should be thinned with turpentine before using, as it would otherwise make an uneven coat.

The machine should never run more than 100 r. p. m., and unless the work is very small 80 r. p. m. would be better. If it is run too fast the japan will be thrown off the work by centrifugal force. About 30 lb. air pressure is sufficient, but a greater pressure may be used by throttling down with the valve.—Contributed by W. J. S., Emsworth, Pa.

HOW TO MAKE A SMALL TAP-WRENCH

A small tap-wrench may be made of two pieces of pipe, a T fitting and two bolts. On one end of a piece of ⅜-in. pipe, A, cut a standard thread and file a $\frac{7}{16}$-in. machine bolt, B, to fit it snugly. Then file the head of the bolt to go inside the ⅜-in. T, indicated by D. File a groove, C, in the top of the head. Screw this pipe into the T tightly.

On a similar piece of ⅜-in. pipe, E, cut a long, loosely-fitting thread and stick a ⅜-in. bolt, F, into the end. This bolt should fit loosely, so it will remain stationary while the handle is being turned to tighten the wrench. Cut a groove, G, in this bolt, also. The tap is inserted in the third opening of the T and is held firmly when the loose handle is screwed up.—Contributed by Homer Keesling, Eden Vale, Cal.

HAND=CUT KEYWAYS IN PULLEY HUBS

The following method of cutting keyways in pulley hubs by hand was resorted to by a correspondent of the American Machinist who had a job that could not be done on a slotter.

A piece with a flange at one end was forged and turned to size; the slot was then

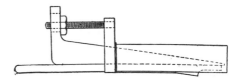

planed at an angle or taper and a wedge piece was made with a gib head having in it a slot through which passed a stud, the other end of which was tapped into the flange on the first piece mentioned. The stud was provided with a nut which held the gib wedge in place, while the drift or broach was driven through. The taper of the wedge was made to suit the taper wanted in the key seat. By turning the nut on the stud at each cut made, the feed was obtained.

A PATTERNMAKER'S KINK

Patternmakers and other wood workers know how difficult it is to plane a small block of wood without rounding the edges. A good way to avoid this trouble is to fasten the plane in the vice instead of the wood. The plane should be fastened in an inverted

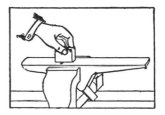

position, and the work can then be rubbed on the surface as shown. In this way a

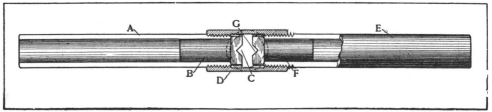

Tap-Wrench Made of Pipe

good true surface to the exact dimensions may be obtained, as the work is always visible and the corners are not rounded in doing so.

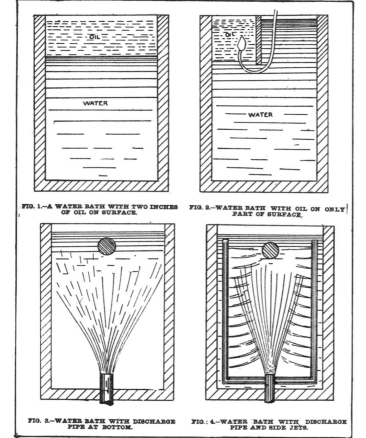

FIG. 1.—A WATER BATH WITH TWO INCHES OF OIL ON SURFACE.

FIG. 2.—WATER BATH WITH OIL ON ONLY PART OF SURFACE.

FIG. 3.—WATER BATH WITH DISCHARGE PIPE AT BOTTOM.

FIG. 4.—WATER BATH WITH DISCHARGE PIPE AND SIDE JETS.

THE SMALLEST BOOK

The smallest book in the British Museum and probably the smallest in the world is "The English Bijou Almanack for 1839." The book is printed in very clear type, but so small that the naked eye can hardly read it. It is illustrated, too, though, as will be observed, the little volume is scarcely

larger than a man's thumb nail. It is kept in a small box with a glass lid.

KINKS FOR TEMPERING

When steel is heated red hot and then plunged into water, the rapid contraction sometimes causes it to crack. This is especially true of articles having small projections, or parts of different thicknesses. To avoid this difficulty a correspondent of the American Blacksmith recommends the use of a quantity of oil on the surface of the water, as shown in Fig. 1. This being a poorer conductor of heat than the water, does not chill the steel so suddenly, and prepares it for the water or brine below.

It is sometimes desirable to harden only the surface of a piece of steel and leave the interior tough. To do this a bath is constructed, with a partition extending below the surface of the water or brine, as shown in Fig. 2. This compartment is filled with oil, and the object to be hardened is fastened to a piece of iron, bent in the form of the letter J, as shown. The steel may then be passed from the water to the oil without exposing it to the air. Linseed oil is generally used for this purpose, although lard oil and sperm oil are sometimes substituted.

The baths shown in Figs. 3 and 4 are the ones generally used when it is desired to keep the contents agitated. This is very necessary for large work, as the hot steel forms steam, which collects in some places and leaves other portions exposed to the brine. This results in uneven cooling, which should always be avoided, as it leaves the steel softer in some places, and often cracks the work.

To free lampblack of grease, says the Master Painter, saturate it with alcohol and then set fire to it. The pure carbon, only, will remain.

SHOP NOTES

A HANDY HOLDER FOR LOOSE SHINGLES

In shingling, where the roof is sheathed tight and especially at the top in putting on the last rows of shingles a shingle holder

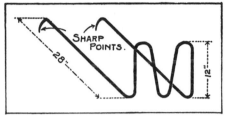

Holder for Loose Shingles

for loose shingles will be found a decided convenience. The holder is made of ⅜-in. steel pump rod and has sharp hooks which can be set anywhere on the roof or hooked over the comb. A half dozen of these holders, says the American Carpenter and Builder, will be plenty for anyone.

DRILLING HOLES IN VERTICAL COLUMNS

For drilling holes in vertical iron or steel columns try the following method:

Obtain an ordinary pipe hanger, which is made in two parts and so constructed that

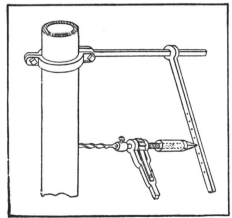

To Drill a Hole of Any Depth

the ends do not meet, and clamp it to the column as shown. Place a 1-in. steel rod, 2 ft. long and having an eye in one end, between the two clamp bars and pass a bolt through the clamp bars and the hole in the end of the rod.

Place a square wrought-iron rod, 1 in. thick, with an eye in one end, on the horizontal bar as shown, says the Engineer. Then put the ratchet in place and by moving the vertical bar nearer the column, the ratchet may be used to drill a hole of whatever depth desired.

HOW TO MAKE A STEAM TRAP OF PIPE FITTINGS

To make a steam trap of old pipe fittings, get a cast-iron pipe 2 ft. long, cap it at both ends, A and E, then drill and tap holes

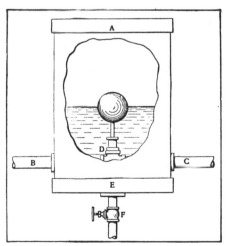

Home-Made Trap

opposite each other for the pipe, B and C. The inlet is at B and the outlet at C. On to pipe C, which should have an extra long thread, screw an old globe valve, D, having previously removed the threads from the spindle of the same.

Attach a float ball to the spindle as shown. Valve F, says the Engineers' Review, is to drain the trap when necessary.

If valve D is properly connected, very little packing need be used on the s[ ]ndle, as the pressure will tend to close the valve. The trap is for low pressure. Whe[ ] it fills with water the float will rise and so let the water out.

HOME=MADE WATER RESISTANCE

A portable home-made water resistance for testing purposes was made in the electrical repair shop of the street railway at Lansing, Mich. The Street Railway Review describes the device. By reference to the accompanying illustration it will be noted that this

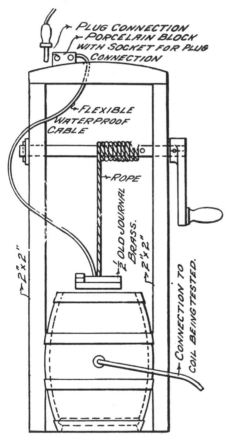

Home=Made Water Rheostat

water resistance consists of a small barrel or keg to the sides of which are fastened vertical 2x2-in. wooden posts. Near the top, these posts are pierced by a horizontal shaft fitted with a crank at one end. On this shaft is wound the rope which supports an old journal brass used for making electrical

contact with the water in the barrel. By means of a flexible cable this piece of brass is electrically connected to a porcelain connection socket fastened to the framework holding the small windlass. A suitable plug with a flexible cable completes the circuit between the porcelain connection block and the source of current. The cable, from a plate immersed at the bottom of the inside of the barrel, is brought through a wooden bushing driven tightly into the bung hole. This cable is of sufficient length to connect with an ammeter or other instrument in the circuit with the coils to be tested.

WHEAT BIN THAT WILL NOT LEAK

A form of wheat bin which may be made large or small, built of any size lumber and will never leak is shown in the illustration from the American Miller.

Build the hopper first. Put in the rafters,

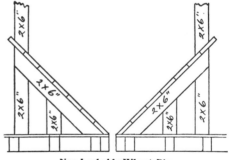

Non-Leakable Wheat Bin

then floor them, running the flooring crosswise and having it extend out past where the studding will be. Cut the studding on a bevel to fit the hopper. The sketch is an end view.

HOW TO LENGTHEN A SPRING

This is a simple matter, but often very convenient. Drive wedges in between the coils, and before taking the wedges out, drive wire nails in between the coils. Then place the spring where it is to be used, says the Engineers' Review, and drive out the nails, letting the tension come on the spring.

Method of Lengthening

RAPID METHOD FOR MAKING RINGS

Having had occasion to make a large number of brass wire rings, I found the following method the quickest and best: The wire to be made into rings was first made into springs, which were then cut along one side, thus forming as many rings as there were coils in the spring. As the springs

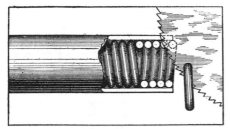

Ring Cutter for Lathe

were wound with the coils touching each other, the elasticity of the wire brought the ends of the rings opposite each other, thus doing away with any offset at the junction.

To cut the rings I used a very thin circular saw, fastened to an arbor and used in a lathe. Then I fastened a piece of brass tubing in the tool post, by means of a straight-tail dog, and fed the coils through by hand, running the lathe backwards at high speed. In this way I cut over 2,000 an hour, the rings dropping out of the end of the tube, as shown in the sketch.

There are many methods of making wire into springs, and any device which makes good close wound springs will do, but for this particular purpose I have found the following method very satisfactory: The wire is wound on an arbor in a lathe, and is fed through two pieces of wood held by the tool post. The pieces of wood should be clamped together so that the friction will draw the wire out perfectly straight, and the tool post should be fed by the screw-cutting attachment of the lathe.—Contributed by A. W. Griggs, 955 Market street, Kenosha, Wis.

WATERPROOFING FOR CEMENT BLOCKS

Shave ½ lb. castile soap into 1 gal. water; let dissolve, but do not make a suds. Apply it while boiling hot to the surface of the blocks, using a brush. After the soap wash dries apply a lukewarm solution of ½ lb. powdered alum in 4 gal. water. Two applications, says Cement Era, will close all pores and make a perfect waterproofing.

HOW TO MAKE A WATER AIR COMPRESSOR

In an establishment consuming an average of 25,000 gal. of water per day, drawn from the city mains through a 1½-in. pipe under an average pressure of 60 lb. and discharged into tanks of 1,000-gal. capacity each, the water was made to supply all the compressed air required for several machines, thus doing away with the expense of operating an air compressor. The system was arranged as follows:

A tank, A, of 1,000-gal. (133 cu. ft.) capacity was placed over the water tank room, and another tank, P, of 66 cu. ft. capacity was placed below tank A, in the water tank room and the piping was arranged as shown.

To operate, the handle of the three-way cock, C, is given a one-eighth turn, causing the water to flow from the water main into tank A, until the float valve closes and in

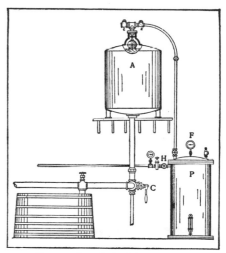

Compressing Air by Water Power

turn discharges the corresponding volume of air through check valve, E, into tank P. The handle of the three-way cock is then turned to its natural position, when the water flows from tank A, to the water tank and in turn draws in air through check valve, G, ready for another filling.

In filling tank A with 1,000 gal. of water 133 cu. ft. of free air is compressed in tank P, to about 2 lb., says a correspondent of the Engineers' Review, and by using 25,000 gal. of water per day it equals 25 fillings or the displacement of 3,325 cu. ft. of free air compressed to about 50 lb. pressure per square inch deducting necessary losses. This air is drawn out of tank P, through a reducing valve, H, under the desired pressure.

HOME=MADE GASOLINE BRAZING TORCH

A gasoline brazing torch which fastens to the wall in front of the work bench and swings back out of the way when not in use, may be made as follows:

Thread both ends of a 2-ft. length of 2-in. gas pipe. In a 2-in. cap drill a hole to re-

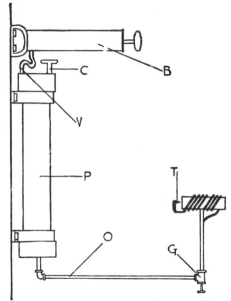

Fastens to Wall in Front of Work Bench

ceive a single tube bicycle valve, V; drill another hole and tap it to receive a ¼-in. pipe, C, 5 in. long, on which weld a piece of iron to form a handle or T for convenience in replacing the piece after filling the tank by way of the apped hole.

Fit the 2-in. cap on the top of the 2-in. pipe. Drill and tap the cap for the bottom for a ¼-in. pipe, O, 2½ ft. long and threaded at both ends. Make the burner of a piece of bicycle tubing, says the American Machinist, with a 2-ft. length of small-sized tubing coiled around it. An angle valve at G controls the supply of oil to the burner. The arrangement of the burner causes a continuous generation of gas by the blast. Make a hole not larger than a pin prick in the cap, T, at the end of the coiled tube. Fasten a bicycle pump, B, to the wall just

above the tank to use in keeping up a constant pressure in the tank.

HOW TO MEND OLD SACKS

Turn the sacks and shake them well. Make some good paste and apply it around the rent, using a brush. Cover the rent with a piece of cloth, says the American Miller, smooth it on with the hand and your patch is complete.

GAS BAG FOR STOPPING MAINS

Flow of gas from the main can be stopped by means of the gas bag illustrated, a device much used by gas fitters. To make the bag use common bed sheeting, cutting it 1½ in. larger than the circumference of the pipe; sew it up, turn it inside out and then dip it in linseed oil so it will hold water.

Put the bag over the hock, A, and put it into the pipe, then remove the hook and fasten the mouth of the bag to a ¾-in. pipe as indicated. Support this ¾-in. pipe by a stake driven into the ground. Pour water through the ¾-in. pipe into the bag until it is full and stops the flow of gas.

To remove the bag grasp it at the mouth with one hand and with the other pull out the ¾-in. pipe. Pull slowly on the bag, thus forcing it to the inner or top surface of the

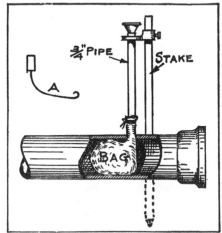

Stop-Bag for Gas Main

pipe and causing the water to run out. From 2 to 3 lb. can be created on the bag, depending on the height of the water column, 15 seconds being necessary to insert the bag and cut off the flow of gas.

For a 10 or 8-in. main, use a 10-in. bag; for 6 and 4-in. pipe use a 6-in. bag and for 4, 3 and 2-in. pipe, use a 4-in. bag.

TANK ALARM FOR LOW WATER

In a water supply system where the tank is located a distance of two miles from the pumping station, and where there is an alarm to notify when the tank is full, but none to tell when it is empty, a correspondent of the Engineers' Review installed a device as follows:

A is a water pressure gauge and B is the pointer. An insulated wire runs from the battery, C, to and through a hole in the top of the gauge shell. A bare end extends down low enough to allow the pointer to form a contact. This causes a current to flow from the batteries through the wire to the hand of the gauge and to the bell by means of the wire, E, which is fastened to the case of the gauge, by either soldering,

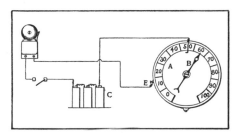

Tells When Tank is Empty

or with brass or copper screw. The switch is for cutting out the bell when the water pressure is low enough for the pointer to hit against the end of the wire.

HOW TO TEST A SQUARE

Draw any line (A-B) with any radius and use any point on the line as the center, C, describing a semi-circle, a c b. If the square is a true right angle, says the Metal Worker, one arm should meet the diameter at b, the other arm at a, and the corner come directly

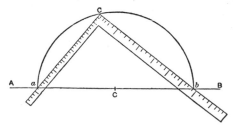

Testing a Square

on the circumference at c. If the test is carefully made any inaccuracy in the square may be detected.

FASTENING LINE WIRE TO TREES

Where it is impossible to set poles for a rural telephone line, a good method of fastening the wire to the trees is as follows:

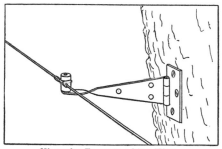

Hinge for Fastening Line Wire

Take a hinge (the longer the better and safer), nail it to a limb as illustrated. Twist the tip one-fourth turn and bolt a porcelain button to it, to which button fasten the wire. When the motion of the tree is parallel with the line, the wire will give and when it is at right angles with the line, the hinge will take up the motion and prevent the wire breaking.—Contributed by F. W. Mintzlaff, Grafton, Wis.

HOME=MADE POST AUGER

For the auger use a piece of 3x¼-in. soft steel 3½ in. long. Cut it as shown; sharpen the wings, A A, not attempting to finish the spur. Then forge a handle hole in one

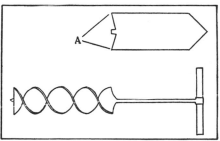

Good Post Auger

end of a piece of ¾-in. round stock 30 in. long; weld this piece to the auger blade, heat the blade and twist it in the vise (to the left). Finish up the cutting edges over the horn of the anvil and make a square point of the spur. A correspondent of the American Blacksmith, who has made fifty augers of this kind, finds them very satisfactory.

METHOD OF MENDING CIRCULAR SAW

Do not throw the cracked circular saw into the junk heap, make it as good as new by the following method:

Drill a ¼-in. hole at the crack near the teeth and another hole at the end of the crack. Countersink the hole near the teeth on both sides and insert a rivet very neatly,

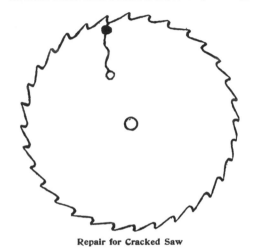

Repair for Cracked Saw

finishing the heads of the rivet down even with the saw blade. Should the crack be an extra long one, says the American Blacksmith, two rivets may be necessary

GAS STOVE FOR WORK BENCH USE

This handy device for heating soldering irons, etc., is made of a piece of ½-in. gas barrel, 8 in. long. Cap one end and to the other fit a reducing socket having a short length (2½ or 3 in.) of ¼-in. barrel in its smaller end. The outer end of this ¼-in. barrel should take the rubber tube, the inner end being reduced by forging to leave a small hole as indicated by the dotted lines.

Cut an aperture, to admit air, on the ½-in. barrel as close to the reducing socket

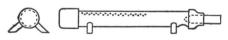

Gas Stove for Work Bench

as convenient and at the cap make four rows of holes to allow the air to escape. Screw in four pins ¼ in. in diameter to

serve as legs, says the Model Engineer, London. Provide a sheet iron box to stand on the bench to retain the heat and a bar of ⅜-in. round iron across the interior to support the soldering irons.

PREVENTING BLISTERS IN PHOTO-GRAPHS

Blisters in photographic prints or plates are frequently ascribed to the hot weather, though they sometimes develop in cold weather, to the mystification of the amateur.

The cause is the difference in temperature between the atmosphere and the baths used in developing.

In summer one will work along with the atmosphere, wash water and toning bath high but uniform, and then plunge the prints in a fresh hypo bath that has become as cold as ice owing to the fall in temperature which always results when hypo is dissolved in water. The result, says Camera Craft, is a case of blisters. And the same result may be accomplished in winter, merely by having one of the baths much colder or warmer than the others.

WHEEL FOR LAYING OUT ORCHARD

This device is made of two 1x4-in. boards, 10 ft. long, and an old wheelbarrow wheel. Establish base lines on the orchard ground

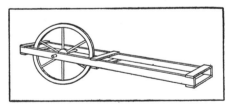

For Laying Out an Orchard

when it is ready, then draw the wheel from one tree point to a point at the opposite side of the field and so back and forth until the ground is marked one way. Then mark it the other way and where the wheel marks cross is the place for a tree. Dig a hole there, says the Rural New Yorker, and set the tree on a line each way with the marks. By this method every tree will be exactly in line.

Nitric acid of 1.2 specific gravity will darken cherry. Let stand 12 hours, then wash off the acid and dry.

TURNING A FLYWHEEL

This device is similar to one described in our April, 1906, number, but is for moving a heavier machinery load. To prevent the grip on the wheel from slipping the inside

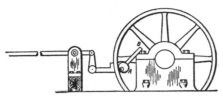

Device for Turning Heavy Wheel

jaw of the wrench was turned in a lathe and an eccentric cam, A, with a short lever, B, made. When the long arm is raised, the full throw of the eccentric is turned against the inside of the rim of the wheel, holding the jaws of the starting device firmly. With this device the engine cannot be turned backward unless the device is anchored to the floor. One man is required to adjust the eccentric, which is detachable, and another to manipulate the long lever.

A correspondent of the Engineers' Review, who uses this method of starting, has a rope transmission with 13 grooves for 1½-in. rope, and to protect the metal between them, he inserted a copper plate, long enough to lap three grooves, under the jaw of the wrench.

HOME=MADE BATTERY=CALL TELE-PHONE

The wiring and connections of two battery-call telephones are shown in the accompanying sketch. No transmitters are used, the receivers being used for that purpose, and the receivers and bells are thrown in and out of circuit by means of the hooks,

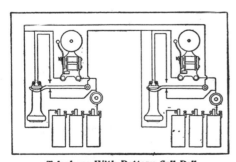

Telephone With Battery Call Bell

which hold the receivers. When the hook is down it closes the circuit at the lower contact and brings the bell in circuit, and when it is up it touches the upper contact and connects the receiver. When either push button is pressed both bells ring, as they are in multiple with both sets of batteries.

By connecting the bells and receivers in this manner only two line wires are necessary, and if a ground connection is used, only one wire will be needed.—Contributed by Richard E. Jenness, Kirkwood, Missouri.

TO REPAIR A GAS=HOLDER LEAK

File a ⅝-in. bolt flat 4 or 5 threads from the end and drill a small hole through the

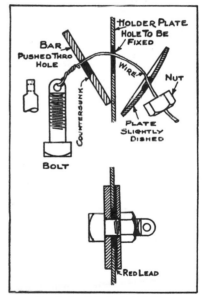

Repair for Hole in Gas Holder

end. Fasten a wire in the hole, string a bar on the wire and place the whole on the inside of the holder, as illustrated. Use a steel plate and nut on the outside and make the joint with red lead.

HARDENING DRILLS FOR GLASS

Prepare a solution of zinc dissolved to saturation in muriatic acid, says Machinery, and reduce by adding an equal quantity of water. Dip the drills in this and use without tempering.

PORTABLE LATHE FOR MACHINE SHOP

A portable lathe is one of the conveniences used in the Columbus (Ohio) shops of the Pennsylvania lines. A small motor is applied to an ordinary 16-in. lathe, as shown in the illustration. By the arrangement of the switches either 120 or 240 volts can be

THE TWEEZERS FOR PICKING UP SMALL ARTICLES

Lay the object on the back of the hand—usually cleaner than the palm—and then pick it up with the tweezers. In this way, the tool gets a good grip on the object, such as a screw or pivot, says Machinery, and is not so apt to slip.

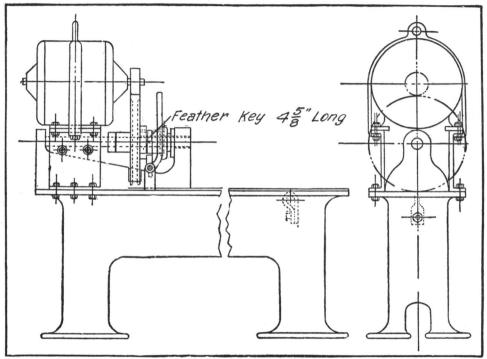

Portable Electrically-Driven Bolt Lathe

used. A small amount of field resistance gives a considerable range of speed.

This lathe can be moved about convenient to whatever engine is being served. It is provided with two hooks by which it can be picked up by an overhead crane and placed wherever desired. There is a combined clutch and brake provided with the handle, convenient to the operator, so that when the clutch is thrown out, the brake is applied, stopping the lathe spindle but allowing the motor to run. In calipering holes for bolts the portable lathe has reduced the expense 40 per cent in the time it saves.

Aluminum cannot be successfully soldered. Holes may be filled with solder, but two separate pieces cannot be soldered together.

PROTECTING WAX FINISH

Every drop of water allowed to fall on wax finish will leave a white spot. Try protecting the wax, suggests the Master Painter, with a coat of the following: Zanzibar copal varnish, 6 parts; boiled oil, 6 parts; turps, 10 parts, all by weight. Mix together well and apply.

REMOVING BROKEN STUD BOLTS

Drill a hole in the bolt, being careful not to drill too small. Then drive a square nail set or any square tool into the bolt and screw it out with a wrench. This method is easy and rapid.—Contributed by C. I. Mitchell, Temple, Texas.

CEILING FAN MADE OF PIPE FITTINGS

A ceiling fan costs from $6 to $32.25; here is one made of pipe fittings at a total cost of 99 cents and which works to perfect satisfaction. The parts required and their cost are: Two drilled flanges, A, 10 cents; 5-in. pulley, B, 25 cents; ½-in. pump rod,

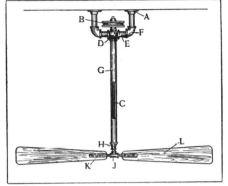

Ceiling Fan That Costs 99 Cents

C, 8 cents; cross, D, 4 cents; two nipples, E, 4 cents; two elbows, F, 6 cents; ¾-in. pipe, G, 10 cents; ¾x½-in. reducer, H, 3 cents; ½-in. tee, J, 4 cents; two couplings, K, with male connections, 9 cents; fan blades, L, made of ⅜-in. pine, 16 cents. The fan should be mounted 7½ ft. from the floor and the pulley connected by belt as shown.

I have made several of these fans, painting and gilding them, so that they compare favorably with factory-made ones in every way.—Contributed by Ora S. Harmas, Fennimore, Wis.

◆ ◆ ◆

PROTECTION FOR HITCHING POSTS

Most horses seem to take particular delight in chewing up hitching posts if made of wood and unprotected, but when covered with tin washers fastened by nails as shown in the sketch, the most voracious animal will soon refrain from this pastime.

The tin washers referred to are the kind generally used by roofers in laying paper roofing and can be fastened with ordinary steel wire nails.—Contributed by Stoke Richards, Santa Clara, Cal.

HOW TO MAKE A SHAFT HANGER

Almost any machinist who has a forge can make a good hanger, which will have all the adjustments found in an improved ball and socket hanger.

A piece of wrought iron, about ½ in. by 3 in. for ordinary size shafting, is bent to the shape shown in Fig. 1, if a drop hanger is desired, and if a post hanger is to be made, the iron frame can be of the form shown in Fig. 2. A side view of the drop hanger is shown in Fig. 3.

In making a drop hanger, a piece of iron like that used in the frame is bent over at the ends, as shown at A, Fig. 1, and fastened by means of ⅝-in. bolts, B. The center is tapped for a ⅝-in. set screw, C, which is directly over a similar set screw in the frame. Both set screws are provided with jam nuts so that they may be held from turning after being adjusted.

The bearing consists of a piece of common iron pipe, D, equal in length to four times the diameter of the shaft and countersunk on opposite sides at the center to receive

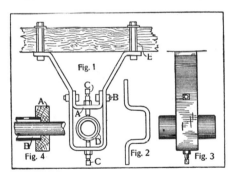

An Adjustable Hanger

the set screws, C. A hole should be bored through the pipe near each end to allow pouring the babbitt. To do this make two pieces of wood as shown at A, Fig. 4, and slip one over each end of the pipe with the shaft in the center, thus leaving a space, B, to receive the babbitt. Thoroughly smoke or chalk the shaft to prevent the babbitt from shrinking on it, and if the inside of the pipe is very smooth make a number of grooves with a cape chisel.

In fastening up the hanger make the hole E (Fig. 1) somewhat larger than the bolts, F. This allows lateral adjustment of the hanger. The vertical adjustment can be obtained by the two set screws, and if one end of the bearing should be a little too high, it can be lowered by loosening the

nolts, B.—Contributed by Lee R. Clarke, 116
S. Eighth Ave., Bozeman, Mont.

HOW TO MAKE AN AUTOMATIC LAMP CORD ADJUSTER

Procure an old curtain roller, A, and cut
off the solid end. Fasten it in the wooden
spool, B, which is drilled to receive the

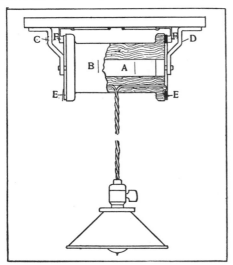

Automatic Lamp Cord Adjuster

wires from the incandescent lamp. Make
two sheet brass brackets, C and D, one having a round hole, and the other a slotted
hole to prevent the spring shaft from turning. Then make two brass rings, E E, and
fasten on ends of spool. Solder the lamp
wires to these rings and make two sheet
brass brushes, F F, to make contact with
the rings.

The lamp may then be lowered or raised
the same as a window shade.—Contributed
by Wm. D. Probst, 1036 Erie St., Youngs-
town, Ohio.

EMERGENCY GASOLINE SUPPLY FOR AUTOS

Every automobilist should carry with him
a length of small rubber hose for use in
case the gasoline feed pipe running from the
supply tank to the carbureter should rup-
ture. Also he should carry an extra can of
gasoline—say a gallon or two gallons—the
spout of the can being fitted with a cork
stopper. To one end of the length of hose
must be fitted a short length of small pipe.
Then in the emergency mentioned, says the

Automobile, all that is necessary is to
stretch the loose end of the rubber hose
over the fractured end of the gasoline pipe
and push the other end of the hose, having
the pipe, through a hole made in the cork
stopper of the extra can of fuel and by prop-
ping up the can he will be able to supply the
motor with gasoline during the home run.

THE CAMERA AS A DRAFTING TOOL

Sometimes a perspective view of assembled castings is required when it would not
be advisable to call in a skilled artist. For
instance, when bids for a casting are required, the patterns being furnished, and it
is desirable to send the foundry people blueprints showing the nature of the work. A
good and cheap way, says the ·American
Machinist, is to use the camera as a drafting tool.

To do this take a photograph of the pattern and make a blueprint from the negative. Outline in pencil, emphasizing points
of particular importance. Then dip the
print in sodium hydrate or in common lye.
This will turn the blue into pale yellow and
leave the pencil outline in bold relief. Then
trace, free-hand, the outline on tracing cloth.

A STETHOSCOPE FOR MACHINES

When a physician examines a patient,
about the first thing he does is to produce
an instrument which looks like the earpiece
of a phonograph, and proceeds to adjust it
to his ears and apply the extremity to the
various parts of the body. A modification
of this instrument, which is known as a
stethoscope, has been found valuable for
locating troubles
in machines.

When a noise
is heard which
cannot be lo-
cated the stetho-
scope can be
used as shown
in the sketch.
The instrument
in this case
should have a
longer hose than
those used for
medical purposes to allow easy access to all
parts of a machine.

It should be remembered that in a machine which is not running properly sound
is produced first, and then heat. Sometimes

when the parts get hot it is too late to remedy the trouble, as they may be so badly cut that they are ruined. To detect the sound quickly before much heat is produced, apply the stethoscope as shown in the sketch, moving the free end to different parts to find the precise point the noise comes from.

An instrument of this kind, made by a correspondent of Machinery, consists of simply a piece of rubber tubing, and when the end is placed to one ear and the other ear closed with the finger the device is very effective.

A WATER SPREADER FOR ROOFS

It often happens that shingle or slate veranda roofs having only a slight pitch become worn at the down spouts, where the deluge of water in time works down through the joints of the roof covering.

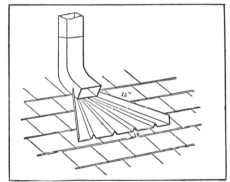

Spreader Attached to Spout

To remedy this trouble, a correspondent of the Metal Worker devised the spreading deflector shown in the sketch. It should be made of sheet copper or galvanized iron, and should be about 15 in. long by 18 in. wide.

HOW TO MAKE FILLETS FOR PAT= TERNS

It is a mistake to leave out the fillets on any pattern, even on hurry-up jobs, which require no finishing. The object of the fillet is not to beautify the work, but to strengthen the casting, and it is much more necessary than rounding the outside edges, which is often done on patterns in which the fillets have been neglected.

This will be more clearly understood by referring to Fig. 1, which shows the cavity left in the sand after a pattern without fillets has been drawn from the mold. It will be noticed that a sharp edge is left in the sand at A, which is easily washed away by the molten metal, thus making a dirty,

porous casting. The corner opposite A offers no protruding edge and, as far as a

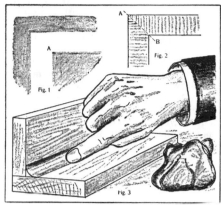

Making a Putty Fillet

clean casting is concerned, requires no rounding, but, as will appear later, it is well to round it for other reasons.

Fig. 2 shows the casting which would be produced by pouring the mold shown in Fig. 1. When the molten iron cools it crystallizes, the lines of crystallization being at right angles to the surface as indicated by the vertical and horizontal lines. The effect of this crystallization is the same as would be produced by gluing a number of very thin pieces of wood face to face, and then gluing the ends together at the beveled corner. It is evident that the weakest point would then be at the corner. This is exactly the case with the iron. If sufficient force is applied to a casting of the form shown in Fig. 2, it will invariably break along the line of A-B, although the section of the metal at that point is greater than at any other.

It is a curious fact that rounding the pattern at A (Fig. 2) will strengthen the casting and, as would naturally be expected, the addition of a fillet at B will further increase the strength. The rows of crystals will then swing round from a common radius much as in the position of soldiers when making a turn. Thus instead of the rows of crystals meeting on a line as at A-B they will arrange themselves in wedge-shaped segments, thus leaving the metal more homogeneous.

Having thus seen the necessity of fillets in patterns, there are doubtless many who would be interested in a quick, easy method of making them. This is shown in Fig. 3, the only tools necessary being the hands, and the only materials a lump of putty and a dish of turpentine.

Dip the index finger in the turpentine and

rub along the part which is to receive the fillet. Then roll a piece of putty out long like a lead pencil and lay in the corner. Dip the finger in the turpentine again and then rub on the putty as shown. If a large fillet is wanted, use the thumb and if a very small one is required, the little finger can be used. Pressing on hard also reduces the size of the fillet. After thus forming the fillet allow it to stand about an hour, when it will then be ready to shellac. When the pattern is finished the fillet cannot be distinguished from the best leather fillets and if properly applied will last as long as the pattern.

HOW TO CASEHARDEN IRON OR SOFT STEEL

Procure a quantity of old boots and heat same in a sheet iron box until thoroughly charred. Place the articles to be casehardened in the box and cover them with the charred leather. Reheat and keep at a dull red heat for an hour or more and then plunge the contents in cold water or brine.

If a blue color is desired, the articles after being treated as above should be ground and polished and then placed in a pan of sand. Apply heat and when the desired color appears drop the articles in cold water.

HOW TO MAKE A FARM-LEVEL

A serviceable farm-level which does not cost over 50 cents to make is shown at Fig. 1. The level should be 4 or 5 ft. high with a crossbar 3 ft. long at the top. To the ends of the crossbar tie small glass tubes and connect them with a piece of rubber tubing 4 or 5 ft. long, which fill with colored water up to the line A B. When the instrument is set so that line A B exactly corresponds with the upper edge of the crossbar, the latter will be level. This instrument is as accurate and nearly as convenient as a level costing $15 to $25, says the Yearbook of the Department of Agriculture.

A more expensive and more convenient farm-level may be made by fastening a 30-in. carpenter's level to the head of an ordinary camera tripod, using two right-angled screw hooks as at A, Fig. 2. The level will cost about $1.25.

HOW TO REPAIR A LEAKY HAND-HOLE

A leaky handhole located in the rear end of the boiler, where the plate had been allowed to leak until the head of the boiler had corroded away so that it could not be kept tight, was repaired by a correspondent of the Engineers' Review as follows:

A steel ring ⅜ in. thick and 1½ in. wide was procured from the boiler shop and put on. To do this the ring was bored for ½-in. rivets and corresponding holes were drilled in the boiler head and countersunk on the inside, in order to bring the heads even with the plate and leave a clear place for the packing. The countersinking was done by placing the drill chuck in a piece of ⅜-in. pipe and running it through the front handhole; and by fitting the countersink in the chuck and the outer end of the pipe in the ratchet, one man did the turning while the other kept the countersink in the hole, and from running out of center.

When driving the rivets, a cupped piece of pipe was used to hold them in place in the same way, until they were headed. Then by the use of a gasket that did not require "following" the job was completed satisfactorily.

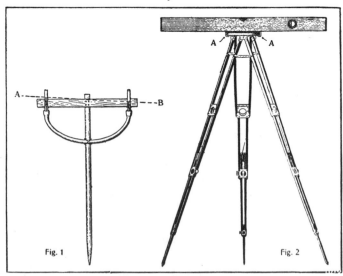

Fig. 1   Fig. 2

Inexpensive Farm Levels

THE CONSTRUCTION OF A HOME=MADE MOTORCYCLE

At the present time motorcycles are playing a great part, not only for a pastime but for practical use as well, and it is the earnest desire of most young men to own one. As I have had practical experience in this line I feel able to lay before the readers of Popular Mechanics a general outline with illustrations showing the construction of a practical machine.

In designing a home-made machine it is well to follow the lines of a regular motorcycle as much as possible, the location of the motor, transmission, etc. The first consideration is that of finding a suitable frame, one that is of heavy construction, with reinforced joints and with a slight or no drop to the crank hanger.

There are several bicycle motors with all necessary attachments on the market which

The gasoline tank is clamped to the horizontal bar on top and with small pipe connecting it to the mixing valve or carbureter. The battery box and spark coil are located by clamps on the rear slanting bars, directly behind the seat. The electric wiring should be carefully executed, placing a switch on the grip of the handle bar, by which the circuit can be opened or closed by the thumb or forefinger. This gives immediate control of the engine, and is very necessary, especially when riding in crowded thoroughfares where it is vitally important to stop quickly. The writer has narrowly escaped serious injury in a collision, due to a defective and poorly insulated switch, by which he was unable to break the circuit.

The battery box is made to hold 4 dry batteries, from which the current passes

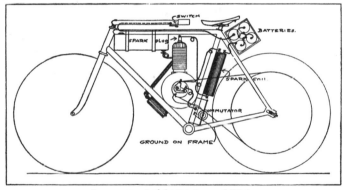

Arrangement of Apparatus and Wiring

sell for $45.00 to $65.00, according to horsepower. Included with the other attachments is the metal driving-pulley rim which is to be attached to the left side of the rear wheel, which must also be fitted with a coaster brake. This metal rim is provided with legs or clamps which are to be bolted fast to the wooden rim. A spring saddle will be found much more comfortable than the ordinary bicycle saddle and will add but little to the expense of the outfit.

The motor is to be clamped to the front slanting bar, for which clamps are provided; care must be taken to have the engine driving pulley in a true line with that of the rear pulley rim. The belt should be stretched on and the idler wheel put in place, then wheel the bicycle along the floor and note if the belt runs straight and true, if not, shift the engine until the pulleys are in line.

through the switch and commutator and thence to the induction coil, from which it leaps to the spark plug in the engine cylinder. A diagram of this wiring is given in the sketch.

After making all these connections and everything else is in place, place the rear wheel of the motorcycle in a rack which raises it from the floor and start the motor to see if all is in working order. There is always a lot of final adjusting to be done after the machine is assembled and should be done as each occasion arises. First, test the spark by closing the circuit with the switch and after disconnecting the spark plug wire, hold it about ¼ in. from any part of the plug and slowly turn the rear wheel until the spark leaps across the space, the revolution of this wheel causing the commutator on the engine to make and break the circuit, which induces the spark. If no spark is seen, then there is a defect in the wiring at some place.

When this feature is in working order, mount the machine, turn on the gasoline supply, open the throttle half way, place the spark advance lever at a little more than midway, open the compression cock (if one, or if the motor has an automatic valve lift, no attention is required to this) and placing the feet on the pedals start the motor and rear wheel in motion. Do not try to start the motor by slow pedaling, as in most cases a rapid revolution is necessary to obtain the first explosions after which the compression cock is closed and the engine will speed up at once. As soon as it does, regulate the speed with the spark advance lever which will be found to govern the speed absolutely. If the motor does not catch a few explosions at first, regulate the spray valve until it does, as that is the vital point for a perfect mixture.

It is well to experiment with the engine in this way until one is familiar with the levers before taking it on the road, after which, with some final adjustments to the belt, etc., no trouble should be had.

To complete the machine in regard to appearance, mud guards may be added; heavy tires and long straight handle bars will add greatly to its good looks.—Contributed by Prentice P. Avery, Ridgewood, N. J.

PRIMING A STEAM PUMP

A pump which was used for fire protection purposes only and which was required to be under steam pressure at all times, made the engine room so hot that the steam was shut off. One day at an unexpected visit of the inspector, the engineer succeeded in turning on the steam without being observed, but though the pump started up he could tell it was getting no water. Fortunately, the inspector did not ask to see the

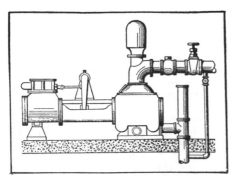

Pump Connected for Priming

pump throw a stream. After his departure the engineer made an examination and found that the foot valve on the suction pipe leaked and the pump had "run down."

To prevent trouble of that kind occurring again, says the Engineers' Review, he piped up a connection from the service pipe to the suction as illustrated. With this arrangement, if the pump ran down again, it would be an easy matter to prime the suction pipe.

HOME=MADE COOKING UTENSIL

As handy a dish as one can have for the kitchen is made from an empty coffee can. Take a piece of tin about 1 in. by 3¼ in., roll into a tube and solder, making a tube

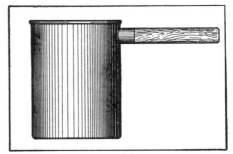

Inexpensive and Convenient

1 in. long and 1 in. in diameter. Now whittle out a soft wood stick 5½ in. long, to fit the tube tight. Secure the two by driving a small nail through both, filing off the end of nail. Now solder the end of the dish near the top. You can handle this utensil over a stove without burning the hands. When the dish is worn out, unsolder and put on a new dish.—Contributed by T. L. Reed, La Porte City, Iowa.

CASE=HARDENING CAST IRON

Pulverize equal weights of saltpeter, prussiate of potash and sal-ammoniac and mix them together. Prepare a dipping solution by adding to each quart of cold water 1 oz. prussiate of potash and ½ oz. sal-ammoniac. Heat the cast-iron pieces red hot, says Machinery, roll them in the powder, then plunge them into the liquid.

Oiling of smoothly polished castings, such as cylinder heads of steam engines, more than doubles the loss of heat by radiation. —Kent.

GOOD METHODS FOR BENDING PIPE

A "hicky" (B, Fig. 1) is a useful device for making bends in small pipe, up to ¾-in. To make a hicky, bullhead a 1¼x1-in. tee on the end of a piece of 1-in. pipe, 4 ft. long.

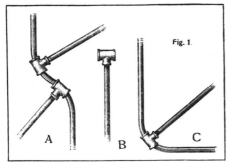

Bending Pipe with "Hickies"

Then lay the pipe to be bent on the floor, or leave it in place, slip the tee on the hicky over the pipe to a point near where the bend is to be made. Start the bend with a slight pressure on the lever, then move the hicky along the pipe a little and apply pressure again. Repeat this operation until the bend is made as desired (C, Fig. 1). To make an offset, use two hickies (A, Fig. 1), holding the first bend in position with one and using the other to make the offset.

For bending pipe up to 2 in. a good method is shown at Fig. 2. Lay two 10-ft. planks up against a horse or window-sill, placing them 3 ft. apart. Nail a piece of 4x4-in. timber to the under side of the planks, and provide another piece, which leave loose so it can be moved back and forth as desired, says the Metal Worker. Insert one end of the pipe to be bent under the lower 4x4-in. piece and adjust the other

To Bend 2-In. Pipe and Up

4x4-in. piece to the point on the pipe where the bend is to be made. Then apply strength to the projecting end of the pipe to make the bend.

HOW TO CONVERT A LEAD PENCIL INTO A WIRE GAUGE

An article in the July number of Shop Notes describes a method of finding the resistance of any copper wire by means of the slide rule. The method there given is entirely correct, but as a wire gauge is required to determine the size of the wire and a slide rule needed for the necessary calculations, and as many persons possess neither of these instruments, I thought the following method would prove acceptable.

The only device required by this method is a common lead pencil on which is marked off two spaces: one 1 in. long and one ½ in. long. To obtain the resistance per 1,000 ft. of any size wire first remove the insulating covering for a distance of a foot or more, depending on the size of the wire, and then wind the wire on the lead pencil as shown in the sketch. Count the number of turns per inch using the 1-in. space for large wire and the ½-in. space for fine wire. When

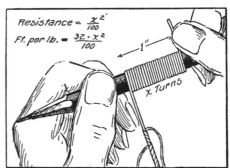

$$Resistance = \frac{x^2}{100}$$
$$Ft.\ per\ lb. = \frac{32 \cdot x^2}{100}$$

Lead Pencil Used as Wire Gauge

the number of turns per inch is determined, square that number and point off two decimal places and you then have the resistance per 1,000 ft. at 20° C.

When the resistance is known the number of feet per pound can be found by multiplying by 32. Of course all these results are only approximate, but they are sufficiently accurate for practical purposes.—Contributed by A. Willatowski, 165 Alexander St., Atlanta, Ga.

FILLING TIRES WITH SAND

When it is impossible to inflate the punctured tire of your auto, try filling it with sand, if any is available. The sand will cushion the tire in a measure and keep the dead weight of the machine off that wheel.

DRILLING OVERHEAD HOLES

Anyone who has ever had occasion to drill holes in a ceiling, or any other place where the job has to be done overhead, knows what tiresome work it is. A strong man will feel exhausted after holding his arms overhead for five minutes without doing any work and when the work of feeding and turning the

Simple and Easy

drill is added, it is almost impossible to continue working for more than three or four minutes at a time.

Having had occasion to do some overhead drilling, I found that the men's labor could be greatly reduced by means of the device here illustrated, which consists of simply a board, which acts as a lever, with the fulcrum at the round of the ladder. The board to work well, should be in a horizontal position and if the round is not in the right place, it may be changed by moving the lower end of the ladder, or if this will not produce the desired effect, a few blocks of wood placed between the brace and the board will bring the board to a horizontal position. The pressure should be applied to the board as far from the round as possible, thus increasing the leverage.

When the ladder is inclined too much it is hard to reach the handle of the brace. In that case the brace can be placed on the other side of the ladder and the board can be raised by placing your shoulder below it. —Contributed by A. J. Saxe, Engineer, Railway Exchange Building, Chicago.

CLAMP TO HOLD WIRE WHILE SOLDERING

This clamp may be made any size and of almost any material, soft iron being preferable, however. It is used for holding wire

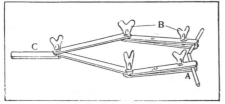

Clamp for Use in Soldering

or small metal pieces while soldering or brazing. The hand screws, B, should be somewhat harder than the arms and clamps. The machine is very flexible and rods can be held at any angle by adjustment. A indicates the vise jaws, and C the handle. It is of especial convenience in soldering as one or both hands may be free to spread the solder or flux.—Contributed by David R. Shearer, Lenoir, N. C.

DEVICE TO PREVENT AUTOMO= BILES FROM BACKING

In hilly localities it is often advantageous to equip an automobile with the device shown in the sketch. A large ratchet lever,

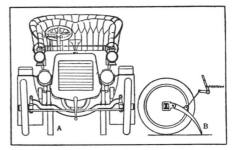

To Prevent Auto from Backing Down Hill

A (shown in detail at B), is pivoted from the axle with the point suspended in the air normally, but capable of being lowered when desired, thus preventing the machine from backing.

TO REMOVE STAINS FROM NEGA= TIVES

A good formula for removing stains from negatives is as follows:

Iron sulphate ....3 oz.
Sulphuric acid ....1 oz.
Water ..:............3 oz.

Another method is to allow the plate to soak several days in a solution of hypo.

MARKING CORRECTIONS IN BLUE= PRINTS

The simplest and best way to mark corrections in blueprints is to use a saturated solution of common sal soda for a writing fluid and do the writing with an ordinary new and clean steel pen. The marking will stand out clearer and whiter than the lines of the print.—Contributed by M. L. Schiaffino, 2 Belen St., Guadalajara Jal, Mexico.

SHOP NOTES

LAYING OUT AN ANGLE WITH SCALE AND DIVIDERS

To lay out any angle without other tools than a scale and dividers, strike an arc with a radius of 3.58 in. and count every $\frac{1}{16}$ in. on the arc a degree. For many purposes a radius of $3\frac{9}{16}$ in. will do, the error being one degree in 360.

EXPANSION JOINT SUBSTITUTE

As long steam pipes change their length a considerable amount, due to the expansion and contraction which takes place during changes of temperature, an expansion joint is needed to take up this motion, which would otherwise break a fitting or cause a

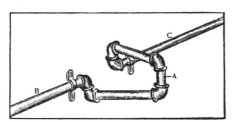

Expansion Joint Made of Pipe and Fittings

leak. When an expansion joint is not available, however, the device here shown will prove an excellent substitute. The nipple, A, is of such a length that the center lines of pipes B and C will coincide. Four common ells and two street ells will be the only fittings required, the cost of which will compare favorably with an expansion joint.—Contributed by Frank J. Borer, 230 Rankin St., Elizabeth, N. J.

CEMENT FOR WOODWORK

The following cement will be very hard when dry, and will adhere firmly to wood: Melt one ounce of rosin and one ounce of pure yellow wax in an iron pan, and thoroughly stir in one ounce of Venetian red until a perfect mixture is formed. Use while hot.

ANOTHER QUICK REPAIR FOR LEAKY PIPE

To repair a leaky pipe with the pressure on, simply wrap the inner tube from a bicycle tire around the leak, stretching the rubber tightly and winding around the pipe in a manner similar to that employed by physicians in bandaging a limb. Continue in this way until the leak stops, and then

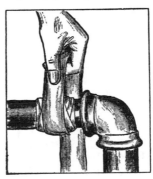

tie a knot in the rubber. This repair will often hold for years, and it only takes a few minutes to apply it.—Contributed by F. D. Munger, Oconomowoc, Wis.

WATER MUFFLER FOR GASOLINE ENGINE

A pail of water makes a very simple but most effectual muffler for a gasoline engine. The illustration shows how it is used. The pail is partly filled with water and the end

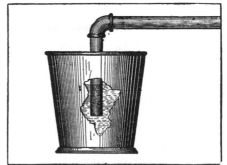

Cheap Gas Engine Muffler

of the exhaust pipe is carried below the surface, thus causing the exhaust to bubble up through the water.—Contributed by Walter Weber, 643 W. 46th St., Chicago, Ill.

INEXPENSIVE AND USEFUL RATCH= ET WRENCH

The ratchet wrench illustrated was originally designed for use in car repair work for removing nuts from the bolts of split gears, but is also useful for removing square or hexagonal nuts so located that they are hard to get at.

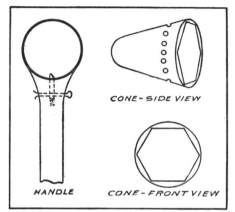

Details of Ratchet Wrench

A cone-shaped device takes the place of the jaws in the ordinary form of wrench. This cone on the interior is hollowed to the form of a hexagonal pyramid which will fit most of the nuts generally in use. The cone fits into a circular opening at the end of the handle. A small steel pin inserted in the handle and held in place by a split key serves as a ratchet and engages with small indentations in the surface of the cone, says the Electric Railway Review. The wrench will work either right- or left-handed, depending on which side of the opening in the handle the cone is inserted. It is said that this wrench can be made for about 75 cents.

HORSEPOWER OF A GAS ENGINE REDUCED BY HIGH ALTITUDES

A gas engine giving 10 hp. in Chicago will give only 8 hp. in Denver and if moved to the summit of Pike's Peak would give only 5 hp. This is due to the difference in atmospheric pressures of the places mentioned.

Other conditions remaining the same, an engine while consuming the most gas will give the most power. By consuming, in this case, is meant actual combustion and not simply the wasting of gas which occurs when the mixture is too rich.

In Denver, where the atmospheric pressure is less than in Chicago, the amount of air taken into the cylinder during each cycle will be correspondingly less and will therefore be unable to support the combustion of as great a quantity of gas. The amount of compression is reduced as well and this also results in loss of power.

FASTENING ON A GUITAR BRIDGE

The method I adopted for gluing on a guitar bridge I believe is original and a valuable kink for those players placed in a similar position. Soon after purchasing the instrument the bridge became detached, there being a tremendous strain exerted by the strings, and it was returned to the dealer to be repaired. He glued it on and in addition put in two screws with nuts, one at each end of bridge; yet it again came off soon afterward. As the dealer ran a first-class repair shop, I decided that it would be useless to go elsewhere, but to try the job myself.

I cut off about 6 in. of the largest diameter hardwood curtain pole I could find and planed a flat surface about ¾ in. wide. Into this I drilled six holes a trifle smaller than the root diameter of a $\frac{1}{16}$-in. wood screw having a round head, and at a distance apart corresponding to the holes in bridge. This block, A in sketch, was inserted in the sound hole of the instrument and placed under the string holes. Placing a strip of wood, B, drilled with corresponding holes, under the heads of the screws,

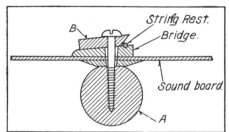

Gluing Bridge on Guitar

they were screwed into the block as hard as possible. Of course, the glued surfaces of bridge and sound-board were first cleaned with sandpaper and slightly warmed. By this method I secured a pressure impossible by any other means adaptable to the conditions, and costing practically nothing. Of course, any block of hard wood would answer the purpose, but curtain poles happened to be plentiful at the time.—Contributed by R. E. Bates, Mansfield, Mass.

HOW TO DRILL BRICK, CEMENT, STONE, ETC.

Seeing an article in Shop Notes describing a method of making a drill for small holes in brick and cement, reminded me of a drill for making larger holes, which I have used

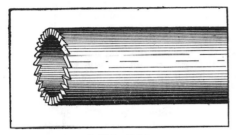

Drill for Brick

with great success in perforating walls over a foot thick.

All that is needed is a piece of ¾-in. gas pipe with the end cut off square and cut with teeth as shown in the sketch. The teeth may be cut with a three-cornered file, and should be of a liberal number and all the same length so that each tooth will do its share of cutting.

In using this drill strike light, quick blows with a machinist's hammer, at the same time revolving the pipe.

If a very deep hole is to be drilled, use a short pipe at first to get the hole started, finishing with a longer piece, and if the teeth become very dull, remove the drill and sharpen with a file.—Contributed by Stoke Richards, Santa Clara, Cal.

DEVICE FOR FILING FLAT

In filing flat—a very difficult operation—the device illustrated will be found convenient. The illustration is an end view.

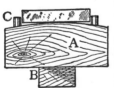

A block, A, of metal or wood and slightly rounded on the top is caught in the vise by the part B. Pins, C, hold the piece to be filed on the rounded top as shown. The file is worked backwards and forwards on the work, says the Model Engineer, London, and the rounded top allows the job to rock to accommodate the motion of the file, and no difference how the file is pushed about, one is always filing flat.

COLD WEATHER VESTIBULE FOR SHIPPING ROOMS

In transferring freight from the shipping room to a box car in winter so much cold air enters with the opening of a door that it is often uncomfortable to work in the room. One company, says Machinery, got around this difficulty by devising a handy vestibule which folds up bellowslike against the side of the building when not in use. The device is shown in the sketch.

A light rectangular framework, B, surrounding the shipping door is fastened to the outer wall. A similar framework, A, is connected to this by two swinging arms, D, on each side, and between these two frames is fastened the tube, C, of heavy close-woven duck, or some other similar material. When the box car is in place, the weight of the outer framework, A, acting on the arms, D,

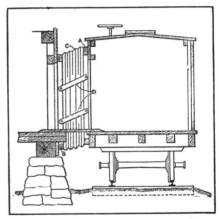

The Vestibule in Place

tends to hold it firmly against the side of the car, thus forming an enclosed passageway between it and the building tight enough to prevent the wind from entering to any great extent.

TO CLEANSE MERCURY

Put a 10 per cent solution of nitric acid in an iron ladle and add the mercury. Place the ladle over a blacksmith's forge, says Machinery, until the nitric acid boils. The dirt will rise to the top and the mercury, perfectly clean, remain at the bottom. Do not let the mercury boil, the fumes are poisonous.

HOW TO MAKE A MILLING CUTTER WITHOUT BACKING

The ordinary milling cutter, shown in Fig. 1, has the teeth backed off, or, in other words, cut away for clearance between the tooth and the work at all places except the cutting edge. This is a condition that is

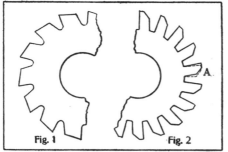

Fig. 1   Fig. 2

Backed and Unbacked Milling Cutters

necessary in all machine tools, and is usually very difficult to obtain. This is especially true of milling machine cutters where the backing is usually done by hand in a special lathe, or in very expensive machines used by tool manufacturers.

To obviate the necessity of backing, the cutter can be made as shown in Fig. 2. Then when it is tempered the teeth will spring back, as shown exaggerated at A, and give a slight clearance at the backs of the teeth.—Contributed by L. G. Harren, 14 Barnett St., New Haven, Conn.

SPARK PLUG EFFICIENCY

A spark plug that emits a long-distance spark outside the cylinder, will not always do the same within the cylinder in the middle of a highly compressed charge, says the Automobile. It may be weak or fail entirely at the critical time. The vigorous spark is the effectual one.

ONE MAN TO CARRY LONG LADDER

One man can carry a long, heavy ladder with ease by using the device illustrated herewith. Little blocks slide along a shaft for adjustment to the ladder's width and

into these blocks the ends of the rails fit. Then by taking the other end of the ladder, one can wheel it to any point desired. The wheel should be made of a piece of plank.

INFLATING AUTO TIRES

For the proper inflation of auto tires a good registering pump is necessary. Press the valve in with the pin in the cap to make sure it does not stick. Raise the pump piston to the top of the cylinder and push all the way to the bottom, says the Automobile, giving full steady strokes. Each time the plunger descends the gauge pointer will fluctuate more or less beyond the center of equilibrium, according to the rapidity of the stroke. To find the constant pressure, a full, slow stroke should be given, and near the end the plunger should be held stationary, equalizing the pressure in the pump and tire. The gauge pointer will then slowly find its balance and remain stationary, pointing to the figures of the real pressure in pounds.

If the tire is inflated with air at 68° F., the increase of pressure by reason of the temperature of the air in the tire being raised by frictional heat will not be sufficient to cause it to burst.

TO PRESERVE HEADS OF STEEL TOOLS

When the head of a cold chisel or other tool becomes flattened as shown at A, do not continue using it but heat to a dull

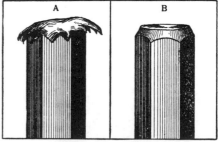

A   B

Effects of Crystallization

red and then dress the head as shown at B. Simply grinding the head, without heating, will not be satisfactory, as the steel is usually crystallized at the flattened end and it is necessary to heat it in order to restore its original life and strength. For this reason the heads of steel tools should be heated occasionally whether flattened or not.—Contributed by Hiram Stitt.

CEMENT FOR SLATE

Switchboards and other articles made of slate, which have become cracked, can be repaired by using a cement made of slate dust and a solution of silicate of soda. If this is worked thoroughly into all the cracks and given a smooth surface it will hardly be noticed when dry and will not crumble or break.—Contributed by Raymond W. Johnson, Wade Park and E. Madison Aves., Cleveland, O.

HOME=MADE ASH-HOE

A worn-out firing scoop makes a light and convenient ash hoe, says a correspondent of

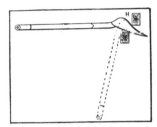

t h e Engineer's Review. Heat the scoop red hot at the point indicated at H in the illustration, having previously prepared a place for bending, as shown. Bend, bringing the handle into the position indicated by the dotted lines, and let the scoop cool. Remove the old shovel handle and replace it with a long hoe handle, which rivet in place.

COLORINGS FOR CEMENT BLOCKS

For red sandstone add 22 lb. of an aggregate iron oxide, called mineral paint, to each barrel of the dry mixture of cement. For lighter shades use less of the coloring matter.

To get a brown shade add Germantown lampblack to the above. For a pleasing gray use the lampblack alone, 2 lb. to the barrel of cement.

A good blue is produced by using 19 lb. of ultramarine to a barrel of cement, and for green use 23 lb. of the ultramarine.

For yellow use 23 lb. of yellow ochre to a barrel of cement; use the same quantity of brown ochre to procure a good brown.

In using these coloring materials mix in a dry state till no streaks are visible, then add water and mix and tamp as before. While the blocks are moist the color will be much darker than when they are dry, it must be remembered.

Always use the least amount of coloring possible to give a good shade, warns the American Carpenter and Builder, as most of the pigments used are of a clayey nature, ill-adapted to stone making.

WHEEL STAND FOR THE SHOP

When working with wheels, washing, painting, or striping them, a wheel stand is a handy device to have in the shop.

To make a wheel stand cut off an old ⅜-in. axle, B, 18 in. from the shoulder and bend it 1½ in. from the shoulder, leaving the front round, a little higher than the collar so the wheel will not run off. Make the other end to fit 6 in. into an iron pipe, A, 8 in. long.

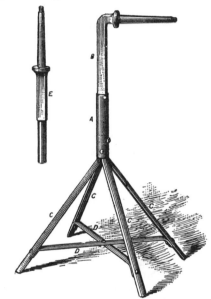

Home=Made Wheel Stand

Make the feet of four pieces of old 1-in. tire, C, 18 in. long. Swage 2 in. of one end of each foot to fit into pipe A from below and bolt together with ³⁄₁₆-in. stove bolts. Take two pieces, D, 23 in. long, and swage and bend them off 1½ in. at both ends to fit against the legs. Rivet them together where they cross at the center. This will leave the round side of the tire up, says the Blacksmith and Wheelwright. The straight piece, E, can be substituted for B and used for face striping spokes. The paint glass may be laid on the end of the hub for convenience.

The electrical conductivity of distilled water is 6,754,000,000 times less than that of copper.—Culley.

HANGERS FOR SUPPORTING PIPE

For supporting pipe do not use a hanger like the one shown in Fig. 1; it is liable to bend off at A, being affected by the expansion and contraction of the pipe. This defect, says the Engineers' Review, can be

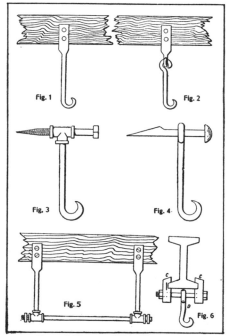

Fig. 1   Fig. 2

Fig. 3   Fig. 4

Fig. 5   Fig. 6

Several Forms of Pipe Hangers

overcome by the method shown in Fig. 2.

Two simple hangers that give good satisfaction are shown in Figs. 3 and 4, while where several pipes of small diameter are run together, the hanger shown in Fig. 5 is good. Hooks like those shown at C C in Fig 6 can be used where I-beams instead of wood joists are used. A hook should be made at the top of the binding bolt at D.

CEMENT FILLING FOR COM-
MUTATORS

The shellac and plaster-of-paris cement commonly used for commutators soon deteriorates as a result of the heat. A better cement, and one which will not carbonize, can be made by mixing plaster-of-paris and a solution of silicate of soda.—Contributed by Raymond W. Johnson, Cleveland, O.

The popular notion that hot water freezes more quickly than cold with air at the same temperature is erroneous.—Trautwine.

SOLDERING ALUMINUM

For soldering aluminum make a solder of 80 per cent tin and 20 per cent zinc, using stearic acid as a flux. Tin the surface of the aluminum with this solder, moving the copper bit backwards and forwards over the metal and flowing the solder, says Machinery. The film of oxide that prevents the ready soldering of the aluminum can then be cleaned off and the metal soldered with either the above-named solder or tinsmiths' solder.

GASOLINE STORAGE TANK FOR
STEAM AUTOMOBILES

Owing to the reduction in price of steam runabouts, there are at present a great number in use all over the country; one fault is the limited storage capacity of the gasoline tank, which furnishes fuel for about 25 to 30 miles. To reduce the possibility of running short of gasoline on the road, I have designed and constructed with great satisfaction a tank to hang on the inside of the dashboard, between the gauges. The same should be constructed of copper with crimped edges, and hung on iron bands bent

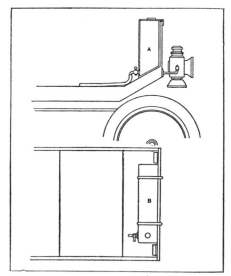

Storage Tank for Automobile

as per the drawing. Have a screw filling cap on top and a tap with short hose on the bottom. The tank can be filled and emptied in its position on the dashboard by use of the hose.

In the drawing A is an elevation and B

a plan view of the tank in position.—Contributed by Prentice P. Avery, Box 311, Ridgewood, N. J.

VOLTAGE INDICATOR FOR SELEC= TIVE RINGING GENERATORS

Constant voltage of the ringing generator is an important matter in exchanges where selective ringing is used on subscribers' lines. A good indicator for showing the variation in voltage is made of lamps placed so as to be constantly under the observation of the wire chief, says the American Telephone Journal. The indicator may be installed as follows:

Connect two switchboard lamps, one to the positive lead and the other to the negative lead as shown in the sketch, inserting the resistance between the lamp and the ringing main. Mount the lamps on the wire chief's test table so that he will see them every time he looks up. As he becomes accustomed to making observation he will be able to detect the slightest variations in pulsations or brilliancy of the lamps. Two 40-volt lamps connected in this way through a 400-ohm resistance have been burning steadily for two months and are as bright as ever.

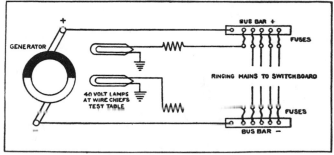

Indicator Lamps Connected

BRACKET FOR USE IN BENDING WOOD

The best woods for bending are ash, hickory, white oak and elm. Ash after being subjected to a steam bath is very pliant and is used extensively for handles. The tight bark or pigment hickory is the best species of this wood for bending, though select parts of three others—peccanut, mocktanut and

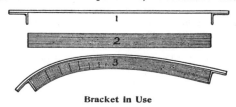

Bracket in Use

shellbark—are used also. White oak when treated by steam bends readily and the bending qualities of elm when given the same treatment are said to excel all others.

In the bending process, the wood does not stretch, but contracts, says the Wood-Worker, and to force the contraction it is necessary to support the side the strain is on and hold the ends from giving. Fig. 1 shows a device for this purpose. It is a piece of strap iron with an iron bracket riveted on each end. Fig. 2 shows how it is fitted to the piece of wood to be bent and Fig. 3 shows the timber after bending, the outside of the curve being of the same length as before and the inside shorter.

HOW TO REMOVE OLD STUDS

While repairing a pump in the plant where I am employed, I had occasion to remove and replace numerous studs on the same.

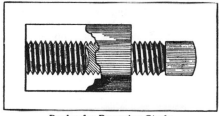

Device for Removing Studs

When there is no shoulder on the stud, a common way to remove it is to use two nuts and by jamming one against the other the stud may be turned by working a wrench on one of the nuts. But in the case of the pump this method could not be used, as the studs, which were all $\frac{5}{8}$-in. diameter, were so close together that there was no room to work a wrench.

I then made the device shown in the sketch. A long nut is made out of hexagon steel and tapped to fit the studs. A set screw is then placed in the nut, and when this is screwed up tight against the end of the stud, the friction of the nut is greater than that of the casting which holds the stud. A wrench may then be used on the long nut, which projects above all the studs, thus allowing a complete revolution of the wrench.—Contributed by John Weldon, 433 Columbia St., Brooklyn, N. Y.

VENTILATING FAN FOR THE SHOP

Make a fan of galvanized iron, screw it to a wood pulley and drive a brass tube through the center of the pulley. Tool a piece of cold rolled ½-in. stock, cut a thread on each end and bolt it to a piece of iron,

Home=Made Ventilating Fan

which in turn bolt to the planer gib. Drill several holes in the iron so the fan can be set over when raising or lowering the head. In the case illustrated the belt is at an angle. This fan could be applied to any power-driven machine, or all of them could be supplied with fans.—Contributed by A. Churchill, 832 E. 32nd St., Portland, Ore.

A SIMPLE HOME=MADE JACK

In putting a new base under a dynamo a jack was necessary for lifting the machine, and the one illustrated was improvised. A ¾-in. bolt 8 in. long, threaded its entire length, and a nut and a piece of pipe were the materials used.

The head of the bolt was placed on the floor beneath the dynamo. Then, by screwing upon the nut, the dynamo was lifted a

Handy Jack

certain amount, and blocked in position. The jack was then raised higher by placing blocks beneath the head of the jack, and the dynamo was again lifted. This mode of lifting was continued until the dynamo was raised sufficiently high to permit of inserting the new base and the removal of the old one.

For the nipple a piece of 1-in. pipe was used, says the Engineers' Review, and stood the strain nicely. A washer between the nut and the nipple improves the jack, and the head of the bolt should rest in a countersunk plate to keep the bolt from traveling.

WIRING FOR GAS ENGINE

It is often difficult to start a gas engine which is ignited by a dynamo and for this reason batteries are used in connection with the dynamo. In the wiring diagram shown in the sketch A is the dynamo, B a two-point switch, and C the spark coil. This wiring is intended for use with make and break engines and will not do for jump-spark engines.

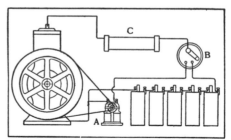

Wiring for Gas Engine

To start the engine place the switch on the right-hand point. This throws the batteries in the circuit, and allows starting the engine with very little effort. Then after the engine has run a few seconds the switch can be turned to the left-hand point, thus throwing out the batteries. With such small demands the batteries will last a long time. —Contributed by H. H. Fountain, 207 9th St., Brooklyn, N. Y.

Greasing the molds, or painting them with coach varnish twice a month will keep cement blocks from sticking. Use the best grade of black coach varnish.

In 1905 the copper product amounted in value to $137,498,727. This is the largest product of copper ever recorded in the United States.

TAR ON THE HANDS

An exchange recommends rubbing the hands with the outside of fresh orange or lemon peel, and wiping dry immediately. It is astonishing what a small piece will clean. The volatile oils in skins dissolve the tar, so that it can be wiped off.

HOW TO PUTTY CRACKS IN FLOORS

Some of the readers of Shop Notes may have had trouble in filling cracks in floors, previous to painting. It seems that no matter how tightly the putty is pressed in with the putty-knife, it will rise out of the cracks and project above the surface of the floor a few days after the paint has been applied, thus producing a very undesirable appearance.

This is usually caused by the presence of dust in the cracks and by applying too much pressure to the putty. As it is almost impossible to fill the cracks without applying considerable pressure to the putty, it becomes necessary to remove the dust or dirt. The necessity of this operation is illustrated in the accompanying sketch. Fig. 1 shows a crack in the floor with a quantity of dust at the bottom. This dust is compressed by the application of the putty, as shown in Fig. 2, and as the compressed dust is somewhat elastic, it tends to expand to its original volume. This results in raising the putty from the cracks as shown in Fig. 3.

In order to prevent this defect, run the pointed end of a file or other pointed object

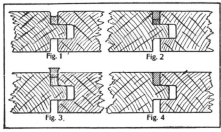

Fig. 1   Fig. 2

Fig. 3.   Fig. 4

Correct and Incorrect Methods of Puttying Cracks

through all the cracks, thus removing all the dust. Then apply turpentine to the cracks by means of an oil can. This soaks into the wood and causes the putty to stick better, at the same time softening the putty and allowing it to fill all parts of the cracks as shown in Fig. 4. Cracks puttied in this

way will remain filled for years and will be practically invisible.

EMERY WHEEL HOLDER FOR LATHE

Having a lathe and emery wheel, but not a wheel holder, I devised the following center for holding the wheel in the lathe:

My emery wheel is 1 in. thick and has a 1-in. hole, so I turned a piece of soft steel

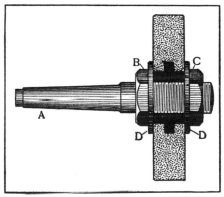

Center with Emery Wheel Attached

1 in. in diameter and 6 in. long to fit the center hole in the lathe, as shown at A in the cut. The other end was threaded for the nuts, B and C, one of which, B, was pinned to the shaft. Both nuts were supplied with washers, D D, as shown.

If desired, a straight piece of steel may be used in place of the tapered piece, but it will then be necessary to either use a chuck or make center holes in each end and use a dog.—Contributed by Donald Reeves, Oak Park, Ill.

STRENGTH OF WOODEN TANKS

The hoops on a wooden tank determine its strength. Flat hoops are less satisfactory than round. Round hoops do not rust so quickly, and are not weakened so much by a little rust as are flat hoops; also, when the tank swells, they are not apt to burst, but sink into the wood, instead.

Cypress, cedar or white pine, free from imperfections and thoroughly dry, are the species of wood advised by the fire insurance authorities for cylindrical wooden tanks. Michigan pine, free from sapwood, is most durable where the tank is exposed to freezing.

STEP LADDER FOR STAIRS

An ordinary step ladder cannot be used on stairways, but by adding the attachment

here shown it can be used in that position with perfect safety. Fasten on an extra pair of legs somewhat shorter than the original legs and arrange so that either pair may be used when wanted. Hooks and eyes may be used on the long legs to hold them against the ladder when using on a stairway, thus making the device easier to move up and down stairs.—Contributed by John Weldon, 433 Columbia St., Brooklyn, New York.

LOOSE PISTON ROD INDICATOR

It sometimes happens (in fact, quite often) that when a piston rod is screwed into the crosshead it will work loose and commence backing out while the engine is running. The clearance is often very small and generally the first hint the engineer gets of something being wrong is a gentle tap, tap, tap of the piston on the cylinder head. In cases where an engine gives this kind of trouble, the expedient illustrated in the sketch will prove useful, says a corre-

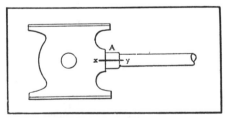

Loose Piston Rod Expedient

spondent of Power. Here A is a jam-nut and X Y is a black stripe of paint, say, ½ in. wide, drawn across the crosshead boss, the jam-nut and along the side of the piston rod. This stripe can be seen quite plainly while the engine is in motion, and if the rod or nut commences to turn, the broken stripe will be noticed immediately.

READING THE WEIGHT OF AN ANVIL

The figures on an anvil indicating its weight form a puzzle to many a smith and mechanic who has not learned how to read them. The figures state the number of gross hundredweight of 112 lb., quarters of hundredweight and the extra pounds, says the American Blacksmith. For instance, the figures 2-1-18 on an anvil mean two hundredweight of 112 lb. each, or 224 lb., plus one quarter hundredweight, or 28 lb., plus extra pounds, 18, amounting in all to 270 lb.

DEVICE FOR CLEANING BOILER TUBES

A simple and good device for cleaning scale from boiler tubes may be made as follows:

To a piece of ¾-in. rod, 18 in. long, weld an angle or cross bar at either end, the bottom piece to be 8 in. long and made square

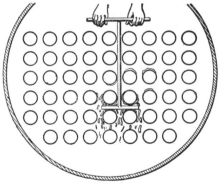

Scale Cleaning Device

to cut the scale, says the Engineers' Review, and the upper piece 12 in. long to serve as a handle.

In using the tool, the bottom or shorter end is shoved down between the tubes and is then used auger fashion. By so doing, the bottom bar is turned crosswise to the tubes, which pushes the scale out from both rows of tubes on either side. By moving along the tubes one is able to clean the entire lot in a very short time. This device removes the scale from the top and bottom tube at the same time, letting the scale fall to the bottom of the boiler, where it can be easily removed.

In tapping out nuts or cutting threads with a die, use good lard oil.

TEMPORARY REPAIR FOR A LARGE PULLEY

A novel method of making a quick repair for a large pulley was used in a large textile finishing plant, where a pulley 84-in. diameter and 36-in. face suddenly broke, at

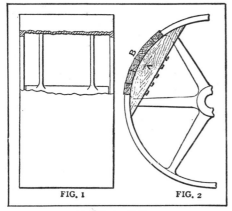

FIG. 1   FIG. 2

Repair for Pulley

a time when the plant was behind in orders, and simply had to run in the shortest possible time. None of the supply houses in the vicinity could furnish a new pulley of the required size, so the master mechanic had to make a temporary repair, which is described by a correspondent of the American Machinist as follows:

The piece of pulley rim broken out was approximately the section between two sets of arms, and was roughly from 2½ to 3 ft. across, as shown in Fig. 1. As the rest of the pulley seemed to be in good condition, he had the carpenters get out some 3x12-in. ash, and prepare four pieces to fit the inside of the pulley rim as at A, Fig. 2. These were placed on each side of the arms, and each pair well bolted together, clamping them firmly to the arms. Some pieces of 4-in. ash were then sawed 36 in. long, and bolted to and across the pieces of 3x12, allowing the bolts to pass down between the pieces, countersinking the heads and using nuts and washers underneath. B, Fig. 2, shows the pieces in place. In the meantime a small engine had been moved into a convenient position for driving a section of this shaft, and the pulley and the cross slide from the shop planer had been rigged to hold the tool for turning, so it was a matter of a few minutes only to turn off the section of wood down to the size of the pulley.

Then the nearest coupling was loosened, and the pulley and section of shaft removed to some convenient horses for balancing. It took 136 lb. of lead to do this, and as it was run in between the pieces of 3x12 ash, there was little fear of its getting loose.

After erection, the main belt was replaced and the plant ran on the same as usual for over two months before it was removed to be replaced by the new pulley, and even then it seemed just as good as the day it was repaired.

HOW TO FORGE A GOOD WRENCH

The directions for forging this wrench, as given by a correspondent of the Blacksmith and Wheelwright, are as follows: First take a file or good buggy spring, according to the size of the wrench wanted, as in Fig. 1. Forge this down 1 in. or 1½ in. from the end, as shown in Fig. 2. Then forge a T on each end and keep the corners round (Fig. 3). Then turn each T on the horn of the anvil and bring one end around a trifle farther than the other, as in Fig. 4. In finishing trim off the ends and square up to suit the nut (Fig. 5). In this way

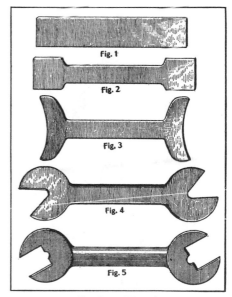

Forging a Wrench

the grain of the steel is forged around each prong, thus making it a good, strong wrench. Never punch a hole and cut it out, as this will make the prongs cross-grained.

CEMENTING A WATCH CRYSTAL

Anyone can cement a loose watch crystal in place and so avoid the necessity of going to the jeweler's with it. Remove the bezel from the case, place the crystal in position and melt enough sulphur flour to run in around the glass. Heat the bezel and crystal over an alcohol lamp until the sulphur runs down in the groove and around the glass, then let it cool. When cooled, remove all the sulphur that remains outside the groove. This makes a water and dust proof joint and also holds the crystal firmly.—Contributed by M. D. Schaefermeyer, Hayden, Colo.

THE RAIL=SPLITTER'S KIT

A rail-splitter's outfit, such as was used by Abraham Lincoln, is shown in the accompanying illustration. The kit consists of several ironwood wedges (tough wood with a fine grain); a couple of iron wedges to start the splitting process, an ax and a "beetle." The "beetle" (shown in the background) is usually made by the rail-splitter himself, says Wood Craft, and is used for driving the wedges.

In splitting rails, the ax is struck into the end of the log and the two iron wedges

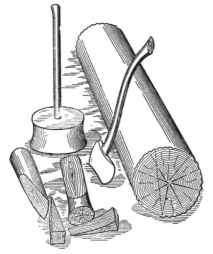

For Splitting Rails

are then driven into the opening made. As the opening extends along the length of the log the wooden wedges are driven in until at last the log is in two parts. These large pieces are cut up into smaller ones in the same way.

HOW TO MAKE A REVERSING RHEOSTAT

A reversing rheostat for changing either the direction or speed of a motor by the operation of one handle can be made by following the diagram shown in the sketch. A and B are copper contacts, A being insu-

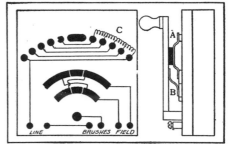

Reversing Rheostat

lated from the handle and B connected to it. The resistance coils, C, give the necessary resistance for decreasing the speed.

When the handle is in the center the motor will not move, but when moved to either side the motor will revolve, the direction of the revolution being changed by swinging the lever over to the opposite side.—Contributed by Donald Reeves, Oak Park, Ill.

POWER FROM WINDMILLS

While windmills, as far as we can determine, have very rarely been used for compressing air, there is no reason, however, why they should not be adapted to this purpose. A windmill with a 12-ft blade is commonly rated at 2 hp., and one with a 16-ft. blade is rated at 4 hp. If this power were utilized for compressing air, the results obtained would be as follows:

2 hp. will compress 9.6 cu. ft. of free air per min. to 100 lb. gauge.

2 hp. will compress 11 cu. ft. of free air per min. to 80 lb. gauge.

4 hp. will compress 19 cu. ft. of free air per min. to 100 lb. gauge.

4 hp. will compress 22 cu. ft of free air per min. to 80 lb. gauge.

The above results were calculated on the assumption that 15 per cent be allowed for friction in the air compressor, but as stated by a correspondent of Browning's Industrial Magazine, the allowance for an apparatus of this kind should probably be greater.

It is not considered practicable to use wind power for the generation of electricity.

HOW TO MAKE A SUN DIAL

As sun dials are coming into use again, it might interest the readers of Shop Notes to know how they are made. In making a sun dial it is very important that the angle of the screen or upright piece (see Fig. 1), should be equal to the latitude of the place

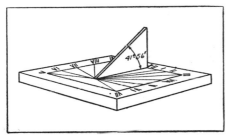

Fig. 1--Sun Dial for Latitude of Chicago

where the dial is to be used. A sun dial which will give the time accurately in one locality, will therefore be inaccurate when moved either north or south any considerable distance. For instance, the dial shown in Fig. 1, which is designed for use in Chicago, would be unsuitable for New Orleans, but if moved straight east or west its time-keeping qualities would not be disturbed.

The latitude of any place can be found by consulting suitable maps. The correct angle for Chicago is 41° 56′ or practically 42°, and for New York it is 40° 43′. The object of making the angle of the screen equal to the latitude, is to have the edge of the screen parallel with the earth's axis, a condition absolutely essential in an accurate dial. It is therefore necessary that the dial, after being made, should be placed in an exactly horizontal position and also that the screen should point directly north and south, the large end being placed toward the north. The screen should also be set exactly perpendicular to the face of the dial.

The material of the dial may be metal, well-seasoned wood, or any other substance which will not warp or change its shape, and it can be made with a round or square base, as may be desired. In marking the divisions of the hours there are two general methods; one in which the divisions are determined by trial and the other in which they are calculated by mathematics and geometrical constructions.

In the former method the dial is placed in the sun in the correct position and the edge of the shadow marked at the end of

each hour. It is necessary to take a reading each hour because the spaces are not all equal, as in a clock, but are shorter at noon and longer in the evening and morning, as shown in Fig. 2. While the consecutive hour spaces are not equal they are all symmetrical from the 12 o'clock mark in the center. Thus the space from 12 to 1 is equal to the space from 11 to 12; 10—11 is equal to 1—2; 9—10 equals 2—3, etc. This rule may be applied in checking the results to see that they are accurate.

The latter method, although more ingenious, is not practical, as the theoretical results obtained by calculation are subject to sources of error such as refraction. It is well known that the sun is visible for some time after it has set, this phenomenon being due to the bending of the rays as they pass obliquely through the atmosphere, and the theoretical division of the spaces on a dial will therefore be inaccurate.

The correct divisions of the hours being

Fig. 2--Dial Spaced for Latitude of New York

obtained, they may be either painted or scratched on the surface of the dial, which will then be complete. If desired, the half and quarter hour divisions may also be marked, although they may be readily calculated by the eye when not so inscribed.

◆ ◆ ◆

To soften putty on glass and frames of windows, paint it over with nitric or muriatic acid. In an hour's time it may be easily removed.

CUTTING A BELT

A driving belt 8 ft. long, for a lathe, was cut out of a piece of leather 6 in. square by a mechanic by the following method:

The corners were cut off, leaving the

Cutting a Small Belt

leather circular. Then he cut around the circumference for about 1 in. to the required width of the belt, and fixed a bradawl in a bench, with a knife opposite, at a distance of the width (⅜ in.) of what he wished the belt to be, and another bradawl to steady the cut through, as indicated in sketch, and placing the end of the belt which he had cut between knife and bradawl, drew the whole belting between this space, the knife cutting the belt to an even width.

◆ ◆ ◆

GUARD FOR BELT

To prevent a belt from swinging and striking the frame of the generator, a correspondent of the Engineer's Review at-

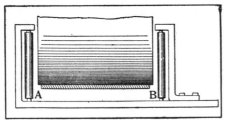

Guide for Belts

tached a guard as shown in the illustration. The guard is made from ½x1½-in. iron; the rollers, A and B, are made of ¾-in. pipe and are set with about ½ in. clearance on each side when the belt is standing.

◆ ◆ ◆

For filling holes in castings, use a metal made of 9 parts lead, 2 parts antimony and 1 part bismuth. This metal expands in cooling.

AIR CUSHION IN BELT

In a plant where a 57-k. w. generator was used as a motor to drive a line of shafting, the paper pulley on the motor being 16 in. by 12 in.; the pulley on the line shaft, 72 in. by 12 in., making 190 r. p. m.; the belt of five-ply rubber of good quality and the distance between centers about 17 ft., a pounding occurred at a certain point at each revolution of the belt, increasing in force each time. It was not convenient to stop the motor, and though the belt was not loose, a tightener was applied as indicated in the sketch, in the hope of stopping the pounding, but without success.

At noontime, when the motor was stopped, examination showed that the outer layers of canvas and rubber were detached for almost the entire length of the belt, while the edges still held together, and a cushion of

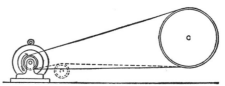

Location of Tightener

air a foot long and 3½ in. thick had formed in the interior of the belt, causing the pounding. The belt was then perforated with a ½-in. belt punch throughout its entire length, the holes being located a foot apart and staggered. This did not stop the pounding immediately, but gradually diminished its force until only a click could be heard, says a correspondent of Power, and for many days after one could feel the air being forced out through the holes at one point.

◆ ◆ ◆

The heat of one pound of coal will convert from five to eight pounds of water into steam in ordinary locomotive practice.

◆ ◆ ◆

TO KEEP CONTENTS OF WOODEN PAILS FROM TASTING OF THE WOOD

Water or anything else for "internal use" kept in a wooden pail is apt to taste of the wood. To prevent this, says the Practical Carpenter, fill the pail with boiling hot water and let stand until the water is cold; then empty the pail and wash the inside with a solution of soda in lukewarm water, with a little lime added, after which scald the pail and rinse carefully.

SACKHOLDER FOR VEGETABLE PICKERS

A sackholder which I improvised last year, when something of the kind seemed a necessity, is shown in the accompanying illustration. I raise many acres of winter vegetables and employ many pickers, and

Tripod Sackholder

the holder saves time and labor. When the sack is full, a pull on one leg of the tripod lets the whole weight of the sack on the ground, and it may then be easily unhooked from the filler. In large acreage, there should be one holder at each side of the patch.—Contributed by Chas. H. Sebree, Monrovia, Cal.

HOW TO MAKE POISON FLY PAPER

Take 1 lb. quassia chips, put them into 2½ qt. water and let stand for 24 hours. Then pour off the liquid and boil it down to 1 qt. Now put the same chips used before into 1½ qt. water and boil down to 1 pt. Pour off the liquid while warm and put in 10 oz. dark brown sugar. When the sugar is dissolved, mix the two liquids. When cool, soak pieces of blotting paper in the liquid for a minute, then take them out and drain and dry them. The paper can be laid away for use at some future time, if desired. To use, place a piece of the paper in a small plate, put a little water on it and set it wherever convenient. —Contributed by F. S. Cummings, 289 Forsyth Av., Detroit, Mich.

DETAILS OF HOME=MADE SHOWER BATH

The home-made shower bath for factories described in Shop Notes for June, 1906, interested so many people and elicited so many inquiries that we publish the accompanying sketch giving further details of its construction.

The bath consists of a cylindrical casing 42 in. in diameter and 90 in. high, made of No. 22 galvanized iron. The casing is intended to rest in a copper tray or bottom

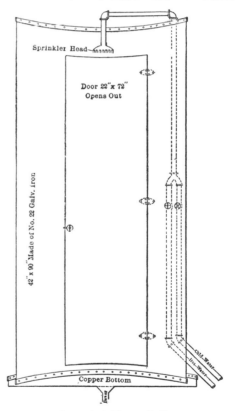

Convenient Shower Bath

which is connected with the sewer and prevents water from overflowing upon the floor.

At the top of the casing is a shower head with hot and cold water connections. In the side of the casing is a door 22 in. x 72 in., which opens out.

CHEST FOR STOVE JOBBER'S KIT

For carrying the stove jobber's kit a small metal chest, such as illustrated, is most convenient and suitable. The top part is for the tools, comprising one brace with chuck and drills, center and rivet punches, cold

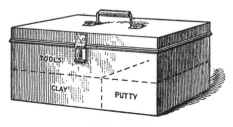

A Handy Kit

chisels, screwdriver, hammer, pliers, hand snips, files and a small trowel.

The bottom, says a correspondent of the Metal Worker, has spaces for fire clay and stove putty and compartments for wire, stove bolts and similar supplies.

PORTABLE FORGE FOR THE SHOP

The accompanying illustration shows a portable forge, which was designed and constructed in one of the large railway shops, where it has proved to be very useful and convenient.

Either coal or charcoal can be used for fuel, says the Railway Review, and by making slight alterations and adding a suitable tank, oil may be used.

The top frame, a plan detail of which is shown in the illustration, should be made of ¼-in. sheet steel, but the hood may be made of lighter material. The device is intended for use in shops where compressed air is used, which can be supplied by means of nipples permitting a coupling direct to the compressed air connections.

FASTENING STEEL TOOLS IN THEIR HANDLES

When the steel tool comes out of its handle, fill the handle with powdered rosin and a little rottenstone, says the Practical Carpenter, then heat the tang of the tool red-hot and push it into the handle. When cold the tool will be held firmly in place.

TO REMOVE DISCOLORATION FROM IRON AND STEEL

When iron or steel has been colored blue by exposure to heat, try rubbing it lightly with a sponge or rag dipped in sulphuric, nitric or hydrochloric acid, until the discoloration is removed. Then wash the metal, dry by rubbing, warm it and give a coat of oil so it will not rust.

When boilers leak along a seam or about a flue, try putting a pint of cornmeal in the boiler.

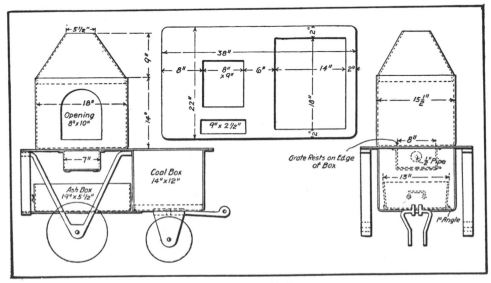

Home-Made Portable Forge

SHOP NOTES

UNDERCUT COMMUTATORS

It has been found to be good practice to undercut the mica, to the depth of about 1-32 in. between the commutator bars on all of the larger types of both direct and alternating current commutator type railway motors. It is claimed of commutators so treated that the heating from poor commutation, which in the untreated commutator is caused chiefly by unequal wearing of mica

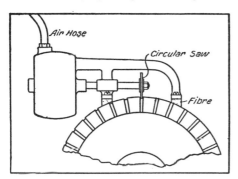

For Undercutting Commutator Insulation

and copper, is reduced to a minimum, also that it is not necessary to use as heavy a spring tension, which cuts down brush friction and its consequent heating. It also reduces the breakage and chipping of carbons by cutting out the hammer effect which is produced by running over a roughened surface with a 7- or 8-lb. spring tension.

The method adopted by one of the largest manufacturers is clearly shown in the illustration, and needs but a few words of explanation. The armature which is to have its commutator under-cut is set up on a couple of horses, and the tool (see sketch) is started in the groove at the inside end of the commutator.

The tool consists of a small air motor with an extended shaft and an outboard bearing. On the outer end of the shaft is placed a small circular saw, about 1-32 in. by ¾ in. Two blocks of fiber, cut to the arc of the commutator, are riveted to the outboard bearings, to act as guides, also as gauges to prevent the saw from cutting too deepl-

After the mica is under-cut the commutator is cleaned up and polished in a lathe; then the armature is subjected to a bar to bar resistance test. A current is applied to the winding on any two adjacent bars and the voltage read; comparative readings are then made on all of the bars around the commutator, 1-2, 2-3, 3-4, 4-5, etc.

A good substitute for the air motor would be a heavy flywheel with a pedal arrangement and a flexible shaft, similar to a dentist's drill, only larger.—Contributed by G. D. H.

TO DRILL CAVITIES OF ANY DE-SIRED SHAPE

This may be easily done by employing a steel finger, A, shown in plan at B. The finger is made of tool steel, hardened, and is made concave along the edge, to fit the radius of the drill. To make the cavity, first drill a hole the required depth and then move the work along and drill again, using the steel finger to guide the drill and prevent springing or breaking it. Continue in this way until the desired shape is obtained.

The manner of holding the finger in position is not shown in the cut, as each problem presents different conditions and requires individual treatment. In my work a cylindrical piece requires a cavity in one end, so I made a collar to fit the cylinder

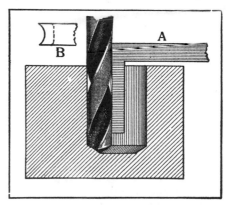

Drilling an Oval Shaped Cavity

and then fastened the finger to the collar with a cap screw. The finger was enlarged and slotted to receive the cap screw and thus allowed the necessary adjustment. But the manner of fastening the finger, A, can be changed to suit the work, and if not objectionable can be fastened to the work itself.—Contributed by L. G. Warren, 14 Barnett St., New Haven, Conn.

HOW TO MAKE AN ALCOHOL BLOW=TORCH

A good alcohol blow-torch suitable for soldering and experimental work can be made from an old bicycle pump and a piece of rubber tubing. Cut the handle and piston off the small tube and pinch one end of the tube together with a vise or a pair of pliers. If not then airtight it should be soldered. Drill a 1-32-in. hole about ½ in. from the

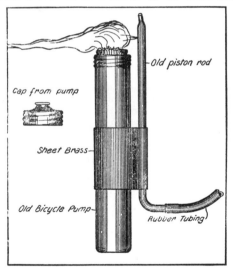

Home=Made Alcohol Blow-Torch

end, or if you have no drill that small, use a brad and small hammer.

Bend a piece of sheet brass to fit the cylinders snugly and solder the tube to it as shown. Then attach the rubber tubing to the lower end of the brass tube. Fill the cylinder with a piece of torch wick and pour alcohol in the top. Then light the wick and adjust the blast tube to give the desired form of flame.

Solder a small piece of tin over the hole in the cap and use it as a cover for the torch when not in use. This prevents the alcohol evaporating.—Contributed by B. Washington, Bar Harbor, Maine.

FRUIT PICKING LADDERS

An ordinary ladder is not suitable for fruit picking, as it cannot be placed near the edges of the tree where the fruit is most abundant. A step ladder is a little better, but is usually very unstable, as one leg is

Ladders for Picking Fruit

usually off the ground. The ladders shown in the accompanying illustration, from the Rural New-Yorker, are the kind generally used for fruit picking, although the single pole ladder at the left is considered dangerous by many. The middle one is perhaps the most preferable, as it has a wide base and wide steps.

DEVICE FOR RURAL TELEPHONE INSPECTION

Telephone linemen, who frequently have occasion to call the home office or one of the stations, will find the following device very useful and convenient. This contrivance, which was designed by a correspondent of the American Telephone Journal, has been found to make the inspector's work more easily accomplished than if he carried climbers and put them on and climbed up a pole each time he wished to make a test.

The device consists simply of a triple jointed cane tube, which may be put together

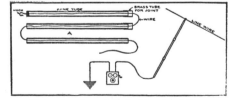

Extension Cane Pole for Tapping Wires

in the same way as a fish pole. It carries a wire or lamp cord through the center, terminating in a hook and fastened in a plug at the upper end. The wire at the lower end may be terminated in suitable snaps for fastening to a telephone or test box. If it is used on a grounded line a ground rod and mallet may be carried, and still the work of connecting to a line and talking is easier than is possible for a person who has to hold tightly to a pole without cross arms. Of course, a double cane would be necessary for a metallic line. This device may be carried in a buggy or on a horse's back, and as it weighs but a few ounces and can be put together in a few seconds, it has given very good results in actual service.

TO REPAIR LEAKY VALVES

When the brass seats of globe and angle valves become worn so that they leak badly the device here illustrated will be found useful. Remove the bonnet from the valve and clamp on the iron piece, A, which is made by cutting out a piece of sheet iron or steel as at B, and bending the three legs down and tapping to receive the three thumb screws.

A bushing, C, will be required, and should

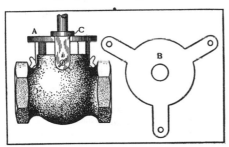

Valve Grinding Jig

have a hole just large enough to admit the valve stem. By making a number of bushings of different sizes the device may be used on different sized valves.

To grind a valve, replace the bonnet with the jig as shown and put a little emery dust and oil on the valve seat. Then turn the stem, first in one direction and then in the opposite direction, at the time applying vertical pressure to make the emery take hold. Valves ground in this way are just as good as new and unless very badly worn or cut by the steam can be easily and quickly repaired.—Contributed by Scott H. Phillips, Fairmount, W. Va.

The world's annual production of raw silk is 61,000,000 lb., of which China produces one-half and Japan one-fourth.

HOW TO MAKE A WATER WHEEL

Make a wooden hub, A (see sketch), and bore to fit the shaft, B. Fasten a number of soup ladles to the hub, as shown, and connect with metal strips, C C. These may be obtained from the handles of the ladles, if of sufficient length, and should be firmly soldered together.

The outside casing may be constructed of wood or heavy galvanized iron and should

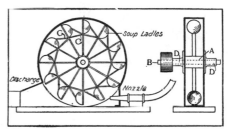

Home-Made Water Motor

be strong enough to support the bearings, D D. These may be made of pieces of pipe with flanges screwed on the ends, the pipes being then poured with babbitt, or they may be made from castings of a wood pattern made specially for the purpose.

The nozzle may be constructed of heavy galvanized iron, well soldered together and fastened to the base, as shown. If the wheel is well balanced and the bearings carefully made a motor of this kind will run up to 3,000 revolutions per minute.—Contributed by Lee R. Clarke, Bozeman, Mont.

RENUMBERING SCALES

A novel method of renumbering scale beams, which through continual use and exposure to smoke, dust or other substances, have become very indistinct, is described by a correspondent of the American Miller as follows:

You can always have nice, visible white figures on your scales without employing an

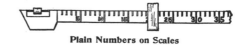

Plain Numbers on Scales

expert painter to renumber them, simply by taking a piece of common white chalk and rubbing it over the numbers on the beam. You can make your one-half pound marks blue and the pound marks white by employing chalk of those colors.

AN UNIVERSAL WASHER

All machinists know that when a nut is tapped out of true and then screwed up tight, the strain will all come on one side of the threads. In the case of milling machine arbors and other devices requiring great accuracy, the threaded portion is liable

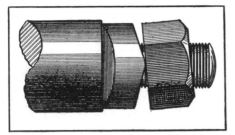

Washer for Inaccurate Nuts

to be damaged, either by being sprung, or by having the threads stripped.

To prevent this happening, I devised the washer shown in the sketch, which is drawn greatly exaggerated, in order to make it plain. Each face of the washer is beveled off at two opposite edges, leaving a ridge across the middle, the ridges on each side being at right angles to each other, so that only one shows in the sketch. The hole in the washer being a little larger than the screw allows the washer to swing and thus take up the inaccuracy of the nut.—Contributed by Wm. Rosenblohm, 997 Hancock St., Brooklyn, N. Y.

CELLAR VENTILATION

The accompanying sketch shows a system of cellar ventilation, which is described by a correspondent of the Rural New-Yorker as follows:

In building the cellar wall, build in on each side a line of 2 or 3-in. drain pipe, emptying

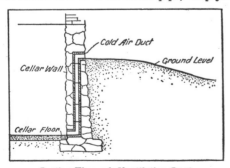

Section Through Ventilating Duct

into the cellar just above the floor, and into the open air just above the ground level. During the summer these can be left open, and the cool air of early morning will flow in, and the cellar will be cool and pleasant all day. During the winter they can be closed except when it is desirable to ventilate or air the cellar, which can be done better and with less danger of frost by opening these ducts than it can be by opening windows.

REPAIRING WASHED OUT TRESTLE

One of our readers, Geo. W. Crumb, of Bloomfield, Mo., formerly president of the Missouri Southwestern Railroad (now a part of the 'Frisco system), tells how, a few years ago, he had to repair a washed out trestle approach to a river bridge on his small line, using 40-ft. piling, a pendulum driver mounted on a flat car and operated by a detached portable engine, drum and ordinary drop head. He says: I discovered that the piston head of the driver engine was so worn that it wasted a large part of the steam and power and that its boiler was unsafe. No machine shop was accessible. To obviate these difficulties, I disconnected the pile-driver engine from its boiler and connected it, by 50 ft., or more, of pipe to the boiler-head of the locomotive. To make it elastic and allow for the "slack" between the locomotive tender and the driver car, I put in a flexible joint, over the coupling (draw-head made with six "ells"), three short nipples and two pieces of pipe, 4-ft. long and a union, making, with the union, four joints, the 4-ft. pieces of pipe extending upward and joined at the top, thus allowing plenty of lost motion, or "slack." Then I put a suitable sheave in a heavy strap shackle, attached it to the top of the trip shackle for the hammer and passed the hammer hoisting rope down from the driver head under the special sheave and back to the gallows head, where it was made fast. This, of course, doubled the pull of the pile-driver engine and made it ample for the 2,000-lb. hammer. The flexible joint worked with very little leakage. The piling was delivered a thousand feet from the washout, at the side of the track, each stick being pulled in front of the leads by the driver engine and the hoisting line raised in the clear and the whole train was then run to the washout (1,000 ft.), adjusted, the piling placed between the leads and driven from 12 to 15 ft. Within two days, in midwinter, in a continuous snow and rain storm, with six men, we drove four bents (16 pieces of piling), put on caps, stringers and ties and ran the train across the break, the piling being all driven in a swollen stream. Of course, large railroads are always prepared for such emergencies.

A SHORT=ORDER BEAM COMPASS

A friend of mine, having need of a beam compass in a land where there was none,

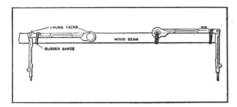

Beam Compass Made From Ordinary Compass

hit upon a scheme as illustrated by the sketch, writes a correspondent of Machinery. He dismantled the compass belonging to his drawing set and fastened the needle-point end firmly to a stick about one-half inch square, and of the desired length. This fastening was accomplished by first notching one side of the stick to admit the hinge of the compass leg, so it might lie squarely on top, and tying it with stout cord. The pencil leg was fastened by a thumb-tack through the eye, another on top to prevent "back-lash," and some rubber bands. This part, by the way, was placed at the side and not on top of the beam. The radius was easily adjusted by removing the two thumb-tacks and sliding the pencil leg to the right location. Once constructed, the compass worked as well as an expensive beam compass.

LAYING OUT SEGMENTS

When it is necessary to saw out a lot of segment pieces, such as are used over door and window frames, says the Wood-Worker, proceed as follows:

Suppose the segments are to be 48 in. long with a rise of 4 in.: Square one-half the length (24 in.), which gives 576; square the rise, which gives 16; add 576 and 16, ob-

Laying Out Segments

taining 592; divide 592 by twice the rise (2×4=8), which gives 74 in., the radius. This rule may be used in any case.

WINDING LONG SPRINGS

There are many methods of winding springs in a lathe, but in the following plan, which has been used successfully by a correspondent of the American Machinist, the length of the spring will be limited only by the length of the wire:

The only thing to be made is a mandrel, Fig. 1, the length depending on the size of wire; for No. 20 B. & S. gage, 1½ in. is long enough. The diameter of the small part, C, to be the same size as an ordinary mandrel for winding the same size spring, the angle to be about 45 degrees, the larger diameter, A, to be as large as possible without giving a permanent set to the spring, and its length to be three times the pitch of the spring.

The end, B, is tapered so as to let the spring slide off easily. It will generally be

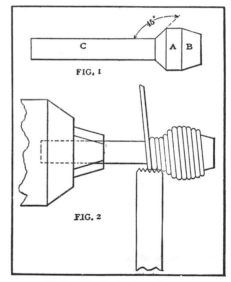

Spring Winder for Long Springs

found that each problem will require some "cut and try" on account of the variations of the temper in the material of which the wire is constructed.

To wind the spring, place the mandrel in a lathe chuck. Select a thread chaser of about the pitch of the spring you are to wind, place it in the tool post in a position to bear evenly on the mandrel. Wind the small straight part of the mandrel full of wire by hand with the free end toward the point. Push the spring thus made over the larger part of the mandrel till you have but 3 or 4 turns left on the small part. Bring up the chaser so as to engage these turns and start the lathe (see Fig. 2).

The pitch of the spring will be modified by the distance between the chaser teeth, the bevel of the mandrel and the angle of the bevel. The shorter the distance between the chaser and the bevel and the steeper the bevel, the closer the spring will be wound.

A HOME=MADE GAS GENERATOR

A gas generator, suitable for use in a country residence, is described by a correspondent of the Model Engineer and Electrician as follows: The generator is designed for producing gas from gasoline by forcing air through a chamber containing the gasoline, thereby saturating the air with

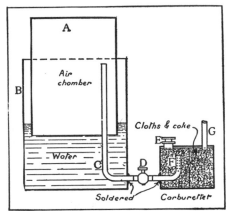

Small Gas Generator for Illuminating

gasoline fumes and making a combustible gas.

The gas made in this way is too rich to be an explosive mixture, i. e., the amount of air contained in it is insufficient to support combustion, but if the gasoline becomes nearly exhausted an explosive mixture is then formed and the flame from the burner is liable to strike back and ignite the mixture in the generator. As the amount of gas contained in the generator is very small, the effect of such an explosion would probably be of little consequence, but it is well to take all precautions and keep the carburettor well filled with gasoline.

The burners used with this device must be of the incandescent type. The ordinary fish-tail burners are useless; they would burn without shedding any light. With burners with mantles the light produced is equal to electric light.

The generator may be described as fol-

lows: A and B are two dust bins; B is 4 in. larger in diameter than A. A is put open end downwards into the water in tank B, care being taken to get them water-tight and air-tight. About 1 in. from bottom of B is a piece of tube, ⅜ in. diameter, with a bend as shown at C, and runs the same height as dust bin. A tap at D (this regulates the air from chamber to carburettor, and also gas from carburettor to burners). If it does not make enough gas, all that is required is to put a weight on top of A. The drawback of the apparatus is that when all the air is used the tank A has to be pulled up and the burners lit again. The tube F in the carburettor is perforated with holes. The carburettor is a biscuit tin with a few sponge cloths hanging down from wires soldered to the top of tin. It is then filled up with coke the size of walnuts; this helps to soak up the gasoline. E is a plug for filling and G is the supply to burners.

ELECTRICALLY PRODUCED STEEL

The enormous amount of energy that is now going to waste in the unused water power at Trallhatta, Sweden, will soon be converted into electrical energy, to be used in the production of steel in the large mill about to be constructed there. The plant will be operated under the Kjelin patents, in which the ore is reduced in large electric furnaces. As the ore deposits are very extensive and the available water power enormous, the steel will no doubt be produced at a great profit. The first plant will be from 10,000 to 15,000 hp. and will turn out about 500,000 tons annually.

VENT NECESSARY IN WATER MUF= FLER FOR TWO=CYCLE GAS ENGINE

The water muffler described in Shop Notes for October will work all right with a 4-cycle engine, but if used in connection with a 2-cycle engine it may happen that the partial vacuum produced in starting would draw water into the cylinder and cause trouble. To prevent this, drill a small hole in the pipe above the water level.—Contributed by D. H. Reeves, 645 Iowa St., Oak Park, Ill.

At Portland, Oregon, recently, 25,000,000 ft. of lumber was loaded: 20,000,000 ft. on vessels for foreign ports, and 5,000,000 ft. for home ports. That city is said to be the greatest lumber port in the world.

REMOVABLE ANCHOR BOLT FOR ENGINE FOUNDATION

The anchor bolts generally used for engine foundations cannot be removed and for that reason cannot be renewed when broken. The accompanying sketch shows a new form of anchor bolt which was used suc-

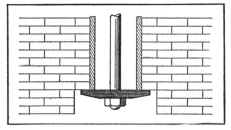

Lower End of Anchor Bolt

cessfully by a correspondent of the Engineers' Review.

In this case a different method of putting in the anchor bolts was employed than usual. The bottom of the bolts were not secured firmly in the foundation, but spaces were provided for them, and they were put in place after the foundation was furnished. This method of placing anchor bolts is a good one, as it allows for removing them in case one becomes broken at any time after the engine gets to running, without damaging the foundation.

HOW TO CLEAN A BOILER

A very useful and efficient boiler cleaning hoe can be made as shown in Fig. 1. The bottom is made to conform to the curve of

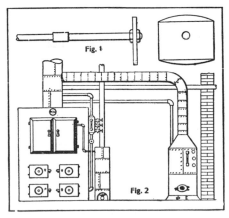

Boiler Cleaning Hoe and Auxiliary Boiler

the boiler shell and is made just large enough to pass through the front manhole, says a correspondent of the Engineers' Review.

A small boiler to assist in cleaning a large one will soon pay for itself in time when the large boiler comprises the plant. Fig. 2 shows such an auxiliary boiler for cleaning. The boiler should have the steam piped to the feed pump of the large boiler, and a feed line from the same piped to the small boiler. On cleaning day let the water out of the large boiler and open it up. Have about 40 to 50 lb. steam pressure in the small boiler and attach a hose to the discharge pipe of the feed pump, and proceed to wash out the boiler.

It can be seen that with an arrangement of this kind the engineer or fireman can wash a boiler out clean under a good pressure.

DISPOSING OF OIL ENGINE ODORS

Offensive odors from oil engines can be disposed of by turning a portion of the jacket water into the exhaust line and conducting it into a cesspool, says a corre-

Destroys Offensive Odors

spondent of the Metal Worker. Make the cesspool about 8 ft. deep by 5 ft. in diameter, of field stone, with a brick arch and a cast-iron rim and cover, as illustrated. Between 2 and 3 ft. above the bottom of the cesspool take a 5-in. pipe out of the side and carry it up a distance of 10 or 12 ft.

To avoid the treacherous back kick when starting the motor the automobilist should learn to crank with his left hand, which throws the hand and arm out of the path of the recoiling crank.

HOME-MADE REVOLVING STOOL

The materials required for this handy revolving stool are: A piece of hard wood 1½ in. thick and cut out in a circle for the top, B; a piece of hard wood 1½ in. thick, octagonal in shape, for a base, C, for the legs and flange; three legs, D, 17 in. long, sawed from an old rake handle; a piece of 1-in. pipe, E, 8½ in. long with a 1-in. thread on one end and a 6¾-in. thread on the other end;

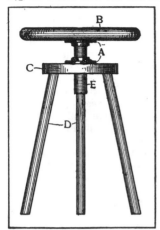

Home-Made Stool

two flanges, A, to fit the threads on the pipe; eight stove bolts, 2 in. long, to hold the flanges to the top and base, and three 3-in. screws to hold the legs in the base.

Countersink the holes for the heads of the stove bolts and the screws. When all the parts are put together sandpaper the wood until smooth and apply a coat of varnish. The stool will cost about 30 cents.—Contributed by Godfrey Aman, Dolgeville, New York.

HOW TO MAKE A CLAMP HANDLE FOR A FILE

In filing large work, such as elevator guides, connecting rods for large engines and other surfaces which are longer than the file, it is necessary to provide means for holding the file without lifting any portion of the file from the work.

Such a device is shown in the accompanying illustration, where the dimensions are given for a file 1⅝ in. wide. A file is placed in the clamp and the nut tightened, and it is then ready to use.—Contributed by John Weldon, 433 Columbia St., Brooklyn, N. Y.

WHY BRICKS ARE MADE SMALL

How much easier it is to criticize than to do better! We view the results of another's life labor and seem to discern at once some chance of improvement, which has evidently been overlooked by the expert, who has given all his time and energy to the problem.

A recent example of this tendency is illustrated in the proposed large size building brick. Instead of the ordinary standard size brick, which is only 8 in. by 4 in. by 2¼ in., a brick 3 ft. long, 8 in. wide, and 2½ in. thick has been suggested. It has been pointed out that bricks of this size would require less labor in laying; would make stronger and better walls, and among other advantages, would be immune against earthquakes.

Brick manufacturers discovered many years ago that there are many advantages and disadvantages to be found in either large or small bricks, and after a careful study of all the conditions, decided to compromise on a brick which should have as many advantages and as few disadvantages as possible. This investigation resulted in the adoption of the present standard size, which is 8 in. by 4 in. by 2¼ in.

There are many reasons why the large brick mentioned above would not be practical. In the first place it would be almost impossible to handle a "green" brick of that size, without bending and stretching it, and the process of burning would be more difficult, and would invariably result in warping and distortion. Bricks of that size would not conform to the standard size window boxes, door frames, and other building material.

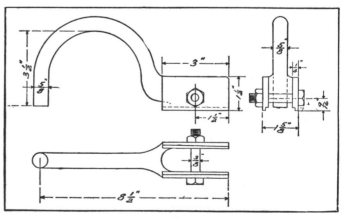

File Handle for Large Work

A HOME=MADE FOOT=POWER EMERY WHEEL

The accompanying engraving shows a foot-power emery wheel stand which I made and am using in my shop for grinding small tools such as cold chisels and drill·bits, says a correspondent of the American Blacksmith. I used ¾-in. gas pipe for the legs and top pieces, and four ¾-in. elbows. The pipes were threaded and screwed into the elbows and the legs were then bent as shown in the engraving. I then used ½-in. pipe flattened at the ends and arranged

angular shaped hole into which a piece of ¾-in. pipe 5 in. long is fitted. For the crank shaft I use a ¾-in. rod, and after drilling a ¼-in. hole through the hub of the wheel and shaft, fasten them together. Any practical craftsman can make an emery wheel stand with little or no cost. An emery wheel suitable for this stand would be about 8 in. in diameter by ½ in. thick. If a suitable belt or fly-wheel can be secured from some discarded farm implement it will save the

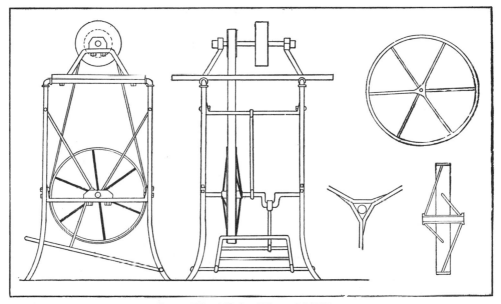

Emery Wheel Made of Pipes and Fittings

them as leg braces, putting them together with ¼-in. bolts. The top of the frame is 14 in. square from center to center of elbows and is bolted on a 14 by 18 in. board for the table. The brackets which hold the shaft for the emery wheel are made of 1 by 1¼-in. iron and are bolted on top of the table. The shaft for the emery wheel is a piece of ⅝-in. round stock with a 2 by 1¾-in. piece shrunk on and used as a pulley. A 2½-in. washer is also shrunk on this shaft as a wheel flange. This is turned up in a lathe. The small wheel shaft runs in two small boxings on the top of the brackets. The large wheel, or fly-wheel, is 26 in. in diameter with a rim 2 in. wide and ½ in. thick. The spokes are of ½-in. rods and are arranged as shown in the engraving. They are six in number and each set of three are welded in such a manner as to leave a tri-

trouble of making one. This is a very handy tool, and will often save time in starting up the engine or using the old grindstone.

Although the height and size of this stand may be altered to suit various conditions, the following is about right: Height of stand, 38 in. Dimensions at top, 14 in. square; stock for legs to be ¾-in. gas pipe. Leg braces: ½-in. gas pipe bolted with ¼-in. bolts. Treadle is made of 1¼ by 2-in. stock bolted firmly together. The large wheel is 26 in. in diameter.

- ◆ ◆ ◆ -

The Government is to make a test of Chinese labor for digging the Panama canal. In the test 2,500 Chinese will be employed. The work is said to be too hard for the large number of Jamaicans now employed, and a sufficient number of Spaniards cannot be secured immediately.

TO PUT A BELT ON A RUNNING PULLEY

In many shops it is the practice to throw on the belts while the machinery is running rather than lose eight or ten minutes by shutting down. Where the belt comes on at the top of the pulley it can usually be thrown on from the floor by two men using stout poles having spurs in the end and a

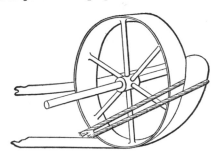

Method of Putting Belt on Running Pulley

finger on the side, says a correspondent of the American Machinist. One man holds the belt up on the face of the pulley and the other catches the edge of the belt with the pole finger and pulls it on. Where the belt runs on from the other side of the pulley, or in cases of very tight belts, the following plan is better:

Take a piece of common bale rope up on the ladder, slip it around the belt and bring the two ends even as in the sketch. Steady the belt with one hand while the man on the floor pushes it up onto the pulley with one of the poles, then with the other hand pass the two ends of the rope twice around the shaft close to the hub of the pulley and in the direction of the rotation. Be careful and keep clear of set screws by keeping just a little tension on the rope. Step down a step or two on the ladder and grasping the ends of the rope in one hand, give the man on the floor a signal for a concerted effort, and with a pull the belt is on and the rope may be removed if it has not already removed itself. Under no circumstances should the rope be wrapped around the hand; be content to merely grasp it firmly. If it catches on the side of the belt, you won't have to be told to let go. Clean shafting and a cool head are required for the successful performance of this operation.

When throwing on a belt, if the pulley or belt is wet, wipe both fairly dry before attempting to throw the belt. If the belt is of rubber, with the rubber partly worn off,

get it back on the pulleys as soon as possible, as if wet it will draw up several inches in a short time.

STEADY FLAME VARIABLE BLAST APPARATUS

In keeping a steady blast with foot bellows and a blowpipe the india-rubber diaphragm generally used does not always give the best results, especially in maintaining a small flame. The apparatus illustrated is an excellent substitute and by its use the strength of the blast can be regulated with ease to suit a full jet of gas, says the Model Engineer, London, or the smallest flame required for fine work, and will not change, no matter how much work is expended on the bellows.

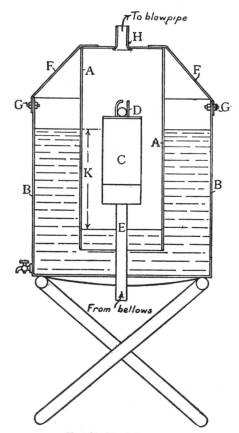

Variable Blast Apparatus

To make the device, invert a long tin can, A, in a larger tin, B; through the bottom of B pass an upright pipe, E, and make the joint tight. To the top of E solder a small tin, C, by its lid. To the bottom of C sweat a piece of sheet copper with a $\frac{5}{16}$-in. hole in the middle of it. The edges of this hole should be knife-sharp. Make the ball-valve, D, a $\frac{1}{2}$-in. steel ball and seat it in the hole in the copper with a smart tap of the hammer. Sweat three brass wire guides into the copper and bend one of them over to keep the ball from being blown off its seating. Test the valve by filling the tin with water and holding the ball down tight to its seating, to keep the water from running out. If the valve is tight, proceed by soldering tin C into its lid at the top of E. Solder four straps of sheet tin, F, onto A and fasten them to the top edge of the large tin, B, by four small bolts, G.

In operation, water is poured into B, and when the bellows are not worked, it partially fills A. As soon as air is blown in, it expels the water from A, and a steady blast is delivered to the blowpipe through the pipe H. This blast depends for its strength on the head of water, K, due to difference of water level in A and B, and this difference can be varied at will by pouring more or less water into B.

The blast cannot be stronger than the pressure due to the head of water, K, as any superfluous air pumped in only bubbles harmlessly out from under A and escapes.

It is advisable to have the difference between the tins A and B large enough, or the escaping air blows the water over the edge of B. A large square biscuit tin answers perfectly. The whole should be mounted on a camp stool, with a hole cut in the seat for the pipe E to pass through.

WASHING PHOTOGRAPHIC NEGA= TIVES AND PRINTS

The customary process of washing negatives and prints is tedious and consumes considerable time. A correspondent of the Photographic Times describes an easier method which he has used with excellent success.

Fasten a small oil can nozzle (A, Fig. 1) to a long piece of rubber tubing, B. Fasten the other end of the tubing to the hydrant as in Fig. 2, or to the bottom of a small tank elevated above the table on which the washing is done.

After the plates or prints are rinsed, turn on the water and spray them with the fine stream. Plates may be held in the hand or the rack, but prints should be placed on

a pane of glass and turned frequently. All traces of hypo, which would cause the pictures to fade or turn yellow easily if allowed to remain, can be removed in this

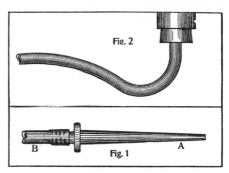

Fine Spraying Nozzle

way in from eight to twelve minutes. If the stream is too strong, however, it will cause blisters.

When many are to be washed, have a tray of clean water in which to place the prints between times. After the treatment, soak them for a few minutes and dry.

OUTLINE DRAWING MADE WITH HELP OF CAMERA

The use of the camera as a drafting tool was described in Shop Notes for September, 1906; the accompanying illustration is reproduced from an outline of a pattern actu-

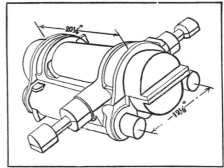

Made by a Camera

ally made by the process, and shows what accurate results may be obtained in this way at small cost.

At a mild red heat, good steel can be drawn out under the hammer to a fine point; at a bright red heat, it will crumble under the hammer, and at a white heat it will fall to pieces.

FACING A LARGE CASTING BY HAND

The illustration shows how a large furnace hopper for a blast furnace was faced by hand. In describing this operation, a correspondent of the American Machinist says:

The boring mill in our shop having only a 10-ft. swing, we had to rig up for the job. We found a large pulley, which we keyed into the inside with wooden keys, C. A piece of shafting was then obtained and secured in the bore of the pulley. A collar, P, was put on this and an old bearing to which was attached the beam. We then secured an old slide rest to the beam at E. With two men to turn the beam and feed the tool in by hand, the job was done in about half a day. The hopper was in six sections bolted together, and as the surface of A was very rough, we had to take several cuts.

Low brass is more likely to fire-crack than is high brass; the amount of it used is comparatively small, says American Machinist, and is confined to drawn or spun articles which cannot be successfully made from high brass.

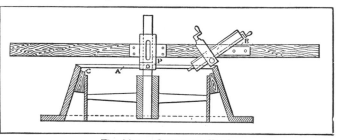

Finishing a Casting by Hand

A safe way of discovering a leak in a gas pipe is suggested by a fireman. It is to use a small brush and ordinary lather. The escaping gas will blow bubbles, however small the leak may be, and will thus show the exact place.

* * *

Zinc dust, when properly packed, is not liable to spontaneous combustion, as is generally believed, according to a German scientist. Wetting of the material is without danger, and ignition and explosion only occur in the presence of air. Many steamship owners refuse to transport zinc dust, because of the idea that it is dangerous.

TRIANGLE FOR DRAWING SCREW THREADS

Drawing screw threads is often rather difficult for the draftsman, but by the use of the triangle illustrated, the task can be made much easier and the threads more uniform.

This triangle is made of an ordinary 45-degree celluloid triangle, like that shown in Fig. 1. Make the lines A B' and B' C' on the triangle, as shown in Fig. 2, scribing them with any sharp instrument and at an angle of about 4 degrees with the horizontal. With a sharp knife cut the celluloid away almost down to the lines, says Machinery, and finish off to the lines with a fine file, making smooth, straight edges. Either horizontal or vertical threads may be drawn without changing the position of the triangle, and right or left-hand threads are drawn by simply turning it over.

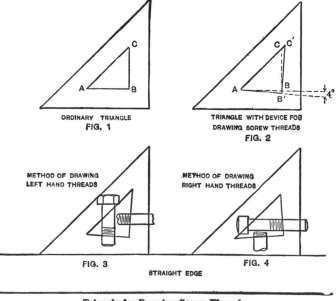

Triangle for Drawing Screw Threads

THE OBJECT OF TRUSSES

Readers of the articles on strength of materials will understand that the span of a beam may be so large that a single beam could not be had of sufficient size to hold the load without bending too much, says the Practical Carpenter.

Such a case is shown in Fig. 1, which can be remedied by supporting it with an upright post or column in the middle, as shown in Fig. 2; this would practically make two short beams of the long beam and con-

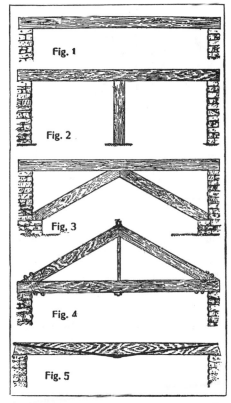

Fig. 1

Fig. 2

Fig. 3

Fig. 4

Fig. 5

sequently greatly increase the strength of the long beam.

In cases where a post would not be admissible in the center a support may be had by using two braces as shown in Fig. 3. Here the pressure instead of acting downward on a post acts downward in a diagonal direction, transferring the pressure to the walls or other supports of the long beam. A little thought will show that these braces (used for the same purpose as the center post in Fig. 2) are subject to compression the same as the post.

When the load on the long beam is

concentrated at the center or evenly distributed the pressure on each of the braces is the same.

In many cases a clear opening is desired and no braces can be used underneath, but the same support can be had by placing the braces above the beam and suspending from them a rod holding up the center of the beam as shown in Fig. 4.

It makes no difference if a weight is placed directly on top of a board or if a string is tied to the board and the weight suspended by the string, the pressure on the board is just the same.

In Fig. 4, instead of being supported directly on the braces, the beam is suspended from the braces by means of the rod; hence the pressure on the braces is just the same as in Fig. 3 (that is, with the slight addition of the weight of the rod itself).

Fig. 4 shows the simplest form of a truss, but all trusses are on the same principle of transferring the load to the support.

In the truss shown in Fig. 4 the load is placed on the beam, but when used for roofs the load is placed on the slanting braces or rafters, as they are called.

Where the span is comparatively short, the beam may be trussed as shown in Fig. 5. Here two iron rods ¾ or 1 in. in diameter are placed on the beam as shown—one on each side. A piece of flat bar-iron, about 3 in. wide and ½ in. in thickness, with ends turned over about ¾ in., forms the middle support for the beam. When the nuts are tightened the tendency will be for the middle of the beam to go upward, thus counteracting the downward bending.

ALARM FOR STEAM GAUGE

This is a handy device for firemen, as it will sound an alarm when the pressure becomes either too high or too low, thus obviating the necessity of constantly watching

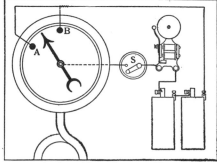

High and Low Pressure Alarm

the gauge. An ordinary door bell out-fit will supply nearly all the parts necessary for constructing this alarm, except that a switch, S, should be substituted for the ordinary push button.

The contacts, A and B, are placed at the two extremes of the permitted pressure variation and are connected to the bell circuit as shown. The switch, S, is closed normally, but when the alarm is sounded it may be opened until the required pressure is obtained.—Contributed by Robert Glaubke, Malott Park, Ind.

A HOME=MADE BAND-SAW

A good, practical band-saw, as made by a correspondent of The Blacksmith and Wheelwright, is shown in the illustration. The frame is made mostly of wood and braced with iron and the wheels are from an old bicycle. The tires are 1¼-in. solid rubber. The top wheel is fixed on a shaft having

Home=Made Band-Saw

a tight and loose pulley, while the bottom wheel is fastened in an iron fork, which can be raised and lowered by the screw and hand wheel.

Cordite used in the cartridges was found to be the cause of the bursting of several rifles during target practice of the Canadian militia.

HOW TO MAKE A DRILL

A serviceable drill can be made of old lumber and pipe at very little cost. The parts used in its construction are as follows: A, piece of lumber (2 by 8 in.); B and C, pieces of wood set into A; D, iron rod to strengthen frame; E E, wooden brackets supporting B and C; I, set nut set into B; F, piece of old pipe or iron

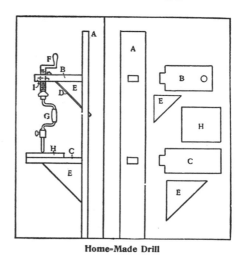

Home=Made Drill

threaded to set gauge nut; G, old brace or made of pipe fittings, with a set screw, K, to hold the drill; H, table to which the work is fastened.—Contributed by F. B. Ewing, Santa Clara, Cal.

TO SANDPAPER A CORE BOX

In the accompanying sketch, A is the core box, B a cylindrical piece of wood, turned a little smaller than the diameter of the required core, and C 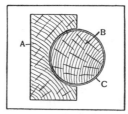 is a piece of sandpaper glued on B. The wooden cylinder, B, is fastened in the lathe and revolved at high speed, the core box being then brought up against it, as shown. If there are any shoulders in the core box the cylinder should be shaped accordingly and a separate piece of sandpaper glued to each section.—Contributed by Donald Reeves, 6453 Iowa St., Oak Park, Ill.

All the articles appearing in this department are reprinted in book form at the end of each year.

SHOP NOTES

Contributions to this department are invited. If you have worked out a good idea or know of one, please send it in.

OLD DRILLS USEFUL

The shanks of broken or worn-out drills may be easily restored to usefulness by 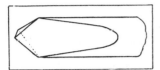 grinding down the end, as shown in the sketch. The drills thus formed are very useful for drilling brass, white metal or other soft material.—Contributed by W. J. S., Emsworth, Pa.

TO FROST WINDOWS

Make a strong solution of epsom salts in hot water and while hot wash it over the glass with a brush. When cool the salts will be deposited on the window in crystalline form, beautifully frosting the window.

Be careful to entirely cover the window with the liquid and do not let it run or the pattern will be spoiled.

ELECTRICALLY OPERATED PLATE BOX

Owing to the great number of undeveloped plates and films which were being spoiled by the careless opening of the plate box, the following device was constructed and is now in successful operation.

Fig. 1--Plate Box for Dark Room

The plate box (Fig. 1) was provided with a home-made latch operated by an electromagnet. When the photographer desires to open the box he presses a push button within easy reach of the box, which com-

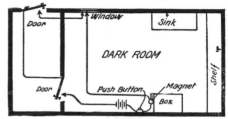

Fig. 2--Wiring Diagram

pletes the circuit and energizes the magnet, thus allowing the lid to be raised. If, however, the window or either of the two doors should be open the current would not be complete and the box could not be opened.

This is accomplished by using ordinary burglar alarm contacts in both doors and window and connecting in series as shown in the wiring diagram (Fig. 2). It will be seen that the opening of either door or window will open the circuit and prevent operating the magnet by the push button.—Contributed by Wm. F. Groose, Photographer, Oconomowoc, Wis.

IMPROVED SOLDERING FURNACE

Any one who has had any experience with this style of soldering furnace will at once  see the advantage of using a bicycle foot pump (attached as shown) over the old rubber bulb with its slow, weak action, leaky valve, and short-lived rubber tube.

A bicycle valve may be soldered on the air valve and the hose connection screwed into that, or the bicycle connection may be removed and the hose simply slipped over tube on tank plug.—Contributed by Ora S. Harmas, Fennimore, Wis.

DEVICE FOR REMOVING REAPER KNIVES

The accompanying illustration, reproduced from the Implement and Machinery Review, shows a device designed to quickly remove worn or damaged sections from reaper and mower knives.

It is a special appliance of much utility,

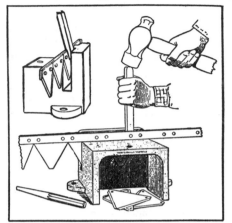

Removing Blades from Sickle Bars

one of its chief recommendations being that by using this tool it is impossible to bend or injure the knife-back. By placing the knife-bar in the block any man or lad should be able readily, by means of the hand tool and a hammer, to remove twenty sections in five minutes. The tool should be held with the shoulder resting on the top of the section over the rivet, so that it may not slip between the section and the block. The simplicity of the tool should commend itself, for there are no screws, bolts, or springs, and it does not require any adjustment. A blow with a hammer, and the rivet is cut through. Its universality is another good point about this new tool, for it is by no means restricted in its sphere of action, since it will remove any section from either a light or heavy binder or mower.

DEVICE FOR REGULATING BACK PRESSURE

A clattering valve on the valve seat as the engine cut off and exhausted caused a correspondent of the Engineer's Review great annoyance; also there was difficulty in regulating the pressure to send the right amount of steam through the factory at the best operating pressure. He remedied the matter as follows:

A long lever was arranged on the valve stem and to one end a cord and spring, S, were attached; a hollow piece of round brass tubing 2 ft. long was soldered to the lower end of the spring. This tubing passed through a clamp as shown, which was made of a piece of brass, cast square and drilled out with a hole somewhat larger than the brass rod. A thumb screw was put in on one side, and to the end of the screw a piece of brass was fitted and filled out concave to fit the rod. The ends were turned over at the top and bottom of the body of the clamp to prevent it from falling out. The concave piece was for the purpose of protecting the rod from the end of the thumb screw. A cord, C, was attached to the other end of the lever on the valve stem, also, for the purpose of fastening the valve open when the exhaust steam was not wanted for heating purposes.

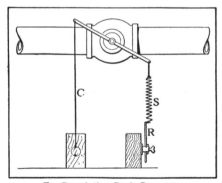

For Regulating Back Pressure

When steam is wanted for the shop the rod R is pulled down until the desired back pressure is obtained, and then clamped in place. This prevents the valve disk from clattering on the seat and the spring prevents unsteady jerking of the cord. Cord C is left free.

DRAUGHTSMAN'S CENTER

A brass thumb-tack with a centerpunch hole in the center of the top will prove valuable when the center of several concentric circles becomes so worn and enlarged that future work will be inaccurate.

The thumb-tack may then be placed in the worn center and the compass used from the hole in the top.—Contributed by John Weldon, Brooklyn, N. Y.

MAKING AND COOLING A 105=TON CASTING

The pattern for a big casting recently poured at Milwaukee was 32 ft. long, 11 ft. wide and 10 ft. high, and ten patternmakers were kept busy four months in making it. The casting was an engine bed, weighing, when completed, 105 tons. It was poured from nine ladles, 108 tons of metal going into the rough casting. Fifteen days were allowed for cooling, but at the end of 20 days the heat given off could be felt at a distance of several feet.

◆ ◆ ◆

POUNDING IN ENGINE

A sharp metallic pounding in a four cylinder engine was found to be due to accumulated carbon in the combustion chamber causing preignition and loosening of the spark-timing mechanism, says a correspondent of the Motor Age.

Ignition was by contact spark, and the spark timing was changed by shifting the inlet valve and ignition camshaft—which performed both functions—along its axis. The arrangement is shown roughly in the sketch, in which A is the camshaft, B one of the ignition cams and C the hub of the two-to-one gear. This gear was keyed on a bronze sleeve, D, which turned in a bearing and in which the shaft slid lengthwise. A feather, E, established the connection be-

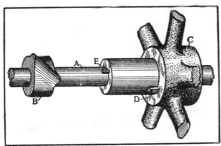

Arrangement for Ignition

tween A and D. On taking things apart it was found that the feather was exceedingly loose in both A and D, and it was inferred that the springs of the inlet valves exerted so much force on A as to cause it to jump rotatively back and forth when the valves opened and closed. A tight feather, which was let deeply into A, cured part of the trouble, and scraping the carbon from the combustion chambers cured the rest of it.

HOME=MADE RIG FOR TRUING COMMUTATORS

An easily made device for truing commutators and one strongly recommended by a correspondent of Power is shown in the accompanying illustration.

This device was used to true up the rectifying commutator on a large alternator,

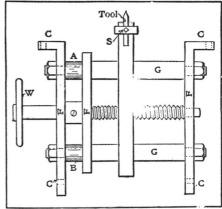

For Truing Commutators

the hole in the brush-holder yoke being used to line up by. The device was clamped in position by inserting the rod A in the brush stud hole, and then bracing the corners C C C C of the frame to foundation, brush yoke and bearing bolts, respectively, with ½x2-in. wrought iron, to insure rigidity. The toolpost guide bars, G G, were made of ¼-in. key steel, turned and threaded at each end for the four nuts shown. The toolpost was made of 1¼x3-in. Swedish iron planed smooth, and with two true, square holes to receive the guides, G G, and work free without lost motion. The tool was of lathe-tool material and attached by inserting in a slot on top of the post and tightening the set-screw, S. The frame, F F F, was made of ½x3-in. wrought iron planed smooth and true. The guides were turned down at A and B to take the two collars, which fitted holes in brush-holder yokes of two sizes of dynamos, the whole device being made reversible. The tool was fed by the long screw, turned by the hand-wheel, W.

◆ ◆ ◆

It is estimated that London sends up into the air 1,000 tons of soot each year. The natives claim that fully a million tons come down.

MACHINE FOR TESTING HARDNESS

One of the most important properties of cast iron is its hardness. An iron which is too hard is brittle, weak and more difficult to finish and the results are inferior to those obtained when soft iron is used.

In order to determine the degree of hardness various machines have been designed,

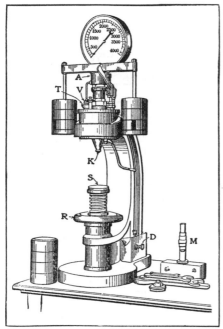

Hardness Tester

some of which depend on the impact of a sharp-pointed object or the effects of scratching, and others on the effects of an ordinary twist drill. In the last named machines a given size drill with a constant pressure applied will make a hole of a given depth in a certain number of revolutions, the number of revolutions determining the hardness of the iron or other material that is being tested.

The machine which is herewith illustrated, by courtesy of the American Machinist, is one which was recently invented by a Swedish engineer, and is regarded by leading technicians as the most reliable machine of its kind that has ever been devised. In this machine the degree of hardness of any substance is measured by the amount of indentation caused by the pressure of a hardened steel ball on the sample to be tested. The pressure is obtained by means of a small hydraulic press, operated by a hand pump, and connected to a gauge which indicates the amount of pressure that is being applied.

A small auxiliary cylinder A, supports a beam on which are suspended a number of weights. These weights are changed to suit the material to be tested, and when the pressure passes a certain point they are raised, thus preventing any excess over the desired amount.

When a sample is to be tested it is placed on the end of the screw S, and the wheel R is then turned until the sample is brought against the steel ball K. The necessary pressure is then produced by working the pump, after which the sample is removed and placed under the microscope M, which has a lens engraved with a scale which is always visible, and thus allows measuring the exact size of the indentation. In order to get the most accurate results the surface of the sample should be polished. After obtaining the exact size of the indentation produced by a given pressure the hardness can be obtained from a table which gives the value in standard degrees.

HOW TO MAKE A SELF=HEATING SOLDERING IRON

A good self-heating soldering iron, having nearly all the advantages of an electric soldering iron, can be easily made by using the devices shown in the accompanying sketch. A is the copper head of an ordinary soldering iron, and is drilled with 1/8-in. holes on the sides as shown. It is also drilled to receive the 1/4-in. pipe, B, which is screwed into the air mixer. The stop cock, C, can be omitted if desired, but is very handy when the gas fixture is high and not easily reached. A 1/8-in. pipe, D, is pushed through an old file handle drilled for the

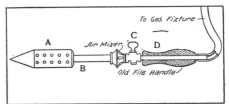

Self-Heating Soldering Iron

purpose, and connects with the hose as shown. The air mixer can be taken from an old Wellsbach light.

When the gas is turned on and lighted and the air mixer properly regulated, a blue flame surrounds the copper and keeps it at just the right temperature.—Contributed by Edw. J. Snyder, Buffalo, N. Y.

ACETYLENE TESTER FOR EGGS

An acetylene lantern has been discovered by a poultry dealer to be ideal for egg-

Testing Eggs

testing purposes. The lantern, which gives a clear white flame of great brilliancy, was first used on an incubator full of eggs by a correspondent of the Poultry Journal as an experiment. A piece of black enamel cloth with a hole in it was fitted over the lens and the eggs in turn held before the lens in the manner illustrated. The intense white light rendered the eggs nearly transparent, so that at the end of the third day of incubation the fertile ones were easily detected, the minute blood vessels showing distinctly.

CLARIFYING RAIN WATER

Many people catch their rain water in barrels placed under the eaves spout. In a long dry spell the roof will become dirty, and the first rain will fill the barrel with dirty water. If the rain is long continued it may clear itself, but will not if the shower is of short duration. In the latter case the barrel will be filled with dirty water.

To clear the water quickly extend the spout within an inch or two of the bottom of the barrel. The incoming water will stir up the water in the barrel, so that it will clear itself in one-eighth of the time ordinarily required. This also applies to cisterns, but the smaller the cistern the quicker the clarifying process.—Contributed by T. L. Reed, La Porte City, Iowa.

To make the elevator pump run smoothly, dissolve a package or two of good washing powder in the water contained in the open tank of the elevator system.

MYSTERY DEVICE FOR SHOW WINDOW

Mechanical devices have always proved attractive when used in show windows and usually increase the amount of sales sufficiently to pay for the cost of making in a very short time. One of these devices, which was recently described in the Keystone, consists of a wooden box with a piece of glass in the upper half of the front and a fan motor on the inside. Numerous bits of tissue paper are kept in motion by the fan, thus giving the appearance shown in Fig. 1. It will be necessary to place the device back in the window far enough to

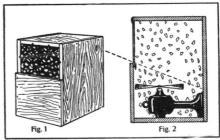

Fig. 1   Fig. 2

The Mystery Solved

hide the fan and keep the angle of vision above the dotted line shown in Fig. 2. An enclosed, dust-proof motor is the best for this purpose, but any ordinary motor can be used by encasing it in a frame of wire netting.

SAW SETTING TOOLS

These tools will be found very convenient for use in spring-setting small rip saws, and can be easily made, says the Wood-Worker. The gauge (Fig. 1) can be made out of a broken scroll saw blade, one of the beveled

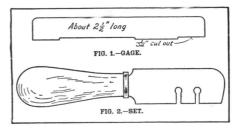

About 2½" long

1/32" cut out

FIG. 1.—GAGE.

FIG. 2.—SET.

For Setting Saws

back kind of, say, 15-gauge thickness. Mine is filed away 1-32-in. for set of saw. The set (Fig. 2) can be made from a large worn-out flat file. Cut two slots, for thinnest and thickest saws.

REFITTING CONNECTING ROD

About the worst form of connecting rod to refit after it has worn out of round is that with the hinged cap shown in the

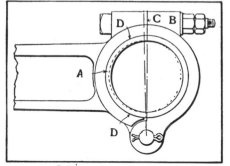

Refitting Connecting Rods

sketch, says Motor Age. The reason for this is easily understood by reference to the dotted lines, which show, slightly exaggerated, the wear which may take place in the brass, A, and the corresponding movement required of the cap to take it up. It is evident that whatever wear A has sustained double its extent must be filed off from the upper portion of B of the cap to produce a fit on the crankpin, and, moreover, the surface, C, must be filed slightly tapering instead of parallel. It is next to impossible, always undesirable, to attempt to refit a crankpin bearing by putting a liner between the brass, A, and its seating. The reason lies in the fact that the pressure per square inch on these bearings is so great that it

is impossible for a brass so treated to stay around after it has been run. Paper is the only lining that can be used, and the paper will crush more or less under the pressure and allow the bearing to squeeze out of shape. For this reason the only way a crankpin bearing can be refitted without replacing the worn brass is to close in the cap to make the bearing round, and then to scrape the brass as true as possible. This is a short operation after the parts are removed, and requires little skill.

◆ ◆ ◆

CENTERING LARGE ARCHES

The accompanying illustration shows the centering of a segmental arch of 50-ft. span, which was designed by a correspondent of the Engineering News.

Owing to the stream becoming rather wild at times, it was desirable to place as little obstruction as possible in the bed of the stream. A truss was considered with supports at each abutment only, but as the cost was excessive, and there were doubts as to its rigidity (the angle of main supports being so flat, due to rise of arch), and not caring to use iron rods, it was discarded in favor of the plan herewith. The centering shown is well bolted, so that it can be moved, the section used being one-third of the whole length of arch.

Possibly some of the readers have had occasion to solve a similar problem lately for segmental arches of 50-ft. span or over, in which case it would be interesting to learn something of the design and what the

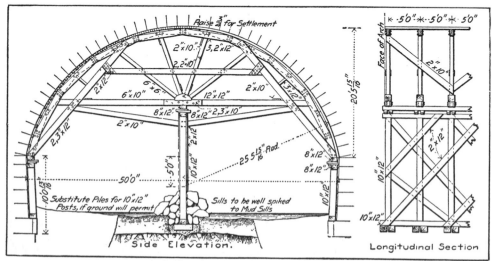

Centering for an Arch of 50-Ft. Span

results were, as some of the stresses in centering for arches are so indefinite it is difficult to proportion the whole economically.

TO DRILL SMALL HOLES IN GLASS

The following method of drilling holes in eyeglasses, which can also be used for drilling other glass articles, is described by a correspondent of the Optical Journal as follows:

Drilling an Eye Glass

Take an old three-cornered file and grind it to a point, being careful not to draw the temper, and make the point sharp as can be with a moderately long taper. Now break off the point by pressing the file with one of the flat sides against a piece of steel or your vise. This will leave the end slightly rough, with three cutting corners. Now slip a strap over the lens where you want to drill the hole and insert the point of the file through the large hole in the strap and rotate the file, using a moderate pressure. When about half way through the lens reverse and drill from the other side, as the lens is apt to chip or break if you drill all the way from one side.

Moisten the drill with benzine to which a small quantity of oil has been added, or turpentine. If worst comes to worst, and neither benzine nor turpentine is handy, moisten the tip of the drill liberally by wetting it on the tongue.

To enlarge the hole use a reamer or a small round file moistened as above. If you use the file turn it backward. Drills may be made in other shapes, as grinding the end of a broken round file to an edge like a chisel or like an ordinary drill. If made chisel edge be sure that the corners are

sharp. When the three-cornered drill gets dull grind a new point and break off as before.

HOME=MADE DRAFT GAUGE

Screw two pieces of 1-in. pipe about 8 in. long into a 1-in. return bend, and put a reducer on the top end of each pipe, reducing it to ¼ in. Remove the plunger from a small bicycle pump and solder a piece of copper on the top of the pump, making it airtight. This is to be used for a float, as it drops down in one of the 1-in. pipes nicely.

Remove the pressure spring from a small steam gauge and attach the gauge to one end of the pipe as shown in the illustration. Solder a fine stiff brass wire to the center of the float, letting the wire extend up

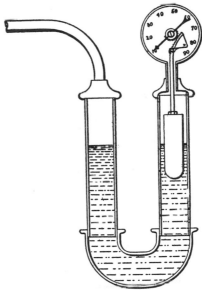

U-Tube and Gauge

through the reducer to which the gauge is screwed and connect the upper end of the wire to the bottom corner of the triangular ratchet of the gauge. Fill the U-tube with machine oil until the float raises enough to turn the hand back to zero, says the Engineer's Review.

Screw a piece of ¼-in. pipe in the other reducer and run to the side of the smoke-box. As the draft tends to create a vacuum, the oil in the ¼-in. pipe raises on the side connected to the smoke flue, and lowers on the gauge side. This causes the float to drop, thus pulling down on the ratchet, and turns the hand upward. Oil is a good liquid to use, as it neither freezes nor evaporates.

HYDRAULIC STUFFING BOX

A short time ago I was called upon to operate a centrifugal pumping plant, says a correspondent of Power. The equipment consisted of a 10x30 Corliss engine and a 10-in. pump with boilers and accessories, which outfit was to throw 4,500 gal. per minute to a height of 50 ft., 12 ft. of which was suction lift.

Trouble commenced upon the first day. The pump was speeded so high that the stuffing-box could not be kept tight and cool at the same time. The speed could not be reduced, and the packing burnt out repeatedly. Water and oil applied in the ordinary manner failed to overcome the trouble.

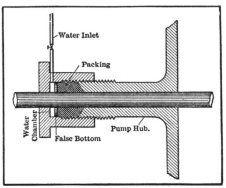

Water-Packed Pump

After several days of heart-breaking delay I had the gland taken off and a false bottom inserted on the air side of the packing, leaving a chamber about three-eighths of an inch deep. This chamber was tapped for a quarter inch pipe, a valve was put on at the gland, and the pipe connected into the main discharge of the pump. This practically made a water-packed pump; the packing was left loose and the pump forced to take water instead of air. We had no more trouble with the gland and the packing lasted almost indefinitely.

I hope that this may be of value to some other victim, as I know of nothing so contrary as a centrifugal pump that is taking air. The accompanying sketch is self-explanatory.

An unloading coal record was recently made at Escanaba, Mich., when 4,200 tons of hard coal was taken out of the steamer "H. S. Sill," in 10 hours, with two hoists.

FRICTION PIPE WRENCH

A simple friction wrench for manipulating polished brass and nickel plated pipe is shown in the accompanying sketch and is constructed of the handle, A, a piece of oak wood 1 in. thick, 3 in. wide, 14 in. long, with end of same rounded as shown at B; a piece of canvas, C, so folded as to make three thicknesses and the same width as

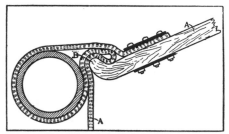

Pipe Wrench for Polished Work

handle and about 18 in. long, so that it will encircle all ordinary work. It is fastened about 3 in. from end of handle by means of two brass plates 3 in. square and five countersunk bolts as shown.

To use the wrench pass the canvas around the pipe or other cylindrical object and tuck the folded end between the canvas and wood, as shown in the sketch. Then, when the handle is pulled down, the canvas will tighten around the pipe and under all ordinary conditions produce sufficient friction to turn it.

The use of this wrench will not mar the surface of the work, nor bend the pipe, because the compression is distributed evenly over nearly the entire circumference.—Contributed by John Weldon, 433 Columbia St., Brooklyn, N. Y.

STEAM SOFTENS CLINKERS

Clinkers in the ashpit can be softened and the grates preserved by the introduction of steam, either alive or exhaust, says the National Engineer. Also, the fire, it is claimed, will burn with a longer flame than where dry air is used.

USING A NEW FILE ON BABBITT

When using a new file, on babbitt or aluminum, rub it with a piece of chalk or soapstone. This fills the teeth of the file so the chips cannot stick in them and cut scores in the work.—Contributed by Wm. Ed. Jackson, Tarrytown, N. Y.

LAMPLIGHT PHOTOGRAPHY

When two or three lamps carefully placed in the right positions are used, splendid negatives can be made by lamplight, says a correspondent of the Photographic Times.

Two 20-cp. oil lamps placed in front and to each side of the sitter at a distance of about 4 ft. will give excellent results. The exposure should be from two to four minutes, according to the plates and lens.

CIRCULATING DEVICE FOR GAS ENGINE

Very often a gas engine, having no pump, will become over-heated after running for a few minutes, especially if the tank is not very large or is made of wood. The reason is, that as soon as the water gets warm it does not circulate as fast or cool the engine as well as when it is cold.

The simple device here illustrated, which consists of ordinary pipe and fittings, will effectually cool the engine without the use of a pump and without reducing its power.

A small pipe, A, connects the exhaust pipe with the water outlet, B, at a point above the check valve, C. At each explosion of the engine there will be a discharge into the water pipe, thereby forcing the water into the tank, where the consumed gas separates and escapes through the pipe, D.—Contributed by E. H. Klipstein, 116 Prospect St., East Orange, N. J.

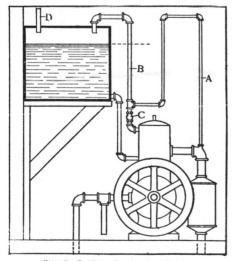

Simple Cooling Device for Engine

LUBRICATE LAG BOLTS

Put a bit of tallow into the hole bored for a lag bolt and it will go easier. The bolt squeezes the tallow ahead of it and greases the hole as it advances.—Contributed by Wm. Ed. Jackson, Tarrytown, N. Y.

HOW TO MAKE A BUFFER AND GRINDER

The materials necessary for making this machine are a pipe flange, A; a bushing, B; five ½-in. nipples, C; three ½-in. tees, D;

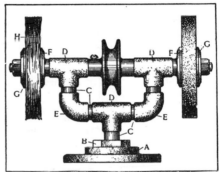

Home-Made Buffer and Grinder

two ½-in. ells, E; two collars, F; two washers, G; a number of cloth discs, H; a small emery wheel; piece of ½-in. shaft; pulley with set screw, babbitt, and sal ammoniac.

In order to prevent the fittings from turning loose, apply a solution of sal ammoniac and water to the threads before screwing up. This will rust the two pieces together and prevent loosening. If the threads are greasy so that the sal ammoniac does not adhere, heat slightly and then dip in sal ammoniac.

The tees which form the bearings should be drilled on top for the double purpose of pouring the babbitt and making an oil hole. In pouring the babbitt it will be necessary to cover the ends of the nipples to prevent the melted metal running down inside the base. This may be done by using a small piece of asbestos. Be sure that the shaft is lined up in the center of the bearings before pouring the babbitt.

The emery wheel is fastened to the shaft by a nut and washer as shown and the buffer is fastened in the same way. To make the buffer cut a number of circular pieces of cloth, H (almost any kind of cloth will answer), and cut a hole in the center of each piece large enough to receive the shaft, assemble all the pieces of cloth concentrically and sew them together near the center.

Then place the buffer on the shaft and screw the nut up tightly.

A GOOD SOLDERING ACID

A soldering acid which can be used to tin and solder cast iron is made by dissolving zinc in muriatic acid and burning the gas generated by the chemical action.

Place the acid in a stone jar having straight sides, something like a closed-circuit battery jar. Add plenty of zinc (you cannot put in too much) and immediately throw a lighted match into the jar. There will be a slight, but harmless, explosion. Have a good supply of matches and if the fire goes out, light it immediately. Keep this up until the acid has ceased to boil, then filter to remove remaining zinc and the matches.

Do not make this acid within doors, as it will rust and tarnish everything metal the room contains.

I have tinned iron castings and wiped lead joints on them with this solution for several years and it is the one and only one I have found to do the work satisfactorily. The acid is good for all soldering purposes, excepting electrical, which is excluded because the preparation is an excellent conductor.—Contributed by V. J. Davis, 314 Fargo St., Buffalo, N. Y.

India has 28,295 miles of steam railroad, of which about half is 5 ft. 6 in. gage.

DIFFERENCE BETWEEN A 2=CYCLE AND A 4=CYCLE GAS ENGINE

The accompanying illustration shows the working cycles of both 2-cycle and 4-cycle gas engines. Although more complicated in construction, the principle of the 4-cycle engine is the simpler of the two and will be described first. The explosive mixture of gas and air is first drawn into the cylinder by the downward movement of the piston, as shown in Fig. 1. The inlet valve, which is shown open, is operated mechanically in some engines, but in the simplest engines it operates automatically, being opened by the partial vacuum in the cylinder.

When the piston reaches the bottom of the stroke, the inlet valve closes so that when the piston returns to the top the mixture will be compressed, as shown in Fig. 2. The electric spark or other ignition device then explodes the mixture, which expands and forces the piston down, as shown in Fig. 3. This is the power stroke of the engine and it is here that the flywheel receives the necessary momentum to carry the engine over the other three cycles.

In Fig. 4 is shown the exhaust stroke in which the upward movement of the piston forces the burnt gases out through the exhaust valve, which is opened mechanically in all 4-cycle engines.

In the 2-cycle engine an airtight crank case is used, in which the explosive mixture of gas and air is stored and partially compressed, previous to ignition. The working cycle is best understood by starting at the compression period (Fig. 5) where the upward movement of the piston compresses the mixture in the cylinder, at the same time drawing in a new supply through the check valve at the inlet.

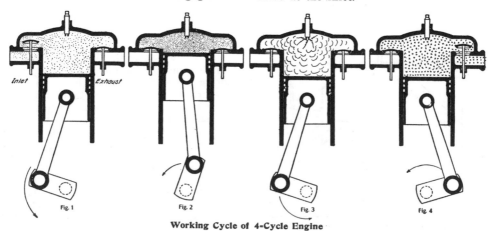

Inlet　Exhaust

Fig. 1　　Fig. 2　　Fig. 3　　Fig. 4

Working Cycle of 4-Cycle Engine

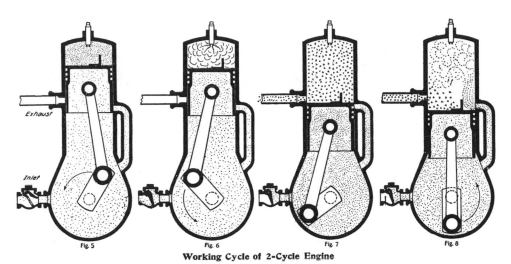

Fig. 5   Fig. 6   Fig. 7   Fig. 8

Working Cycle of 2-Cycle Engine

When the piston nearly reaches the top the spark or other ignition device explodes the mixture (Fig. 6), which expands and forces the piston down, thereby partially compressing the mixture in the crank case. The expansion continues until the exhaust port is uncovered by the piston, as shown in Fig. 7, which allows the burnt gases to escape.

The piston in finishing its downward stroke uncovers the inlet port, as shown in Fig. 8, and allows the partially compressed mixture to fill the cylinder, thereby driving out the remainder of the burnt charge. In this view the function of the small vertical plate on the top of the piston will be clearly understood. If it were not for this plate the entering mixture would shoot across the cylinder and out through the exhaust port, but with the plate in position the gases are deflected and forced into the upper part of the cylinder, as indicated.

◆ ◆ ◆

WHY BOILER MAN=HOLES ARE MADE ELLIPTICAL

In a certain technical college, when the question, "Why are man-holes made elliptical, and not circular?" was put to the class in examination, the majority answered by describing the shape of a man's head or body, or in some other manner going into the details of the human anatomy. The others answered that the reason for making them elliptical is that the covers may be placed on the inside, an operation which would be impossible with a circular man-hole.

A DEVICE FOR RAISING AUTOMO= BILES

The accompanying illustration shows a device which was constructed by a correspondent of the American Blacksmith and used with great success in repairing automobiles.

In choosing material for building, nothing but the best should be used, as a breakdown, liable to occur from faulty material or construction, is likely to result in serious injury to the repair man. The platform consists of two good, strong planks, A. These rest on two V-shaped supports, B, which in turn work on hinges, C, which are secured to the base board, D. The end supports consist of a stationary board, E, at one end and a hinged leg, F, at the opposite end. The leg at F is attached to the main plank by means of a heavy hinge. When the machine is in proper position, this leg is turned under

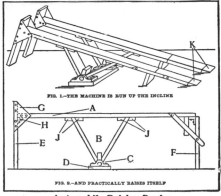

FIG. 1.—THE MACHINE IS RUN UP THE INCLINE

FIG. 2.—AND PRACTICALLY RAISES ITSELF

Automobile Raising Device

the platform and held in position by means of a rod and thumb screw.

The stationary support is attached to the plank by means of a three-cornered plate, G, and a bracket, H. The V-shaped supports are attached to the planks by means of the blocks at J J. The three-cornered plate on each side of each V support takes up the wear at this point and likewise helps to strengthen the support. Should it be necessary, a cleat or two may also be used to strengthen this support. However, this will not be necessary if good, stout stock is used. To facilitate running the machine up on the platform, a small wood block is attached to the floor at K, Fig. 1.

To place a machine on the platform, place the device in the position shown in Fig. 1 and run the machine up the incline. After reaching a certain point, the device will come to the second position when the hinged leg may be swung under the platform and bolted rigidly to support the machine.

WIRE BELT LACING HINGE JOINT

Some mill men have an idea that wire lace is all right in some places, but can not be used where both sides of the belt run to a pulley, as on some feed belts or bottom

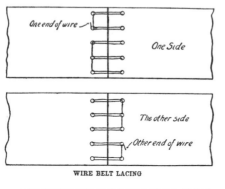

WIRE BELT LACING

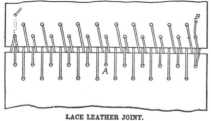

LACE LEATHER JOINT.

cylinder planer belts that run over a pulley on a counter. That this is a mistaken idea you will readily see if you lace your belt alike on each side, like sketch, writes a

correspondent of the Wood-Worker. This is a 2-in. feed belt. Lace the larger sizes same way. Be sure you cut out the small grooves on both sides of the belt and hammer the lace down good and tight. Then you have a job that will last.

With apologies to those who know, and for the benefit of some who may not, I give a rough sketch of a very satisfactory joint made with rawhide lace leather. Start at A, which is half way across belt, and lace both ways. Punch very small hole at B and draw lace end up tightly, to cut off. Then with your knife cut a gash half through the lace close up to the belt. Cut lace end off, say 1/4 in. from the notch, or gash, and hammer end down flat. This will make a good, smooth joint which will last a long time; but if you once get to using good wire lacing, and put it in right, you'll not want any more rawhide lace leather. If you doubt its being strong enough, make it double; that is, lace back across belt again after going once across.

GAUGE FOR PISTON-ROD THREADS

In repairing modern high-speed automatic cut-off steam engines in sizes up to 24-in. diameter of cylinders, a correspondent of the American Machinist experienced considerable difficulty in fitting new pistons and piston rods—particularly in getting the right pitch for the screw thread. In most of these engines the piston rod is secured to the crosshead by a thread on the rod fitting into a tapped hole in the crosshead and with a lock nut behind the boss of the crosshead to make all rigid. To get around this difficulty the piston-rod thread gauge illustrated was devised and it was found that by its use a fair fit could be made every time on the first trial.

To make this gauge, take a piece of 1x1¼-in. flat iron, A, bend its two ends up about ½ in. and file to form two V edges of 60° or the same angle as the threads, in order to fit fairly to the old thread. The distance between the two ends should be about equal to the length of the thread in the crosshead, in order that these V's may approximately represent in the gauge the first and the last thread in the crosshead.

Bend up another piece of the same flat iron as shown at B and rivet it to the middle of A, bringing its free end over and into line with the two V edges and at such distance from them that when a V-point is filed on the free end of B, the old thread will slip in between the three points. Finish piece B by bending and filing the point until a good caliper fit is secured. The gauge so made not only will give the diameter of the thread at one point, but will give the effective diameter at points where it is important that it should be known, and also provides a means of gauging the new thread,

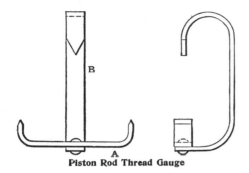

Piston Rod Thread Gauge

which may or may not be of the exact pitch of the old one, but which if made to this gauge will screw in every time and make a fair fit, which is all that the repair man either expects or desires—and, in fact, is all that the builder did in the first place.

HOW TO MAKE A PORTABLE BELL OUTFIT

Make a box with one beveled end, as shown in the sketch, and mount an ordinary electric door bell on the top and a push button on the beveled end. One or two dry batteries will furnish enough current to ring the bell. The outfit may be used at

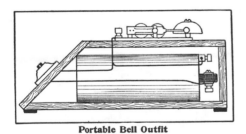

Portable Bell Outfit

the table or for invalids' use, and I have often used mine to imitate the triangle effect in our orchestra.—Contributed by Arthur L. Schacha, 4732 Broadway, Cleveland, O.

A man of average strength can develop .1 hp. with his arms or .4 hp. with his legs for 10 hrs. a day.—Trautwine.

THE ABUSE OF VALVES

Many steam fitters and engineers, upon discovering a leak in a valve, immediately condemn its workmanship instead of trying to learn the true cause of the trouble. Undoubtedly there are cases in which valves defective in construction escape detection until they have been in service for a time; but in most cases the criticism that is directed to the manufacturer does not belong to him, and affects his reputation unjustly. When valves that are thus returned as defective have been received by the maker, and carefully examined and tested, it is found, in the great majority of cases, that the leakage was plainly due to the abuse and carelessness of the persons who installed them.

Effects of Improper Installation and Operation

In discussing this subject, the Valve World gives the following directions for installing and operating valves to obtain the best results.

1. Don't allow any cement or dirt to lodge on the valve seat. Failure to observe this precaution is responsible for more leaky valves than all other causes combined and the trouble can be easily avoided by applying cement to the pipe only and in small quantities, thus preventing any cement getting inside the valve. Remove all the loose rust, scale, or dirt inside the pipe that is to be installed by standing it on end and striking with a hammer and, if convenient, after the pipe is in place, open all the valves and blow live steam through the line.

2. Don't cut threads on the pipe longer than standard, as an extra long thread will allow the pipe to strike the partition, as shown in the cut. This will spring the seat

and make it slightly oval shape, thus making a good fit with the disc impossible.

3. Never apply a pipe wrench on the opposite end of a valve from the end that is being screwed on the pipe, and never clamp a valve in a vise sidewise. This should be particularly observed with the lighter class of valves as it is almost certain to spring the valve and hence cause a leak.

4. Don't try to fix a leaky stuffing box by tightening the stuffing nut with a long wrench, when the trouble can be remedied by renewing the worn-out packing.

5. Avoid undue strains on valves to be installed by placing offsets in the line, when necessary to take up expansion, and don't allow the valves to bear the weight of unsupported pipe.

6. When a valve leaks don't undertake to

tighten it by using some kind of a lever on the wheel. The wheels are so proportioned that sufficient power can be obtained by using the hand alone and any dirt on the seat is only pressed in by the application of powerful leverage upon the stem.

It is far better to remove the dirt from the seat by unscrewing the centerpiece or bonnet. If it is found impossible to remove the bonnet or centerpiece by ordinary methods, heat the *body* of the valve just outside of the thread with a blow-torch, or any other available means that can be applied to the body and not to the centerpiece. Then tap lightly all around the thread with a soft hammer. This method never fails, as the heat expands the body and breaks the joint made by the litharge or cement.

❧   ❧   ❧

MACHINE FOR FINISHING CRANKSHAFTS

The method of manufacturing crankshafts in general has always been unsatisfactory. A large mass of metal must be removed from the center of a forging to form a crankshaft. This work has always been done by drilling holes across the web and then cold-sawing to meet the holes and breaking out lump from the throw; a rough square pin resulting. It was then necessary to center the pin and shaft and balance the forging with jigs so that the pin could be turned up in a lathe. To finish the cheeks of the crank, a powerful milling machine has generally been used.

The machine shown in the illustration, which will turn up a finished crank from

the rough forging, is provided with a patent universal vise for roughing out and a stationary vise for finishing the crankshafts. The vises are easily adjusted to different sizes of crankshafts and will hold the work in a horizontal position for finishing the cheeks, as shown, or in a vertical position for finishing the shaft and crank pin.

By the use of this machine a rough forged crank can be finished all over in one hour and thirty minutes. This remarkably fast work is made possible by the crank being held vertically in the machine, thereby avoiding the rise and fall of the weighty lump of the forging when same is turned in horizontal position.

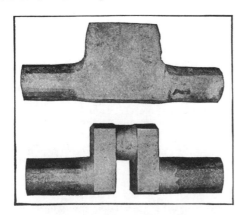

Rough and Partly Finished Work

Crankshaft Machine

TO FIND THE HORSEPOWER PRODUCED OR CONSUMED IN ANY MACHINE

The standard horsepower is equivalent to 33,000 foot pounds per minute, or 550 foot pounds per second, i. e., one horsepower will lift 1 lb. 33,000 ft. in one minute, or 550 ft. in one second. If the weight is increased and the distance proportionately decreased, the power required to lift it will remain the same. Thus, one horsepower would raise 1 lb. 33,000 ft. in one minute, or it would raise 1,000 lb. 33 ft. in one minute, or 330 lb. 100 ft. in one minute.

It therefore follows that the pull or force of any machine multiplied by the distance through which the force acts in one minute divided by 33,000 lb. will give the horsepower. Thus, in turning up a casting on a lathe having a cutting speed of 20 ft. a minute and producing 200 lb. pressure on the cutting edge, the power consumed will be $200 \times 20 \div 33,000 = .121$ hp.

If the cutting speed and cutting force were unknown, the horsepower could be found as follows: Stop the lathe and connect a spring balance to the belt. Then turn the lathe by pulling the balance and note the number of pounds required. Measure the circumference of the pulley and count the number of revolutions per minute. Now, supposing the speed to be 100 revolutions per minute and the belt tension 20 lb. on a pulley of 2 ft. circumference; then the power consumed would be, $2 \times 100 \times 20 \div 33,000 = .121$ hp.

Of course, these results give the theoretical horsepower and do not include the loss occasioned by the transmission, although the extra power required to start the lathe when using the balance will partly compensate for this, as it takes more force to start it than to keep it in motion.

In some machines the force is not uniform. Thus, in a steam engine the pressure on the piston at the beginning of the stroke is several times the pressure at the end of the stroke and even with the pressure remaining constant the force applied to the shaft would be variable, as it would diminish to 0 at the dead center.

The usual method of finding the horsepower of a steam engine is as follows: An indicator is attached to the engine cylinder while running, for the purpose of recording on a piece of paper the exact pressure in the cylinder at all positions of the piston. The indicator consists of a small cylinder, provided with a piston, which is held down

by a spring and connected by a lever to a pencil. The pencil moves on a revolving paper and traces the record of the pressure.

As stated before, there is a considerable difference between the maximum and minimum pressures, so the mean effective pressure is computed from the indicator card and this pressure times the area of the piston times twice the length of the stroke in feet times the number of revolutions per minute divided by 33,000 will give the indicated horsepower.

Thus, a 10-in. by 12-in. engine running at

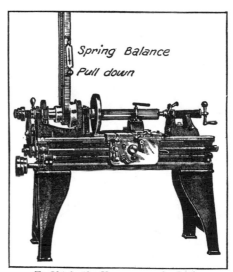

To Obtain the Horsepower of a Lathe

125 r.p.m. with 65 lb. mean effective pressure would give $65 \times 78\frac{1}{2}$ (area of piston) $\times 2$ (stroke $\times$ 2) $\times 125 \div 33,000 = 38.655$ hp.

In some machines the problem of figuring the power is presented in the primitive conditions that determine the value of a horsepower. Thus, a bucket elevator capable of raising material 100 ft. at the rate of 2,000 lb. a minute would require $100 \times 2,000 \div 33,000 = 6.1$ hp.

Stated in a general way the horsepower of any machine equals power times motion divided by 33,000, in which the power is in pounds and the motion in feet per minute.

❖ ❖ ❖

A gale blowing 80 miles an hour exerts a pressure of nearly 32 lb. to the square foot.

CLIMBING TALL STACKS WITH
AID OF KITES

**Novel Method of Repairing 170-Ft. Chimney—Kite
Expert Tells How It Was Done**

By E. E. Harbert

Having occasion to make emergency repairs to the large 170-ft. chimney of the Consumers' Ice Company, Chicago, and find-

After the correct position of the wire was obtained the kite was hauled down and the cord fastened to the roof of a building, as shown in Fig. 2. A releasing device was then sent up, which consists of two wings attached to a frame, supported from the kite string by means of small grooved wheels. This allowed the device to be blown along the kite string in the maner of a "messenger" and was so arranged that the contact with a trigger near the chimney top caused

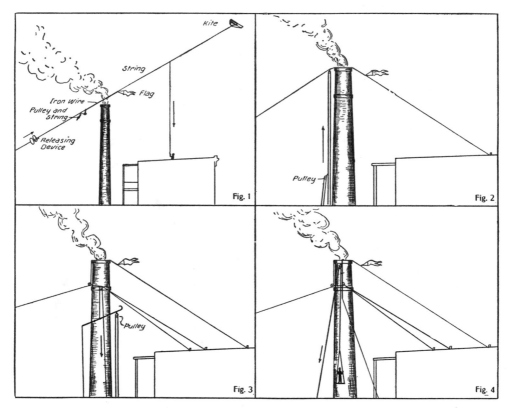

Fig. 1

Fig. 2

Fig. 3

Fig. 4

ing that the cost of erecting a scaffold ran up into hundreds of dollars and would take too much time, I decided to use one of my cellular kites for the purpose of hoisting and attaching a suitable block and tackle.

As one of the requirements of the undertaking was to obtain access to the top of the chimney without discontinuing its use, it was found necessary to interpose a 25-ft. section of iron wire in the kite string, to prevent the intense heat of the chimney from burning it. A flag was placed at the farther end of the wire, as shown in Fig. 1, in order to furnish a guide for locating the position of the wire, which was nearly invisible.

a ball of string to drop to the ground, leaving a double string suspended to the pulley and allowing the elevation of a larger pulley and rope, as indicated.

The large pulley was hoisted a short distance above the collar of the chimney, which was 14 ft. from the top, and the ropes were then brought around each side of the chimney and fastened to the roof of the adjoining building.

This produced a fairly strong support, but not strong enough to bear the weight of a man, and still lacking 14 ft. of the top. A strong wood and iron hook was accordingly made and provided with a pulley at the hook end and a piece of rope attached to the other end, for the purpose of raising the hook and making it catch over the top of the chimney. After the hook was caught on the top, a man was hoisted up and the work of painting and repairing continued in the usual manner.

Although it is often required to reach the top of a chimney in this way the future possibilities of kite-flying are by no means limited to this operation.

The operation of painting and repairing the roofs of church steeples has always been a serious problem and an expensive undertaking. If possible, the top is lassoed from the highest window, thus allowing a man to climb to the top of the spire and attach the necessary tackle, but when there is no window near the top it is necessary to break a hole in the roof. This has often been done in the past, but will probably be superseded by the use of kites in the future. Kites have also been used for stringing telephone wires and have proved very valuable for that purpose.

TUNNEL STERN MOTOR BOAT

American boat builders are following the English practice of tunnel stern construction, which enables the use of a good sized propeller in a craft of small draft. The illustration shows a boat built the past season for use on Lake Michigan and for exploring trips on rivers. The dimensions are: Length, 50 ft.; breadth, 10 ft. 6 in.; extreme draft with fuel and stores aboard, 14 in.

The dining room, 14 ft. by 10 ft., is forward, with folding berths; the engine room and cook's galley with berth for engineer come next, while the after-end has two state-rooms. The bridge deck at the forward end is shaded with an awning and will accommodate a large party. The power is a 4-cylinder gasoline engine. The American Shipbuilder says:

While the yacht is not intended for speed or rough weather service, she made the trip across Lake Michigan in fairly heavy weather and behaved admirably, at the same time making good speed. This type of boat is between a cruising motor-boat and an out and out houseboat, having a part of the speed of the former and the good accommodations of the latter. Such a craft is well adapted for summer use on our great rivers or along the sheltered waters of the coast or the Great Lakes.

NOVEL USE OF RURAL TELEPHONE

A Kansas thresherman, who operates a large crew and several machines, has made use of the rural telephone lines in a way which will prove suggestive with others. The nature of his work calls for a change of location every few days. The first wagon to pull up and move is the office, which is equipped with a telephone. Immediately on arrival at a new place wires are run from the field to the nearest rural telephone line, and connection made. It is then an easy matter to order supplies, repairs, and whatever is needed, from the nearest town.

Arrangements are also made in the same way with the farmer to whom the outfit intends to move next, and help is secured from as many nearby farms or villages as may be required. The actual saving in money to a single contractor during one season amounts to a large sum, and saves hundreds of miles of driving, to say nothing of the increased comforts and convenience.

QUICK SETTING PLASTER OF PARIS

To accelerate the setting qualities of plaster of Paris, add a pinch of potassium sulphate to the water. This hastens the setting without injuring the plaster in any way.—Contributed by Dr. Carl Fossum, Wells Block, Aberdeen, So. Dak.

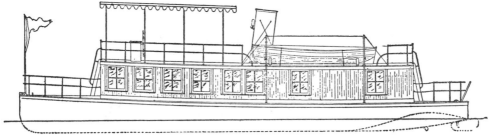

Draft Only 14 in.--Crossed Lake Michigan

THE MANUFACTURE OF DENATURED ALCOHOL

What it is Made From--How Produced--Government Restrictions--Expert Chemist's Advice to Prospective Manufacturers

By Carl Shelley Miner

Probably no piece of legislation in the last decade has created such wide-spread interest, and even excitement, as the Free Alcohol Bill. The public has demanded information about every phase of it. The daily papers, trade journals and magazines have found the subject good copy and have filled their columns with stories, the most notable characteristic of which has been a vast optimism in regard to the future of this "new industry," the manufacture of denatured alcohol. The impression has gone abroad that alcohol may be profitably manufactured from almost any sort of vegetable material, in almost any place, by almost anybody. Wildly exaggerated statements as to the yields from various materials, probable prices and extent of markets have been made, and the result has been to induce a sort of alcohol madness in the public. About one in every ten men has a plan for manufacturing denatured alcohol, and all of them want information to help them plan definitely. This magazine has received scores of letters of inquiry about the process of manufacture, availability of materials and, in fact, every other phase of the whole question. It is in the hope of answering as many as possible of these inquiries that this article is written.* I shall try to enumerate the materials from which alcohol may profitably be produced, to describe briefly the process of manufacture, and to give the prospective manufacturer an idea of the essentials to be most considered in making his plans.

NOT A NEW INDUSTRY.

One thing should be thoroughly understood, that the manufacture of denatured alcohol is not a new industry. The Free Alcohol Bill did not open the market to a new product; it merely enlarged the market of an old one. The manufacture of denatured alcohol is only the manufacture of alcohol. The process of denaturing is no more complicated than the process of

putting cream into coffee. The government decides on a suitable denaturing agent, probably wood alcohol, and the manufacturer mixes it with his product under the supervision of a revenue officer. In view of this fact, it is obvious that the man who enters this field must be prepared to meet the organized competition of the distillers. Worse, it is even rumored that Standard Oil is to take over the large distilleries and attempt to control the alcohol market. However, the raw material is so abundant and so varied that no such thing as cornering it is possible. Roughly speaking, any material containing starch or sugar is a source of alcohol. Many processes have been patented for producing alcohol from cellulose, which includes wood fiber, straw, leaves, etc., but none of them have been successfully operated, although it is said that a company in the south is now producing alcohol from sawdust. It is, however, safe to say that this method will not affect the alcohol market for many years.

SOURCE OF ALCOHOL.

The great source of alcohol in this country is corn, and there seems to be little reason for believing that it will not continue to be. On this account, it will be taken as a type, and the process of manufacturing alcohol from it will be described, and then the variations from that process, necessary for the use of other materials will be discussed. The first step in the process is to change the starch of the corn into sugar, for it is only after this change that the fermentation which produces alcohol can take place. The corn, in either a whole or ground state, is mixed with a little water, and heated by steam, sometimes under pressure, sometimes with the addition of a small amount of acid, until the starch is thoroughly gelatinized, which means that the starch cell is completely disintegrated, so that the malt used to transform the starch into sugar can act more readily. A thick paste is formed, such as the housewife uses for a starch pudding. The mass is then cooled to about 140° F., and some barley malt, made to a cream with a little water, is added. The diastase,

*Should any of our readers wish information which this article does not furnish, the author will be very glad to answer any letters addressed to him, at the Bryant-Miner Laboratories, 353-357 Dearborn street, Chicago.

an unorganized ferment contained in the malt, acts on the gelatinized starch, transforming it into maltose, or malt sugar, and dextrin. It is important that this process shall be carried on under exact temperature conditions, for, on this point depends the relative amounts of maltose and dextrin formed, and it is very important to produce as much maltose as possible, in order to get a satisfactory yield of alcohol. When a small amount of the solution, tested with iodine, shows that the starch has all been acted upon, the solution is cooled to about 70° F. For this purpose air, water, or a combination of the two, may be used.

When the proper temperature has been reached, a little yeast is added, and the solution is allowed to ferment. It seems scarcely correct to say "allowed" here, for the fermentation must be carefully controlled, and it is here that the experienced manufacturer has the great advantage. He has found, by careful experiment, the most satisfactory conditions for producing the largest yield of alcohol. The yeast he uses is a pure culture which produces more alcohol and fewer by-products, fusil oil, etc., than ordinary yeasts. In some cases, he even employs a zymotologist, yeast expert. If he uses a pure yeast culture, he keeps his fermentation vats, and the room containing them, scrupulously clean, to prevent the introduction of wild yeasts. Since alcohol is lighter than water, the progress of the fermentation may be kept track of by means of a hydrometer, an instrument for showing the weight of the liquor.

FERMENTATION AND DISTRIBUTION.

The fermentation is usually completed in from 30 to 40 hours. By this time the sugar and much of the dextrin, has been converted into alcohol and carbon dioxide. The carbon dioxide gas given off during the fermentation is occasionally collected, under pressure, in large tubes, and used for soda fountains, etc., but this has not proved very profitable, and is very seldom done. The liquor now contains from 8 to 12 per cent of alcohol which must be separated from the solid unfermented materials and from the water and the by-products of fermentation. The separation is effected by distillation. The alcohol boils at a lower temperature than the water, and begins to distill over first. The process is not simple, however, for mixtures of liquids are hard to separate even when their boiling points lie far apart, as in the case of alcohol and water. At a temperature a little higher than the boiling point of alcohol a mixture containing much alcohol and very little water distills over, but, as the temperature increases, the amount of alcohol in the distillate gradually decreases, and the amount of water increases, until the boiling point of water is reached, by which time the alcohol has all distilled over, leaving the solid matter, some water, behind. The solid material is either dried and sold for cattle food, or is fed to cattle at the distillery, in a wet state. The distillate is now much richer in alcohol than the original solution, but is not yet marketable. Formerly, it was redistilled until it was of the desired strength.

The modern distiller, however, has a rather complicated form of still which produces 95 per cent alcohol by a single distillation. This still is too complicated to admit of description here, but its principle is the condensation of the vapors within the apparatus, and their re-evaporation by hot ascending vapors, so obtaining repeated distillation in a single still. The distillate is an alcohol of 90 to 95 per cent strength.

Such, in brief, is the method of manufacturing alcohol from corn. There are, of course, many details which it is impossible to consider in an article of this length, but this description covers the essential points of the process. The yield will average about 2½ gal. of 95 per cent alcohol, and approximately 15 lb. of feed from a bushel of corn. This feed is worth, roughly, 1 cent a pound, so that the alcohol can be produced at a cost of 14 cents a gallon for raw material, when corn is 50 cents per bushel. The expense of production will vary with the size of the plant, price of labor, etc., so it is variously estimated at from 2 to 5 cents per gallon.

POTATOES, MOLASSES AND BEETS LARGELY USED.

In Germany, potatoes are largely used for the manufacture of alcohol and the process is almost identical with the process for corn. In this country, unless the price of potatoes drops materially, they can not compete with corn as a source of alcohol.

Molasses and the residues from beet sugar are much more likely to be profitable for this purpose than potatoes. Much of the molasses is manufactured so far from trade centers, that freight charges make it—or at least the lower grades of molasses—a waste product. This material may be easily fermented and gives a good quality of alcohol. Alcohol from this source is manufactured in Cuba for from 12 to 15 cents a gallon. Porto Rican molasses is already being imported into this country so as to be profitably used as a source of alcohol. The process of manufacture is simpler than in the case of corn, for the fermentable material is sugar, and no preliminary malting is necessary. It is sufficient to thin the molasses until it contains from 16 to 20 per cent of sugar and add the yeast.

Fruits, and many kinds of vegetable waste, can be turned into alcohol, but at present most of them can be more profitably used for other purposes. Any of the cereals, many starchy materials such as cassava, rice waste, etc., are sources of alcohol, but on account of their price, it seems unlikely that they will be used in its manufacture.

ADVICE TO PROSPECTIVE MANUFACTURERS.

The man who is preparing to manufacture denatured alcohol must take many things into consideration. First, has he the raw material, containing starch and sugar at a sufficiently low cost? Take corn as a basis, and calculate whether the starch or sugar in the material in question costs more or less than the starch in corn, considering that starch contains 60 per cent of starch. If the material is anything out of the ordinary, so that its composition is not known, have it analyzed, not only for its value as a source of alcohol, but also for the value of the residues that will remain after the alcohol has been distilled. If the material proves suitable, then, is it available in sufficient quantity? The revenue authorities have decided to license no distillery that produces less than 250 gal. of alcohol per day. Questions of markets, transportation, etc., must, of course, be considered. Most important of all, is the probable price that alcohol will bring, and that is quite impossible to prophesy. The demand for denatured alcohol is not going to be as large at the start as many suppose. The papers have recently published an interview in which Commissioner Yerkes is quoted as saying that alcohol is very little used in Europe for power and light. If this is true in countries where denatured alcohol has long been available, it seems probable that it will be some time before it will successfully compete with gasoline as a source of heat or power in this country. There are, however, many other uses to which it may be put, which have been overlooked. Such a one is the manufacture of artificial silk, which in France makes a market for an enormous amount of alcohol.

The possibilities of this business of manufacturing alcohol are so great that very many people will probably rush into it without looking into the matter carefully, but there is no doubt a great chance for the man with small capital who wants to engage in manufacturing and who is willing to give his best efforts to bringing his process to the highest degree of efficiency.

EXTENSION JACKS FOR CAISSONS

The old method of making caissons has several disadvantages. The large steel hoops used for supporting the sides are very difficult to put in place and the increased size of the shaft which is necessary with this form of support, often leads to settling of buildings or other structures in the immediate vicinity.

To overcome these objections, a leading Chicago engineer has designed the extension jacks shown in the accompanying illustration. By using these jacks the shaft

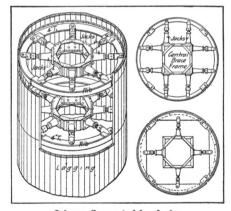

Caisson Supported by Jacks

may be excavated even a trifle smaller than the desired size and the jack screws being then screwed out compress the earth around the sides thereby preventing any displacement or settling. In filling the caisson with concrete each jack may be readily slackened and shifted upward or if necessary the jacks and ribs can be left in place.

Experiments with railroad jag spikes (spikes whose sides are jagged or notched) proved that they can be extracted with less force than the ordinary plain ones.

TREATMENT FOR THOSE SHOCKED BY ELECTRICITY

[Through the courtesy of the United Gas Improvement Co. of Philadelphia, we are enabled to reproduce the text and illustrations from their unique pamphlet on the treatment of persons injured by electric shock; which they have issued for the benefit of the many systems in which the company is interested.—Editor.] Copyrighted.

To give proper assistance to persons shocked by electricity, it is necessary to have on hand the following materials, contained in the company's emergency kit for electric shock cases, as shown in Fig. 1:

(a) A bottle of aromatic spirits of ammonia;

(b) A bottle of ordinary ammonia, with sponge attachment;

(c) A package of bi-carbonate of soda (ordinary baking soda);

(d) A tin cup;

(e) A pair of tongue pliers;

(f) A towel;

(g) A package of antiseptic cotton;

(h) A roll of antiseptic bandaging;

(i) A roll of adhesive tape.

In case of electric shock instantaneous death or only temporary unconsciousness may result. The treatment in both cases is as follows, and it should be carried out in every instance, even though the person is apparently dead, for he might be only temporarily unconscious:

TREATMENT:—*Send for a doctor at once*, in the meantime acting as follows: Carry the patient immediately into fresh air. Place him on his back on a flat surface, with a coat rolled (not folded) under the shoulders and neck, in such a way as to allow the head to fall backward enough to straighten the wind-pipe, as shown in Fig. 2; at the same time open the shirt wide at neck and loosen the trousers and drawers at waist, and have an assistant rub his legs hard.

The sleeves and trouser-legs should be rolled up as far as possible, so that the rubbing may be done on the bare skin, and the shirt and undershirt should be torn down the front so that they may be thrown back,

leaving the chest and stomach bare, as shown in Fig. 10.

Open his mouth, forcing the jaw, if necessary.

If the jaw is rigid it can be forced open

Fig. 1--Emergency Kit

by placing the forefinger back of the bend of the lower jaw-bone, and the thumbs of both hands on the chin, pulling forward with fingers and pressing jaw open with thumbs, as shown in Fig. 3.

Place something (piece of wood shown in Fig. 1) between the teeth to keep the jaws open and to prevent the patient biting his tongue, using something large enough to prevent any danger of his swallowing it accidentally; grasp the tongue with the tongue-pliers, as shown in Fig. 4, having an assistant hold it out while you are helping the patient to breathe, as described below.

In the absence of tongue-pliers, the tongue may be grasped between the index and second fingers, after they have been covered with a handkerchief.

Clear froth from the mouth by putting in

Fig. 2--First Position of Person Under Treatment

Fig. 3--Method of Opening Jaw When Rigid

your forefinger as far as possible and bringing up the froth with a scooping motion. Have the assistant who is holding the tongue slowly pass the bottle of ammonia, with sponge attachment, under the patient's nose about once a minute when the patient is breathing in, and when his arms are being extended above his head, as shown in Fig. 10.

While you are preparing the patient as just described, an assistant should force the air out of the lungs by pressing the *base of the ribs* together about once every four seconds, as shown in Fig. 5. Do not press vertically, but press on the· patient's side (palms of hands over lower ribs) in such a manner as to force as much air out of the lungs as possible.

After the clothing has been loosened, the jaw forced open, as shown in Fig. 4, the froth cleared from the mouth and the tongue

grasped, begin artificial breathing **at once** as follows:

ARTIFICIAL BREATHING.

Kneel far enough behind the head of the patient to prevent interference with the man holding the tongue. Bend the patient's arms so that the hands meet on the chest; grasp the patient's forearms firmly, as close as possible to the bent elbows.

1. Firmly press the patient's elbows against the sides of his body so as to drive the air out of the lungs, as shown in Fig. 6; then

2. Raise the arms slowly with a sweeping motion until the patient's hands meet above

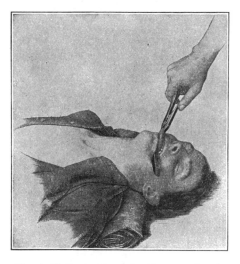

Fig. 4--Method of Inserting Block in Mouth

(or behind) the patient's head, as shown in Fig. 7; then

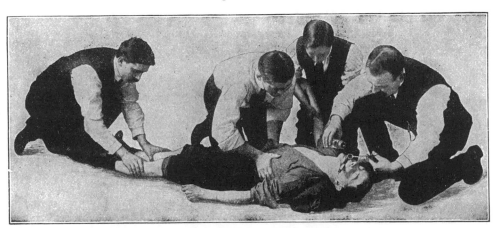

Fig. 5--Forcing Air Out of Lungs

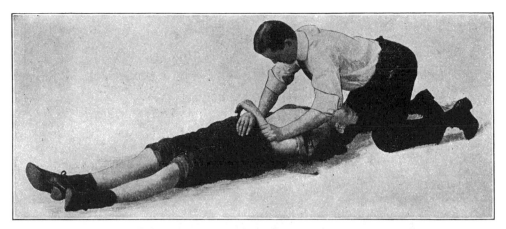

Fig. 6--First Movement in Artificial Respiration

3. While you have the patient's arms stretched out in line with his body, give them a slow, strong pull, until you have expanded or raised his chest as high as it will go, as shown in Fig. 8; then

4. Bring the arms, with bent elbows, down against the sides, and press them firmly as before, as shown in Fig. 6.

This action should be continued about fifteen times a minute until the patient begins to breathe. You must guard against a tendency to make these motions too fast; they must be done slowly. A good plan is to count four slowly—"one," as the pressure is given on the sides, as shown in Fig. 6; "two," as the arms are being extended above the head, as shown in Fig. 7; "three," as the strong pull is given, as shown in Fig. 8; and "four," when the arms are again being bent and returned to the sides, as shown in Fig. 9.

Do not let your hands on the forearms slip away from the elbows; the best result comes from grasping close to the elbows, as shown in Fig. 9.

The operator must appreciate the fact that this manipulation must be executed with methodical deliberation, just as described, and never hurriedly, or half-heartedly. *To grasp the arms and move them rapidly up and down like a pump-handle is both absurd and absolutely useless.*

Each time the arms are pulled above the head and the chest expanded, the assistant who is holding the tongue should pull the

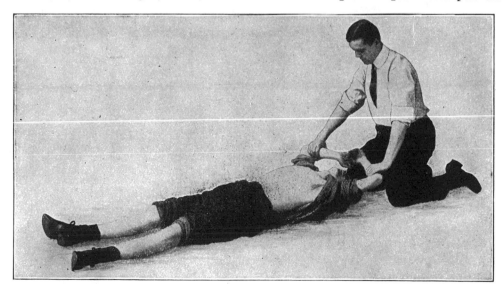

Fig. 7--Second Movement in Artificial Respiration

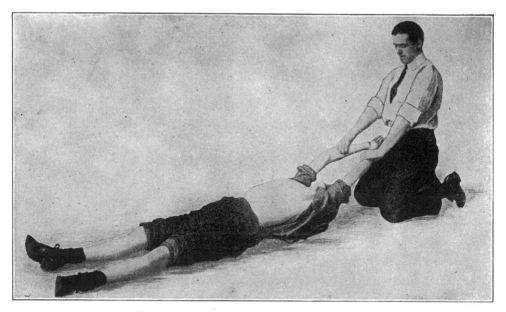

Fig. 8--Third Movement in Artificial Respiration

tongue out and downward, and another assistant should, from time to time, slap the chest with a towel or cloth wet with cold water, as shown in Fig. 10.

When the patient is breathing by himself, the process of artificial breathing can be stopped, but the process of pressing the sides *every other* time he breathes out, should be started as follows:

Do not press vertically, but press on the patient's side (palms of hands over lower ribs) in such a manner as to force as much air out of the lungs as possible, Fig. 5. You can carry out this pressing action most successfully, if, on beginning, you move your hands in and out with every breath, pressing very lightly, until you have established a rhythmical motion of your hands in unison with the patient's breathing; then you can begin to press hard at every other out-going breath.

The object of doing this is to strengthen his breathing. By making the pressure every other time he breathes out, you give

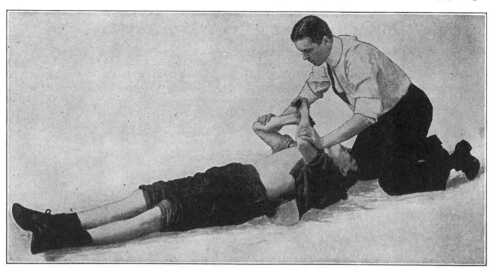

Fig. 9--Fourth Movement in Artificial Respiration

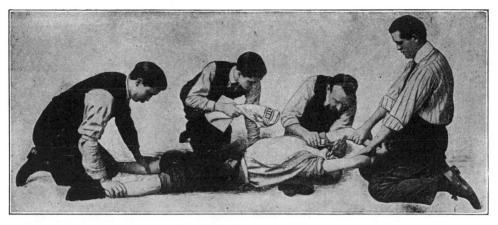

Fig. 10--Positions of Assistants

him an opportunity to take a breath himself, and this natural effort to breathe is in itself strengthening to the action of the lungs.

Continue this pressing action until the man is conscious and breathing well by himself.

The rubbing of the legs and arms should continue as long as the artificial breathing, or pressing action, is necessary, and the holding of the tongue, and the passing of the bottle of ammonia with sponge attach-

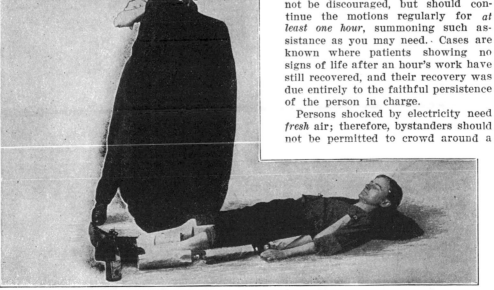

Fig. 11--Treatment After Patient Becomes Conscious

ment under the nose, as long as he is unconscious, as shown in Fig. 5.

After he becomes conscious, give him a half-teaspoonful of aromatic spirits of ammonia in a third of a glass of water. After you have brought him around, surround him with bottles of hot water.

Beer bottles are easily obtained, and should be filled with hot water and covered with a paper or cloth to prevent burning the flesh. Hot bricks, also covered, or gas bags filled with hot water will answer as well.

Then cover him with a coat and watch him. See Fig. 11.

In performing artificial breathing, if the patient does not show any signs of coming to life promptly, you should not be discouraged, but should continue the motions regularly for *at least one hour*, summoning such assistance as you may need. Cases are known where patients showing no signs of life after an hour's work have still recovered, and their recovery was due entirely to the faithful persistence of the person in charge.

Persons shocked by electricity need *fresh* air; therefore, bystanders should not be permitted to crowd around a patient, and no one should be allowed to approach him except those carrying out these instructions.

The recovery of a person unconscious from electric shock may be hastened by the use of oxygen, which should be administered at the discretion of the doctor.

BURNS CAUSED BY ELECTRICITY

Electric shocks are often accompanied by various types of burns, which should be treated as follows:

Have the injured attended by a doctor as soon as possible. In the meantime cover the burned surface with cotton, saturated in a strong solution of bi-carbonate of soda and water (as much soda as the water will absorb), and then wrap with light bandaging. In the absence of soda, carron oil may be used in the same manner.

Even apparently slight burns should be treated by a doctor, as the injuries are likely to prove more serious than those resulting from ordinary burns.

Should the articles contained in the company's emergency kit for electric shock cases not be on hand when needed, after sending for a doctor, every effort should be made to revive the patient, by following the course of movements described until the doctor arrives and the necessary articles are secured.

POINTS FOR INVENTORS

1. When you have made an invention, show a drawing or model of it to two friends in whom you have confidence, and have them sign the drawing or write their names on the model. Don't lose or destroy the drawing or model, for some day it may be needed as evidence.

2. Select a good patent attorney, pay him $5 to find out whether your invention is new and patentable, and have him send you copies of the patents which he finds most closely resembling your invention.

3. If there are real differences between your invention and those shown in the patents sent you, and your invention is better than the others, apply for a patent as soon as possible. If, on the other hand, the differences are slight or superficial, and do not add to the commercial value of the article, don't waste any money in getting a patent.

4. If you cannot afford to apply for a patent, give an interest in your invention to some good business man who will furnish the necessary money to get the patent and build a satisfactory model or sample of your invention.

5. After you have applied for a patent and made a model or sample, prepare either to manufacture and sell your invention yourself, or to sell the patent to some one who will do so. Find out what it will cost to manufacture the invention in quantities, what such things usually sell for to jobbers, retailers and the public. This information is valuable in negotiating the sale of the patent and should be full and accurate.

6. Don't expect to make a fortune from your patent at once. If you cannot sell for cash, sell on a royalty, provided the buyer is reliable and responsible.

7. Don't sign any contracts without first submitting them to your patent attorney, and be governed by his advice.

8. If there are any other points about which you want advice or information write to us and enclose a stamp for reply. Send for our booklet containing suggestions on ''What to Invent'' and ''What to Avoid.''

Popular Mechanics Patent Bureau,
160 Washington Street,
Chicago, Ill.
Branch office at
Washington, D. C.

PATENTS

SECURED PROMPTLY and with special regard to the Legal Protection of the Invention.

HAND BOOK FOR INVENTORS AND MANUFACTURERS SENT FREE UPON REQUEST.

Consultation Free. No charge for opinion as to the Patentability and Commercial Value of Inventors' Ideas.

HIGHEST REFERENCES FROM PROMINENT MANUFACTURERS.

SHEPHERD & PARKER, PATENT LAWYERS

Patents, Caveats, Trade Marks, Copyrights, Reports as to Validity and Infringement.   Patent Suits Conducted in all States.

References: American Water Motor Co., Blum Shoe Co., International Fence and Fire Proofing Co., Winget Concrete Machine Co., Century Chemical Co., By-Products Co., Columbus Pharmacal Co., Richmond Electric Co., M. C. Lilly & Co., N. L. Hayden Mfg. Co., Murray Engineering Co., Alabama Brewing Co., National Leather Tire Co., Stewart Window Shade Co., Berkshire Specialty Co., and Morgan Machine and Engineering Co.

"During the past 10 years Mr. Shepherd, of Shepherd & Parker, has obtained for us a great many important patents. We have no hesitation in heartily recommending him to any one having need of the services of a patent attorney."
HALLWOOD CASH REGISTER CO.

Mr. Parker on November 1, 1903, resigned his position as an examiner in the U. S. Patent Office to enter this firm.

Address, 310 Dietz Bldg., WASHINGTON, D. C.

SHOP NOTES FOR 1907